Jesus' life of prayer and a greater intimacy with the liberating mind and heart of the living Christ."

—Tilden Edwards, Founder and Senior Fellow,
   Shalem Institute for Spiritual Formation

"David Keller invites readers to see Jesus both as a faithful practitioner of the Jewish tradition of his day and a person of deep, abiding prayer. In this way, Lord, Teach us to Pray feeds two hungers of our age: the desire for interfaith understanding, especially among Christians and Jews, and passion for authentic spirituality. Moreover, Keller's approach—daily reflections for 100 days—beckons readers to slow down to dwell richly with the biblical word of the gospels, a life-giving fulfillment of Jesus' own invitation to us to abide in him and his word (cf. John 15:4). Lord, Teach us to Pray combines study with prayer to open up experiential encounters with Jesus whose wisdom about prayer echoes through the centuries to enrich our own lives. Thus, this book is delicious, rich, and healthy food for our spiritual pilgrimage in our own day."

—The Rev. Jonathan Linman, Assistant to the Bishop for Faith and Leadership
   Formation Metropolitan New York Synod, Evangelical Lutheran Church in
   America

Lord, Teach Us to Pray

Lord, Teach Us to Pray

One Hundred Daily Reflections
on Jesus' Life of Prayer

DAVID G. R. KELLER

CASCADE *Books* • Eugene, Oregon

LORD, TEACH US TO PRAY
One Hundred Daily Reflections on Jesus' Life of Prayer

Cascade Books
An Imprint of Wipf and Stock Publishers
199 W. 8th Ave., Suite 3
Eugene, OR 97401

www.wipfandstock.com

ISBN 13: 978-1-4982-2299-0

Cataloging-in-Publication data:

Keller, David G. R., 1937–.

Lord, teach us to pray : one hundred daily reflections on Jesus' life of prayer / David G. R. Keller.

xxxii + 244 p.; 23 cm—Includes bibliographical references and index.

ISBN 13: 978-1-4982-2299-0

1. Prayer—Christianity. 2. Lord's prayer. 3. Jesus Christ—Jewishness. I. Title.

BV230 K45 2015

Manufactured in the USA.

For Emily,
with love and gratitude for the path we walk together!

Table of Contents

Foreword

I am delighted that Cascade Books has discovered *Lord, Teach Us to Pray*. What a gift it will be for so many who want to come to a deeper relationship with Jesus. To know him better and to place him at the center of our lives is at the heart of what we are called to as Christians. This book will also appeal to persons who are not Christians, but who want to know more about him.

David Keller writes from the deep well of his own prayer and life experience as an Episcopal priest and retreat director. Seminarians in a classroom setting have benefited from his focus on making the message of Jesus of Nazareth the core of their learning. Sharing in several dioceses and many congregations David has mentored groups in their efforts to combine prayer and action.

One hundred daily reflections on the prayer and ministry of Jesus of Nazareth form the underpinnings of *Lord, Teach Us to Pray*. Who was this first-century Jew and how did he relate to God, his Abba, in prayer? David invites us to delve into this rich terrain fed by his study of some of the best contemporary Jesus scholars. This background about Jesus' life feeds our minds and David's daily reflections feed our prayer. Then, at moments when we feel compelled to simply stop and rest quietly with God in Jesus, David leads us in six "desert days," spaced evenly throughout the one hundred daily reflections, where in silence we learn to "put on the mind and heart of Christ."

I have a few favorite books I read over and over. This will become one of them. I am going to travel through this inspired text again.

Suzanne Toolan, RSM
Suzanne Toolan is a Religious Sister of Mercy at Mercy Center in Burlingame, CA. She has mentored many people in centering prayer at retreats and in prisons. Suzanne is a prolific composer of liturgical music, including the hymn "I am the Bread of Life."

Preface

He was praying in a certain place, and after he had finished, one of his disciples asked him, "Lord teach us to pray . . . ." (Luke 11:1)

I am always impressed by the fact that it is recorded that the only thing that the disciples asked Jesus to teach them how to do was to pray.[1]

Lord, we want to be like you . . .

When the disciples asked Jesus *"Lord, teach us to pray"* they were not asking for abstract information or methods. They, like Jesus, were devout first-century adult Jews and followed a strict pattern of prayer throughout each day. They were saying, "Lord, we want to *become like you.*" The disciples of Jesus saw a direct relationship between his life of prayer and his active engagement with society. God was present in everything Jesus did. They had followed Jesus throughout Galilee and recognized his intimate relationship with God, whom he called "Abba." They witnessed how God was present and active in his life with unique authority and compassion. Jesus' words and actions were transforming their lives and the lives of people around them: the lame, the blind, persons possessed by demons, lepers, persons who were marginalized by the powerful and wealthy, predatory tax collectors, and even a Roman centurion. They were beginning to understand what Jesus meant when he exhorted people to turn their lives around and embrace the good news that the reign of God was rushing into their faith community and society. It was tangible in Jesus' life. *"But if it is by the finger of God that I cast out demons, then the kingdom of God has come among you"* (Luke 11:20).

---

1. Thurman, *Disciplines of the Spirit,* 88.

The purpose of this book

Although Jesus of Nazareth was a devout first-century Jew, in the twenty-first century he is often lost in the thickets of Christian theology, reflection on the wisdom of his words, and the busyness of church life. But Jesus is more than words about Jesus. What can we know about Jesus as a Jew? What filled his daily life? Why did people come to him in great numbers? At a time in the church's life when "spiritual formation" has become a priority, it is rare to hear anyone ask, "What was Jesus' spiritual formation like and how did it influence his life?" In my experience as a teacher and retreat leader in seminaries and local congregations, most Christians know very little about Jesus' daily life as a first-century Jew or how people in his culture would have understood his teaching and responded to his actions. Yet reflection on this kind of background is an *essential step* toward relating Jesus' life and teaching to our lives today.

This is not a book to read straight through from beginning to end. The purpose of *Lord, Teach Us to Pray* is to lead readers on a three-month journey into Jesus' life of prayer. It offers one hundred daily reflections on the influence of prayer in the life of Jesus of Nazareth. In the process you will explore his daily life and a variety of his relationships and activities in the context of his first-century Jewish faith community and society.[2] In the early church "centuries" were collections of short sayings, paragraphs from longer works, and short reflections in a format for learning and meditation that was more accessible to most people than books. *Lord, Teach Us to Pray* offers a "century" of reflections and invites readers to read and meditate on *no more than one each day*. At first, the reflections follow a roughly chronological pattern in Jesus' life. Then the reflections shift to exploring the patterns of his prayer and the ways his prayer influenced his passionate mission to manifest the breaking in of God's kingdom in the lives of his people. The daily reflections also provide opportunities to discern how Jesus' life of prayer may influence the way each reader prays and lives. *Lord, Teach Us to Pray* attempts to give a portrait of the congruity between Jesus' prayer and his daily life and therefore is not exhaustive in what it includes. It is the product of the author's study of the Hebrew Scriptures and the New Testament from different points of view,[3] yet is written primarily

2. For thorough studies of Jesus' social life and relationships in first-century Jewish culture, see Destro and Pesce, *Encounters with Jesus;* Malina and Rohrbaugh, *Social-Science Commentary on the Synoptic Gospels;* and Malina, *The New Testament World.*

3. For an alphabetical list of biblical scholars and theologians consulted by the author

for persons who do not have a background in biblical studies. All biblical quotations, including apocryphal books, are placed in italics.

Why is becoming like Jesus important today?

According to the Hebrew Scriptures and the New Testament, the original and authentic nature of human life is to manifest God's love in our relationships with all beings and creation. We are created in the image of God and our vocation is to manifest God's likeness in the way we live. The only way to embody this vocation is to pay single-minded attention to our relationship with God. Jesus of Nazareth manifested this intimacy with God in his teaching and way of life. He demonstrated that it was his union with the consciousness and power of God that made his teaching and works possible. His greatest passion was to share his relationship with God with everyone drawn to him. The transparency of God's presence in his life was the authority that made it possible for people to trust him and place their lives in his hands. Their lives were changed by his words and the events they witnessed and, as they shared their memories, various oral traditions evolved that would eventually become parts of the New Testament canonical Gospels. The congruency between Jesus' wisdom and his behavior led to his criticism of institutions and leaders whose values and use of power oppressed people in his society, removed their basic personal freedoms, and limited their ability to fulfill normal responsibilities within family and society. This voice for justice and compassion led to the conflicts that ended with his crucifixion. But his death was not the end of his presence in the lives of those who were open to the same consciousness and power of God that had been present in his human life.

After Jesus' resurrection, the presence of a transformed and risen Christ Jesus filled the lives of persons who formed communities of faith. Members of these new faith communities were empowered not only by the wisdom and human example of Jesus, but also by personal experience of the same consciousness of God that had made the wisdom and behavior of Jesus of Nazareth possible. In the same way that Jesus of Nazareth had desired to be present to persons in his society, especially the poor and marginalized, the risen Christ made himself present to persons who were attracted to newly forming faith communities.[4] They desired the mind of

---

see the bibliography.

4. For more detail see Williams, *Being Christian*, chapter 3.

Christ so that they would no longer live for themselves, but that Christ would live in them. They believed that the goal of their life in Christ was to participate in the very nature of God.[5] Believing that all humans are created in the image of God, their faithful desire was to manifest the likeness of God in their words and behavior. They realized that this was the heart of the Christian path and that it is not possible to walk this path by relying on human desire and effort alone, but by whole-hearted turning toward God and total dependence on God.

The two natures of Jesus of Nazareth

During Jesus' life in the first century and in the two millennia since his death and resurrection people have asked, "Who is this man?" It is clear that he was a man, fully human, and a devout first-century Jew. It is clear from the four canonical Gospels, also, that his relationship with God—whom he called Abba—was one of authentic union. St. Paul, writing to followers of Jesus in the Greek city of Colossae about thirty years after Jesus' resurrection, proclaimed "He is the image of the invisible God . . . . For in him all the fullness of God was pleased to dwell . . " (Col 1:15, 19). The Christian church and its teachers, councils, and theologians have wrestled with the mystery of how "the fullness of God" could dwell in the life of a human being. Christians from a variety of traditions—using a variety of metaphors and language—proclaim that Jesus was both divine and human. In 451 CE the church Council of Chalcedon declared that Jesus possessed both divine and human natures. In Jesus, the presence of God—in God's fullness—becomes tangible within and under the circumstances of his authentic human life. This profound and audacious truth is the heart of the Christian doctrine of "incarnation" and asserts that God is both beyond human understanding and experience and at the same time intimately present in our lives. "And the Word became flesh, and lived among us . . ." (John 1:14). The place where humans encounter and are reconciled with God is here on earth in our daily lives. This encounter transforms and fulfills human living through what St. Paul called "life in Christ." Abundant

---

5. This is expressed clearly in 2 Peter 1:3–4: "His divine power has given us everything needed for life and godliness, through the knowledge of him who called us by his own glory and goodness. Thus he has given us, through these things, his precious and very great promises, so that through them you may escape from the corruption that is in the world because of lust, and may become participants of the divine nature."

human life is accessible because in Jesus "all the fullness of God was pleased to dwell . . . ." In Jesus' words, "I came that they may have life, and have it abundantly" (John 10:10).

Lord, Teach Us to Pray reflects on the life of Jesus of Nazareth as a Spirit-filled and devout first-century Jewish male. My emphasis is made acknowledging and accepting the Christian proclamation that in Jesus' life the human and divine are united without separation. This book's focus on Jesus' life as a Jew does not infer that the human expressions of Jesus' life overshadow his divine nature. I am aware, also, that in recent church theological reflection and teaching the divinity of Jesus has often eclipsed the concomitant nature of Jesus as a human being. At the same time, the Jewish heritage of Jesus and his life as a first-century Jew has very often been buried or denied in myriad discussions of Christian theology, piety, and worship. It is my hope that reflecting for one-hundred days on Jesus' life of prayer—as a devout Jew—will enable readers to ponder and enter into the mystery of his union with God and what that makes possible for our human lives.

The risk and richness of pondering

> "His mother paid attention to all these things in her heart."
> (Luke 2:51b, author's translation.)

Mary of Nazareth had a lot to ponder: a visit from an angel prior to Jesus' birth, lowly shepherds summoned to his birth by angels, gifts given to Jesus by learned visitors from the East, unusual claims about her son by an old man in the Jerusalem temple at the time of Jesus' presentation to God as her firstborn son, a precocious son who stayed by himself in Jerusalem listening to teachers after the Passover Feast rather than retuning home with his family, and Jesus leaving his home and livelihood as an adult to proclaim his unique role in the immanent manifestation of God's presence to restore Israel's life with God. "Who is my son?" "What is going on?" Mary was not always sure, but she paid attention to and pondered all these things in her heart. Mary has been my mentor for decades in helping me trust the movement of God's Spirit in life when I am puzzled, discouraged, or not sure of the outcome. It has not been easy.

It's not easy for any person these days. We live in an age dominated by information and digital interaction. The constant pressure of voices competing for our attention through our smart phones, social media, and interactive devices fill our hours day and night. Constant digital stimulation and communication can inhibit our desire and opportunities for personal relationships. There is nothing wrong with digital communication, conversations, entertainment, education, and efficiency in the workplace. Yet our lives can become so full of activity that life, itself, is emptied of its intimacy and richness. Surrounded by so much noise and personal stimulation we may lose our ability to listen to each other and to life itself. The pace of modern society lures us to remain on the surface of life. And that's the rub. Where is the time and opportunity to ponder and pay attention to the deep structure of life?

Lord, Teach Us to Pray invites readers to ponder Jesus' life of prayer one day at a time for three months. Yes, you can download it to your Kindle or smart phone, but resist the temptation to ponder on the run! It is possible that through reflection on the human life of Jesus—with prayerful attention—we may be led into an awareness of God's divine life in Jesus. All four Gospels agree that Jesus regularly spent time in solitude. Let Jesus and his mother be your mentors. Try not to look for answers to your questions or for affirmation of what you already know to be true. There is risk involved in letting go of the devices and desires of our own hearts. But there is also richness in discovering that life is more than we think.

Two ways of learning

Embedded in *Lord, Teach Us to Pray* are "Desert Days" where readers are invited to let go of the author's reflections, adjunct texts, personal study, and spend a day of quiet reflection and listening (or at least part of a day). This will give readers an opportunity to listen *to* Jesus' life of prayer, rather than study *about* his prayer. It will provide breaks in the process of study to reflect on the significance of Jesus' prayer for the lives of readers and the Christian community. Avoid getting overly serious about this process and turning it into something heavy and cumbersome. In the words of Hildegard of Bingen, let it become more like "a feather, rather than a hippopotamus."

In order to see the context for Jesus' life of prayer it is essential to look at the cultural, historical, and religious backgrounds that embraced his life. But equally important is the discipline of listening in the context of our personal silence. A simple method for contemplative prayer and reflection is found in Appendix E.

Additional resources

The Appendix offers a variety of background material and opportunities to assist your reflection on Jesus' life of prayer. These resources are listed at the end of the Table of Contents. Be sure to look at Appendix F: "Following Jesus through the Gospel of Mark" as you begin your one hundred daily reflections. It is essential to place Jesus' life and ministry in its geographical context and "see" his movement in your mind. "Following Jesus through the Gospel of Mark" combines a detailed outline of Mark's Gospel with three maps so that you can trace Jesus' path from place to place in pencil. This will help you ground Jesus' life in his homeland.

Some advice for the journey

As you explore Jesus' life of prayer and his prayers try to avoid using twenty-first century lenses and your personal understanding and practice of prayer as benchmarks for interpretation. Enter into the first-century contexts of Jesus' life and his prayer. Let Jesus' actions and words reach out and mentor you. Let your mind and heart be drawn into them. Try to avoid the impulse to set a personal agenda for what you hope to learn or experience. Jesus said, *"Let anyone with ears to hear, listen!"* (Luke 8:8)

A prayerful and daily journey

Let this journey be wrapped in prayer as well as disciplined academic study. Let Jesus' life of prayer place you in *a stature of waiting, listening, and dialog. Lord, Teach Us to Pray* is designed to enable you to encounter Jesus and his life of prayer every day throughout the next three months. Let this process be steady, rather than saving your efforts for big blocks of time. Jesus invited his disciples to share his *daily* life. He invites us to follow him in the same way.

At the end of each daily reflection you will find one or more questions for reflection. These questions are an invitation for dialog with what you have read that day as well as encouragement to frame your own questions and responses.

Begin each day with prayer

You may find it helpful to begin and end each day's reflection with a period of silence. The prayer below will help you become centered in God's presence.

> Abba, breath life in me; Amma, I bless you.
> Jesus, show me the way; Jesus, I bless you.
> Spirit, reveal what's true; Spirit, I bless you.

Acknowledgements

Lord, Teach Us to Pray began as a study guide for a course I taught in 1999 called "Jesus at Prayer" at St. John's School of Theology and Seminary in Collegeville, MN. I am grateful to students in that course who encouraged me to expand the guide and make it available to a wider audience. In 2003 I used a revised version for an ecumenical Lenten course called "Jesus' Life of Prayer" at Westminster Presbyterian Church in Minneapolis, MN. Responses and questions from participants in that course, especially Allen Youel, helped me to continue to refine the guide. In 2011 I taught "Jesus' Life of Prayer" for graduate students at the General Theological Seminary in New York City and comments and evaluations from Jeff Geffine, Miguel Hernadez, Steven Lee, and Wen Wen Lin encouraged me to continue to refine the study guide. One student commented, "This is why I came to seminary." In 2012 my wife, Emily Wilmer, and I used an expanded version of the guide in a nine-month ecumenical course for lay persons and clergy in the Asheville, NC area. Responses from participants who had never before discovered Jesus in the context of his own culture led me to seek publication. I am grateful for the suggestions, questions, and affirmation from this variety of seminary students, clergy, and lay persons. Their enthusiasm to explore the Gospels and enter into the life of Jesus as a first-century Jew is woven into *Lord, Teach Us to Pray*. My wife, Emily, Suzanne Toolan, Peg Birk, Joan Hershbell, and Mahan Siler read my final draft and offered great support and comments along the way. Thank you.

The evolution of this book renewed my personal research into the first-century culture and religious life of Jesus of Nazareth and the oral and written sources for his life of prayer. I am especially indebted to the scholarship of Kenneth E. Bailey, Marcus Borg, Bernard J. Cooke, Adriana Destro, James D. G. Dunn, David Flusser, Sean Freyne, Bernard J. Lee, Gerhard Lohfink, Bruce J. Malina, José Antonio Pagola, Pheme Perkins, Mauro Pesce, Bargil Pixner, and N. T. Wright. During three years of study at the General Theological Seminary in New York, (1958–61) Pierson Parker, professor of New Testament, challenged and enabled me to learn about and appreciate

Jesus' life as a first-century Jew and balance that awareness with the church's experience of and theology about Jesus following his resurrection.

Abed El Hawash has been a close friend and colleague for twenty-eight years. He lives in Ramallah, Palestine and his ancestral roots are in Jericho. During twelve visits to the Holy Land Abed has taught me that if I want to understand the life of Jesus of Nazareth it is essential to know the geography and the cultural and religious significance of the variety of places where he lived and visited. In Abed's culture places have memory and power. People are mentored by places. Abed and I have spent the night on the Mount of Transfiguration, collected pine nuts in the forests near Caesarea Philippi, hiked in the fields surrounding the Mount of Beatitudes, shared fish on the shore of the Sea of Galilee near Capernaum, hiked the first-century path through the Wadi Quilt to Jericho, walked from the Mount of Olives to the Garden of Gethsemane, and followed the first-century stone steps leading to the palace of Caiaphas the High Priest in Jerusalem. These and many more experiences together have influenced *Lord, Teach Us to Pray*. I have been truly mentored by Abed and the hospitality of his family and friends.

My wife, Emily Wilmer, has given constant and patient support as this book has evolved. Her enthusiasm about the contents of the manuscript, her questions, and her suggestions are valuable gifts that I will always treasure.

I am grateful to the editorial staff of Cascade Books for recognizing the potential of *Lord, Teach Us to Pray* and to my editor, Dr. Robin Parry. No author could ask for more friendly, timely, and competent assistance.

Introduction:
Finding a Path to Jesus' Life of Prayer

Before you begin the daily reflections it is important to explore the oral and written sources that will lead you into Jesus' life of prayer.

Four reliable sources for discovering Jesus' spiritual formation and his life of prayer

The primary sources used in *Lord Teach Us to Pray* for exploring Jesus' life of prayer are the four canonical Gospels: Matthew, Mark, Luke, and John.[1] Matthew and Luke used parts of Mark (or at least his sources) and they both use another source absent from Mark. This source is called "The Q Sayings Gospel" or simply "Q."[2] No literary form of Q has ever been found. Q is assumed by the common material used by Matthew and Luke that is not in Mark and is included herein as a primary source. A sixth, but secondary, source is a codex scholars have named the "Gospel of Thomas," though it is not really a gospel but a collection of sayings of Jesus discovered among many other documents in 1945 near Nag Hammadi, Egypt.[3] Both Q and the Thomas codex are different from the canonical Gospels because they are collections of sayings without narrative contexts. The canonical Gospels place Jesus' sayings within many narrative situations, including the passion narratives that describe events prior to and during the last week of his life, and his resurrection.

---

1. The phrase "canonical Gospels" indicates that these four gospels were considered normative as representing both the oral traditions (memories) about Jesus' life and teaching before his death as well as the teaching of the apostles as that teaching was transmitted to other teachers in the earliest Christian faith communities after Jesus' resurrection. More information about the canonical Gospels and other early Christian documents related to Jesus' life and teaching is found in Appendix A.

2. For a complete collection of the Q sayings see Robinson (ed.), *The Sayings of Jesus*.

3. The genre-designation "gospel" is not used by the text itself and is arguably inappropriate for a text that lacks narrative, as the Thomas codex does. For the complete collection of these codices, with commentary, see Meyer, *The Nag Hammadi Scriptures*.

Is it possible to discover an "historical Jesus" using "authentic" written documents about his life?

For almost two hundred years biblical scholars have tried to isolate "original sources" in hopes that we may discover "what Jesus really said" and "what actually happened" in Jesus' lifetime and after his resurrection. The twentieth century was dominated by "the quest for the historical Jesus." By looking at sources, comparing patterns, and relating the sayings and narratives to archaeological information and knowledge of first-century society and religious life, scholars have made decisions about their authenticity. All this research has been completed with emphasis on the assumption that reliable sources should be literary (written) sources, even though they were most likely preceded by oral memories of Jesus' teaching and behaviors.

Many scholars have come to the conclusion that it is not possible to discover an "historical Jesus." There are too many "layers" of sources and too little agreement among sayings and narratives to construct an authentic "original" depiction of Jesus' life and teaching. Most scholars, including some respected feminist biblical scholars, agree that, in all six sources mentioned above, the content has been influenced by the faith and life of the earliest Christian faith communities.[4] In other words, there is suspicion that what we read is presented primarily from the perspective of experience of Jesus Christ after his resurrection. One assumption is that each source represents the faith, experience, theology, catechesis, and liturgical life of a specific faith community. A common conclusion is that such post-resurrection experiences and interpretations of Jesus' life and teaching are the closest we can get to an "historical Jesus."

Discovering oral narratives about Jesus' life and teaching that led to the written documents

Yet there is more to the story. Several important things have been overlooked or undervalued in the quest for an historical Jesus. James D. G. Dunn, a respected New Testament scholar, maintains that research related to the formation of the Synoptic Gospels, Q, and the Thomas codex has been focused on the assumption that the earliest reliable sources must be literary, almost excluding any effort to understand and identify the

4. For the perspectives of three feminist biblical scholars and theologians, see Fredriksen, *From Jesus to Christ*; Schottroff and Solle, *Jesus of Nazareth*; and Schottroff, *The Parables of Jesus*.

presence of the earliest memories of Jesus' life and teaching (prior to the resurrection) as those memories were used and transmitted orally.[5] Dunn maintains that the canonical Gospels contain memories of Jesus' teaching and actions from *both* pre-resurrection and post-resurrection circumstances. He points out that Jesus had a profound effect and influence on persons who were attracted to him during his lifetime; he changed their lives and gave them a new vision of life. They were not the same because of their encounters with Jesus. They wanted to follow him and share what was present in his life. They remembered his teaching and their encounters and experiences with Jesus and then repeated them to each other and to other people. Dunn, whose research includes years of study on the nature of oral traditions, maintains that in the collections of sayings (such as the sermon on the mountain), parables, and incidents (such as healings) in all four canonical Gospels you find patterns that are congruent with oral tradition. The fact that they were eventually put in written form does not deny their integrity as oral, and therefore very early, tradition. This means that although we cannot see what Jesus actually said or did (there is no record of that) we can discover what was *remembered and shared* by those who heard and saw Jesus and whose lives were changed by his words, actions, and presences in their lives.

> We declare to you what was from the beginning, what we have heard, what we have seen with our eyes, what we have looked at and touched with our hands, concerning the word of life—this life was revealed, and we have seen it and testify to it, and declare to you the eternal life that was with the Father and was revealed to us—we declare to you what we have seen and heard so that you also may have fellowship with us; and truly our fellowship is with the Father and with his Son Jesus Christ. We are writing these things so that our joy may be complete.
>
> (1 John 1:1–4)

The integration of oral narratives formed while Jesus was still alive with narratives formed by early faith communities after Jesus' resurrection and ascension

At the same time, there is no question that the canonical Gospels, Q, and the Thomas codex (and other documents such as the *Didache*, an early

5. See Dunn, *Jesus Remembered*; and Dunn, *A New Perspective on Jesus*.

manual for worship, teaching, and church order written in the first or second century) contain material that represents memory of Jesus' teaching and life that was part of the life, faith, and experience of faith communities that continued or were formed after Jesus' resurrection. These memories looked back on Jesus' life from the perspective of Jesus' resurrection and continuing presence in the lives of these communities. In this context, the six sources mentioned above (in varying degrees) describe what Jesus may have said or done for the purpose of authenticating the experience of the risen Christ in these communities and explaining the significance of Jesus' life to persons who had no knowledge or experience of Jesus. The areas of greatest congruence in these six sources are the collection of sayings known as the "Sermon on the Mount" and various sayings and parables that describe Jesus' teaching about "the kingdom of heaven." Many scholars agree that the Thomas codex, is valuable for its presentation of 114 sayings (logia) of Jesus from the perspective of an early Christian community, most likely influenced by gnostic thought. They place its origin most likely in Syria after 70 CE, perhaps even as late as the end of the second century. Yet Thomas still shows dependence on the sources used by the canonical Synoptic Gospels.[6] It, like other early Christian texts that were not included in the New Testament, is valuable because it is an example of how the memories of and literary sayings of Jesus were interpreted in a variety of early Christian communities. Other scholars maintain that Thomas predates the canonical Gospels and represents an authentic, possibly the earliest, collection of sayings of Jesus as a teacher of wisdom.[7]

Another New Testament scholar, N. T. Wright, advises caution when assuming that the canonical Gospels represent solely the perspectives, experience, and theology of specific post-resurrection and early Christian communities and evangelists. Rather than assume that the canonical Gospels present Jesus' life predominantly from these points of view, Wright asserts that it is equally possible, and perhaps more probable, that portions of these gospels present the "mind-set" and theology of Jesus himself, which were valued and passed on through oral tradition and eventually written down when the authoritative stewards of eye-witness memories had died. In addition, Wright points to the essential role of narrative context for discovering the meaning of Jesus' parables and sayings. Rather than beginning with "wisdom sayings" and applying their meaning in a general way

---

6. See Pagola, *Jesus*, 473–74, and Schröter, *Jesus of Nazareth*, 33.

7. See Bauman, *The Gospel of Thomas*; and Meyer, *The Gospel of Thomas*.

to life situations as abstract truth, Wright suggests that Jesus' actions, in the context of his first-century Jewish religious environment, will help readers discern the motives for and meanings of his teaching. Wright insists that Jesus' teaching "acts" and "creates a new world." "Actions, especially symbolic actions, speak louder than words. Studying actions, especially symbolic actions, is a far better starting-point for the historian than studying isolated sayings."[8] As you will see, *Lord Teach Us to Pray* will look at many incidents in Jesus' life, as a first-century Jew, and then discern what his actions and relationships may teach us about his life of prayer and his teaching about prayer.

Discovering Jesus' life of prayer in its fullness

As we look for Jesus' life of prayer in the context of his daily life—as it is presented by the six sources mentioned above—it is essential to avoid placing emphasis on only one of the many patterns that characterized his life. Some scholars and modern spiritual writers claim that Jesus was primarily a "wisdom teacher" or the personification of Wisdom. There is no conclusive evidence in the earliest sources that Jesus' identified himself or presented himself in this way. There is, indeed, substantive wisdom expressed in his teaching and behavior as narrated in the canonical Gospels, the Sayings Gospel Q, and the Thomas codex. In the first century, *Sophia* (as expressed in the Jewish wisdom writings beginning in the second century before Jesus) was still understood as a personification of God's creative power, rather than a manifestation of God's concrete being. It is easy to see, after the resurrection of Jesus, how some early Christians saw a direct relationship between *Sophia* and Jesus. Some modern scholars, including feminist theologians, also present Jesus as the personification of Wisdom. Ben Witherington III suggests that Jesus' intimate and unique relationship with God as *abba* enabled him to receive wisdom about "God's true nature" for the purpose of sharing this revelation with his disciples.[9] At the same time, Witherington is clear that an understanding of Jesus should not be limited to his access to wisdom; it was one of several aspects of his unique life. Based on first-century Jewish perspectives on *Sophia*, it would not be accurate to assert that Jesus presented himself as an incarnation of *Sophia*.

8. See Wright, *Jesus and the Victory of God*, 130–41 passim.

9. See Witherington III, *The Jesus Quest*, 189. For a detailed study see Witherington III, *Jesus the Sage*. For a feminist perspective see Fiorenza, *Jesus*.

In like manner, some writers and scholars emphasize Jesus as a Jewish teacher and sage.[10] The source of his wisdom as sage or teacher is his intimacy with God. God's wisdom is manifest in his teaching. The emphasis is not on Jesus *as* "wisdom," but on what his teaching makes possible in people's lives. The sources give ample evidence that Jesus was called "master" and chose disciples. "Master" was the proper term of respect for a teacher and sage. Jesus' method of gathering followers, traveling together with a common purse, sharing meals, teaching in outdoor venues, and choosing a core of intimate disciples fits the pattern of Jewish teachers, rabbis, and sages in the first century. But the emphasis in this type of relationship was not primarily on intellectual mentoring. It was on the intimacy of life between the master and the disciples. It was teaching by example in a variety of situations. The wisdom flowed from experience. Some translations of the Gospels refer to Jesus as "rabbi." This term, referring to a well-trained scholar and interpreter of the Torah, did not come into general use until after the destruction of Jerusalem in 70 CE. José A. Pagola, a Spanish New Testament scholar, maintains that Jesus' role as sage or teacher was directly related to sharing his experience of the way God's kingdom (reign) was breaking into people's lives and exhorting people to participate in what God was making possible. Pagola points out that Jesus' parables, sayings, and proverbs (some original with Jesus and some reflecting traditional Jewish storytelling) were directed to simple and uneducated persons as well as religious and political leaders. Some were very radical, but all were intended to evoke a "change of heart" and behavior, rather than impart information.[11]

Other scholars and writers characterize Jesus as a religious (even political) revolutionary, the founder of "a sectarian renewal movement within Israel,"[12] or an apocalyptic prophet.[13] We will see aspects of Jesus life and mission that demonstrate his disagreement with certain aspects of the Torah, both written and oral. There is no doubt that his mission questioned the ethics of the control of the political and economic elite of his day over ordinary people. He was very specific about understanding his mission as

10. See especially Flusser, *The Sage from Galilee* and Young, *Meet The Rabbis.*

11. See Pagola, *Jesus, An Historical Approximation,* chapter 9.

12. See Borg, *Jesus: A New Vision.*

13. For overviews of Jesus' roles as apocalyptic and eschatological prophet see Wright, *Jesus and the Victory of God,* sections 2 and 3; Keener, *The Historical Jesus of the Gospels,* chapters 17–20; Solle and Schottroff, *Jesus of Nazareth*; and Crossan, *Jesus.*

the breaking in of God's kingdom to restore God's compassion in human relations and his religious community.

All these aspects of Jesus' life are important as we look for his life of prayer and how his prayer influenced his mission. Therefore, it is wise to include all these characteristics and try to discover what they reveal about Jesus, based on the memories of the persons whose lives were changed by his teaching and actions. These memories (embedded in the sources) will help us discover Jesus' life of prayer. An overall pattern will emerge if we allow all the possibilities to have a voice. Even then, as José A. Pagola says, it will be an "approximation."[14]

Current scholars generally agree that the quest to understand the sources for narratives of Jesus' life and teaching must continue to value textual and form criticism along with further study of the presence of oral tradition within the Gospels. Late twentieth- and twenty-first-century study of the Gospels has added valuable data and interpretive insights from social science history, archaeology, newly discovered historical and biblical manuscripts and commentaries, rabbinical literature, and ancient historians.[15] One new emphasis has been reclaiming Jesus' life as the life of a first-century Galilean Jewish male after years, even centuries, of looking at him almost solely from a Christian perspective.[16] As N. T. Wright maintains, the quest for the historical Jesus has and continues to be an important aspect of the life, faith, and mission of the Christian community.[17]

Using a variety of sources, *Lord, Teach Us to Pray* presents a portrait of Jesus' life of prayer

This survey of sources and interpretive scholarship gives the background for exploring Jesus' life of prayer. *Lord, Teach Us to Pray* uses narratives and sayings from all four canonical Gospels to describe the formation of Jesus' spiritual life in his family, his faith community, and his personal prayer. We will try to discover how his prayer influenced his decisions, teaching, and actions. We will approach his life as best we can from the point of view of a faithful first-century Jew. Like José Pagola we will rely on research to fill

14. Pagola, *Jesus*, 16.

15. For an overview of current research see Witherington III, *The Jesus Quest*; Dunn, *Jesus Remembered* cited above; and Freyne, *Jesus A Jewish Galilean*.

16. See Lee, *The Galilean Jewishness of Jesus* and Pagola, *Jesus*.

17. See Wright, *The Challenge of Jesus*.

in details, contexts, and background to give at least an "approximation" of what Jesus' life of prayer was like. This approach does not take every verse "at face value," as if details from different sources (literary or oral) and their reasons for remembering and sharing details about Jesus' life and teaching are unimportant. At the same time, *Lord, Teach Us to Pray* realizes that the perspectives of *all* sources respected by biblical scholars are valuable for searching for what Jesus' prayer was like, how it influenced his life, and became the exemplar for the lives of those who followed him. José Pagola reminds us that Jesus called disciples to *follow him* and share his compassionate engagement in the lives of people. "What makes us Christians is to follow Jesus. That's all. This following of Jesus is not theoretical or abstract. It means following in his footsteps, committing ourselves to humanizing life and so contributing little by little to making a reality of his project of a world in which God and his justice reign."[18]

The patterns in Jesus' life of prayer

The four canonical Gospels reveal a three-fold pattern in Jesus' life that was the source of his life with God:

- quiet listening
- faithful discernment
- compassionate response

Jesus always found time to listen to God, his inner self, and the world around him. This listening heart was the source of the guidance and desires that, along with direct experience of God's love, led and sometimes drove him into compassionate involvement in the lives of others. All this took place in the context and in fulfillment of his religious community. Jesus' life of prayer opened him to the vitality of God's energy and wisdom. He became a manifestation of the Abba he experienced in prayer. This transformed the lives of many who were attracted to him. (And it was they who remembered and shared their experiences with Jesus.) He loved unconditionally. He transformed what he touched. His experience in prayer was tangible in his daily life.

18. Pagola, *Following in the Footsteps of Jesus,* 63.

Jesus' life of prayer was rooted in experience of God and daily life

As we have seen, it is common to reflect on the teaching of Jesus, especially his sayings, as wisdom for living. He has much to say about abundant human life that is, indeed, wise. But his wisdom did not come from his *thinking* about living. He was not proclaiming a "philosophy" or intellectual approach that would guide people's lives. Mirrored in Jesus' life is the wisdom and challenge that *prayer is both a personal journey and at the same time an opportunity to transform society by making God's presence tangible in and for human lives. Jesus' life demonstrates that prayer and living must be congruent because they are integral parts of the same reality.* Following the pattern of first-century Jewish sages and teachers, Jesus proclaims: "My life is my message." His wisdom and teaching had a least three fundamental sources: his experience of God in prayer, his Jewish heritage (both the Scriptures and worship), and the crucible of his daily life in first-century Galilee and Judea. His teaching and living embodied the presence and power of God that came from the womb of his experience of his Abba. This was the source of his teaching (remembered in collections of sayings). His desire was to enable others to share this experience and to "*do greater things than I have done*" (John 14:12).

Although it may be edifying to see Jesus as a wisdom teacher and reflect on his sayings, the wisdom of Jesus did not exist in isolation from his daily life and his engagement with the lives of people around him, especially in Galilee. Without the Gospel narratives his sayings can lose their roots. The same may be said for looking at Jesus' life of prayer. It did not exist in a vacuum, nor was it focused on him, although it included his very personal and intimate relationship with his Abba.

DAY 1

The origin of Jesus' prayer

> *. . . then the Lord God formed the human of dust from the earth, and breathed into the human's nostrils the breath of life; and the human became a living being.* (Gen 2:7)

The author of Genesis 2 describes the beginning of a dialogue between God and humankind. The first human (*'adam* in Hebrew) is formed from *"the dust of the ground"* (*'adama* in Hebrew) and is physically related to the earth at a fundamental level. Then the author declares that *"the breath of life"* enters man's physical body and he becomes a *"living being."* The body of *'adam* and the vitality of God are united in a two-fold yet continuous action through God's initiative. This co-inherence creates *'adam* as a *"living being."*

Ancient Hebrews believed that breath conveys vital power and is a tangible manifestation of the soul and energy of the giver. They did not make a distinction between "life" and "soul." The soul of a human being is the totality of that person and includes the body, which is its "outward form." This lies behind the Hebrew understanding of a blessing (*berakha* in Hebrew). When a patriarch blesses his son he is not wishing him good health and success; he is transmitting the totality of his soul—his physical and psychological being—to his son.

The inspiration of God's life-giving breath into man's nostrils begins what may be seen as a prototype for prayer that is manifested in a variety of ways throughout the Hebrew Scriptures. It takes a dialogic form when God's vital Spirit is personified through breath and enters man's body and becomes the source and sustaining power of human life. Yet the dialogue initiated in Genesis 2—and continued throughout Hebrew Scriptures by God's words and activities in human lives and the nation of Israel—is un-fulfilled without a response. God's initiative is the genesis of a prayerful relationship. In this context, prayer is the flow of God's vital and creative Spirit into a human being and each person's response to that gift.

There is a clear example of Jesus imparting vital energy through breath in John 20:19–23. When the risen Christ breathes on the disciples they receive the Holy Spirit who will enable them to continue his mission. *"'As the Father has sent me, so I send you.' When he had said this, he breathed on them and said to them, 'receive the Holy Spirit.'"* Perhaps St. Paul has this in mind when he says in 2 Cor 5:17 *"So if anyone is in Christ, there is a new creation: everything old has passed away; see, everything has become new!"* and *"Just as we have borne the image of the man of dust, we will also bear the image of the man of heaven"* (1 Cor 15:49).

Jesus' experience of God, his Abba, in prayer mirrors the wisdom expressed in Genesis 2. His entire life flowed from this very basic, yet profound foundation. We know this because he shared this truth with his disciples in two ways. The first is through a parable. Jesus spoke plainly about prayer in the collection of sayings called the "sermon on the mount" in Matthew's Gospel. (We will take a closer look at this teaching from the fifth chapter of Matthew later.) At the end of the "sermon" he tells a parable to encourage his hearers to take his words seriously.

> *Everyone then who hears these words of mine and acts on them will be like a wise man who built his house on rock. The rain fell, the floods came, and the winds blew and beat on that house, but it did not fall, because it had been founded on rock.* (Matt 7:24–25)

But why does Jesus think his words are a foundation for wisdom and wise behavior? The answer lies in his awareness that all his words and actions have their source in his prayerful experience of his Abba. He experienced the flow of God's energy so completely that God became tangible in his life. He told his disciple Thomas,

> *How can you say, "Show us the Father?" Do you not believe that I am in the Father and the Father is in me? The words that I say to you I do not speak on my own; but the Father who dwells in me does his works. Believe me [that is, entrust yourself to me] that I am in the Father and the Father is in me; but if you do not, then believe me because of the works themselves.* (John 14:8–12)

Jesus' words and behavior seem to tell us that his times of prayer were opportunities to respond to God's initiative and place himself in the flow of God's energy. He prayed because he knew that it was the only way to become "a living being." The same is true for every person. Prayer is the source and sustaining power of human life.

When was your first awareness of the vitality of God's life in you?

What does the Genesis 2:7 account of the creation of *'adam* tell you about the nature of human life?

How have you been blessed by God? In what ways are you a blessing to other people?

BIBLICAL TEXTS FOR STUDY AND REFLECTION:

Gen 2:4b–8; Matt 7:24–25; John 14:8–12; 20:19–23; 2 Cor 5:16–21

DAY 2

The first and last words a child heard each day

> *Hear, O Israel: The Lord is our God, the Lord, alone. You shall love the Lord your God with all your heart, and with all your soul, and with all your might. Keep these words that I am commanding you today in your heart. Recite them to your children and talk about them when you are at home and when you are away, when you lie down, and when you rise.* (Deut 6:4–7)

Jesus learned to pray in his home in Nazareth. Like all children in rural villages in Galilee, Jesus was mentored and cared for by his mother until the age of seven or eight. His religious life began at home and the first words he heard each morning and the last words that entered his ears before sleep were Joseph reciting the *Shema*, the foundation of all Jewish prayer: "*Hear, O Israel . . .*" As soon as Jesus could talk he would have been taught the words of the *Shema* and on his twelfth birthday he, too, was then required to recite the *Shema* twice daily for the rest of his life. The recitation of the *Shema* reminded every person that their relationship with God was the foundation of their lives; this relationship formed their common identity and bonded them to each other as well as to God. Jesus grew up learning that he must frame each day listening to God, not only with his ears, but in his heart. Many centuries before Jesus' birth, God had declared through the prophet Jeremiah that *"I will put my law within them* [Israel], *and I will write it on their hearts; and I will be their God, and they shall be my people"* (Jer 31:33). Jesus learned that love of God embraces a person's whole being at all times and in all places. In Jesus' culture, "love" meant unconditional loyalty and attachment to family, neighbor, or a master. To love God *"with all your heart, and with all your soul, and with all your might"* meant attachment to God with every aspect of your life. Gradually, Jesus realized that prayer bonded him to God, not only in his heart, but in his might. Prayer begins in the heart and is expressed in the power of our lives.

There is no doubt that the *Shema* framed each day in Jesus' adult life and that he considered it the foundation of life with God. On one of his visits to Jerusalem a scribe of the Torah asked him, *"Which commandment is the first of all?"* Jesus answered, *"The first is, 'Hear, O Israel; the Lord our*

God, the Lord is one; and you shall love the Lord your God with all your heart, and with all your soul, and with all your mind, and with all your strength.' The second is this, 'You shall love your neighbor as yourself.' There is no other commandment greater than these." When the scribe agreed with Jesus, he replied, *"You are not far from the kingdom of God"* (Mark 12:28–34).

Jesus' adult prayer life and ministry were formed very simply in his Galilean home.

What were your earliest experiences of prayer?

How have they remained with you?

How do they influence your daily life?

BIBLICAL TEXTS FOR STUDY AND REFLECTION:

Deut 6:1–9; Jer 31:31–34; Mark 12:28–34

DAY 3

A rural venue for prayer

Jesus' life as a child in Nazareth influenced his prayer as an adult.

> *Therefore I tell you, do not worry about your life, what you will eat or what you will drink, or about your body, what you will wear. . . . Look at the birds of the air; they neither sow nor reap nor gather into barns, and yet your heavenly Father feeds them. . . . Consider the lilies of the field, how they grow; they neither toil nor spin, yet I tell you, even Solomon in all his glory was not clothed like one of these.* (Matt 6:25a, 26a, 28–29)

> *From the fig tree learn its lesson; as soon as its branch becomes tender and puts forth its leaves, you know that summer is near.* (Matt 24:32)

In Nazareth everyone was close to the land and almost all work was in relation to crops, animals, and family. Most men worked in fields and vineyards, some as owners of small plots and others as day laborers. A few, like Joseph, were craftsmen, building or repairing homes and furniture. As a small child Jesus had time to see and listen to the birds and play near the fields and the terraced vineyards with his siblings and cousins. Children helped with the harvesting of crops. Family life in Galilean villages was shared with extended families.

Until he was eight years old Jesus would have helped his mother grind wheat and add just the right amount of yeast to the batter for bread. When Jesus was older he would have learned to help Joseph craft beams for stone houses and thatch a roof with branches and clay. Nazareth was about 6 kilometers from Sepphoris, the capital of Galilee. Its sophisticated population of about 8,000 dwarfed Nazareth and its 200–400 peasants. It is quite possible that Jesus and Joseph walked across the countryside for work there in the homes and storehouses of tax collectors and administrators of Herod Antipas. Jesus' parables show familiarity with fine homes, banquets, and large storehouses.

Although there is no specific record in the Gospels, we can infer from images in Jesus' teaching that it was in the countryside, planted fields, and vineyards, watching and listening to birds, the color and smell of wild flowers, and intimate village life that Jesus' awareness of God's presence and sustaining care were formed. His response was trust and gratitude. Jesus used images of ploughing, seeds mysteriously germinating, separating wheat from weeds, and the burst of new leaves on trees in his teaching and personal discernment. These are the building blocks that formed the foundation of his life of prayer.

What is your experience of God's presence in nature?

When is nature a venue for your prayer?

BIBLICAL TEXTS FOR STUDY AND REFLECTION:

Matt 6:25–34; 24:29–32

DAY 4

A grateful heart

At that same hour Jesus rejoiced in the Holy Spirit and said, "I thank you, Father, Lord of heaven and earth, because you have hidden these things from the wise and the intelligent and have revealed them to infants; yes, Father, for such was your gracious will." (Luke 10:21–22)

This prayer was spoken by Jesus as an adult as he proclaimed the presence of God's kingdom in Galilee. It reflects a spontaneous expression of gratefulness that he probably learned as a boy because it was part of prayer in every Galilean home. After reciting the *Shema* first thing in the morning, Joseph—like every Jewish father—would continue with the *Tephilla*, the "Grand Benediction." It begins,

> Blessed be thou, Lord (our God and the God of our fathers), the God of Abraham, the God of Isaac, and the God of Jacob, (God great, mighty, and fearful), most high God, master of heaven and earth, (our trust in every generation). Blessed be thou, Lord, the shield of Abraham.[1]

Jesus would have remembered part of the *Kaddish* prayer in his Nazareth synagogue: "Exalted and sanctified be His great Name in the world that He created according to his will. May His kingdom reign, and may He cause His redemption to sprout, and may He hasten [the coming of] His Messiah—in your lifetime and in your days, and in the lifetime of the entire House of Israel . . . ."[2]

Peasant life in Nazareth was simple, but children learned from parents and other adults to be grateful for what they had. Giving thanks to God was commonplace in and outside the home, as well as in synagogue worship. Simple delights—such as seeing the face of a child, good weather for planting a crop, or the end of a hard day's work—could prompt a spontaneous "*bereka*," a prayer blessing God for God's goodness. It came straight from the heart, without forethought. It was an expression of the intent of the

---

1. Jeremias, *Prayers of Jesus*, 74.
2. Toledano, *The Orot Sephardic Weekday Siddur*, 81–82.

Shema to love God in all things and at all times. In Jesus' culture a blessing was a sharing of energy and life. To bless God was to share one's life with the source of life. It was an expression of love that flowed freely, rather than from a sense of obligation.[3]

Gratitude bonds a person to the Giver; it is a natural part of prayer that bonds us to God.

When has your heart overflowed with spontaneous thanksgiving to God?

BIBLICAL TEXTS FOR STUDY AND REFLECTION:

Matt 11:25–26; Luke 10:21–24; Ps 69:30–36

---

3. For a discussion of the ancient Hebrew understanding of blessing see Appendix D.

DAY 5

Sabbath prayer

> [Jesus] *left* [Capernaum] *and came to his hometown, and his disciples followed him. On the Sabbath he began to teach in the synagogue, and many who heard him were astounded. They said, "Where did this man get all this? What is this wisdom that has been given to him? What deeds of power are being done by his hands. Is not this the carpenter, the son of Mary and the brother of James and Joses and Judas and Simon, and are not his sisters here with us?"* (Mark 6:1–3)

The Gospels reveal Jesus' regular worship as an adult in synagogues on the Sabbath. This pattern began during his childhood in Nazareth and remained an important part of his life of prayer. The English word *synagogue* (used in the Gospels) takes its meaning from the Hebrew phrase *bet ha-knesset* and means "a gathering" or the place of gathering. The synagogue in Nazareth would have reflected the simplicity of the homes there. Unlike synagogues in larger communities, like Capernaum, it was small and may have been constructed like a family home, but used for the gathering of the people for prayer and village meetings. In some small villages in Galilee people met outdoors in the village center.

During his childhood, Jesus would have attended synagogue every Saturday morning and sat toward the front with his father and brothers. All males were required to attend regularly. His mother and sisters sat in the rear behind a veil or screen and their attendance was optional. The pattern of synagogue worship usually began with prayers like the *Shema* and blessings like the *Kaddish*. There were always readings from the scrolls of the five books of Moses (known as the Torah[4]) and sometimes a reading from

---

4. The scrolls of Genesis, Exodus, Leviticus, Numbers, and Deuteronomy were known as the Torah. The word *torah* meant both *law*, referring to the commandments given to Moses at Mount Sinai, and *teaching*, usually meaning instruction for fulfilling the intent of covenant made by the Hebrews and God at St. Sinai. The Torah records the origins of the unique Hebrew way of life, beginning with the call and faith of Abraham, the covenant at Mount Sinai, the years of wandering in the wilderness of Sinai under the leadership of Moses, and the evolution of various applications of the law to Hebrew life. This history became the spiritual foundation of the Jewish way of life.

a prophet. The text was read in Hebrew and then translated into Aramaic, the common language of Jesus' day. The translation was usually followed by comments from an adult male. Unlike the liturgies in the temple in Jerusalem, synagogue worship was led by lay men, not priests. This form of worship reminded people that they were a faith community with a unique relationship with God. It was the center of their community life. The intimate prayers in each family and of each individual had their roots in and were sustained by their worship in community and the knowledge and understanding of their sacred Scriptures.

Many synagogues also had two schools with a recognized teacher of young males. Boys began the Torah School at age five to learn to read the Torah in Hebrew. At eleven or twelve they began to study the oral tradition and application of the Torah to daily life. Synagogue worship and study was an effort of the Pharisee tradition to decentralize worship from its focus in Jerusalem and bring it closer to most people's lives. Although Jesus' left his family and home in Nazareth, he remained faithful to his Jewish faith community for worship on the Sabbath.

What places, worship, and persons influenced your earliest experiences of God's presence?

Biblical texts for study and reflection:

Matt 4:23–25; 9:35–37; 12:9–14; 13:54–58; Mark 1:21–28, 39; 3:1–6; 6:1–6; Luke 4:16–21, 31–37, 44; 6:6–11; 13:10–17

DAY 6

A timeless time apart

Luke's Gospel tells us that immediately after Jesus' time of temptation and discernment in the desert—following his baptism—that he was *"filled with the power of the Spirit, returned to Galilee, and a report about him spread through all the surrounding country. He began to teach in their synagogues and was praised by everyone. When he came to Nazareth, where he had been brought up, he went to the synagogue on the Sabbath day, as was his custom"* (Luke 4:14–16).

Although material evidence of a synagogue in Nazareth during Jesus' lifetime has not yet been discovered, we can assume the presence of a synagogue in Nazareth during Jesus' childhood and adult life. Scholars have documented the presence of over four hundred synagogues throughout Palestine in the first century and there is recent archaeological evidence of ruins identified as first-century synagogues in nearby Magdala and Capernaum. It is very likely that Jesus and his family gathered somewhere with other villagers for celebration of the Sabbath. The Gospels declare that it was "his custom" to worship on the Sabbath.

As we have seen, the Sabbath was central in the life of first-century Jews, whether or not they lived near the temple in Jerusalem. The Sabbath provided time for essential relationships of family, worship of God, and attention to their religious identity. It was a time apart from endless days of work to recall the history of their relationship with God and their promise to live according to the Torah. Sabbath worship was filled with thanksgiving for God's continuing care, the blessings in life, and listening to the words of the Torah and the prophets.

Life in peasant villages like Nazareth could easily be dominated with labor and "making ends meet." Every other day of the week was focused on basic necessities and paying heavy taxes. But Sabbath rest was a release from the pressure of time and productivity so that people could be renewed and refreshed by remembering who they are. It was a sacred time away from time, itself, to look at life and each other and bless God for these gifts. Although Jews prayed toward Jerusalem, each Sabbath centered their lives in God's presence wherever they lived so that they could begin each new week of family life and work with renewed perspective.

As an adult, Jesus' continued to participate in Sabbath worship and there are accounts of Jesus attending synagogue with his disciples. *"He left that place* [the area east of the Sea of Galilee] *and came to his hometown, and his disciples followed him. On the Sabbath he began to teach in the synagogue, and many who heard him were astounded"* (Mark 6:1–2). At the same time, Jesus did not hesitate to heal on the Sabbath and was criticized when his disciples plucked grain on the Sabbath because they were really hungry. He saw the Torah's requirements as wise guidance and pastoral support for human life, rather than compulsion or rigid obligation. He reminded his critics that God requires "mercy and not sacrifice" (Matt 9:13a).

The Sabbath should never be separated from God's loving desires for people. Its purpose is to enrich and ennoble people's lives by reminding them that their home is in God who loves them unconditionally. *"The Sabbath was made for humankind, and not humankind for the Sabbath"* (Mark 2:27a).

How do you integrate Sabbath into your life each week?

BIBLICAL TEXTS FOR STUDY AND REFLECTION:

Luke 4:14–15; 6:1–5; Matt 12:1–14; Mark 6:1–12; 2:23–28

DAY 7

Roots of prayer

> *When he came to Nazareth, where he had been brought up, he went to the synagogue on the Sabbath day, as was his custom. He stood up to read, and the scroll of the prophet Isaiah was given to him. He unrolled the scroll and found the place where it was written: "The Spirit of the Lord is upon me, because he has anointed me to bring good news to the poor. He has sent me to proclaim release to the captives and recovery of sight to the blind, to let the oppressed go free, to proclaim the year of the Lord's favor." And he rolled up the scroll, gave it back to the attendant, and sat down. The eyes of all in the synagogue were fixed on him. Then he began to say to them, "Today this scripture has been fulfilled in your hearing." (Luke 4:16–19)*

Although Mark and Matthew also record the return of Jesus to Nazareth on the Sabbath day, only Luke describes Jesus reading from the scroll of Isaiah. Some scholars conclude that Luke has scripted this part of Jesus' visit to connect the activities of his ministry with Isaiah's vision of a servant who will bring justice and freedom to the people of Israel (Isa 61). There is no doubt that Jesus' ministry parallels Isaiah's vision and Luke's description, scripted or not, gives us plausible information showing how Jesus' adult behavior in the synagogue gives us clues to Jesus' spiritual formation during what are called the "hidden years," from adolescence to adulthood.

There is little reason to doubt that he was raised in the manner of any other young Jewish boy in his day. Although he was under Mary's physical and spiritual care until the age of seven or eight, Joseph would have taught him the *Shema*, the ten commandments, and short portions of the Torah. As we have seen, Jesus would have sat with Joseph in the synagogue on Sabbath day. As an adolescent, under Joseph's care, Jesus could have been sent to the "reader" of the synagogue, like other boys in Nazareth, to learn more about the Torah, its oral tradition, and the psalms. The incident from Luke indicates that Jesus "stood up to read," which means he had learned enough Hebrew, the written language of the Torah, Psalms, and Prophets to read and study those texts. On his fifth birthday Joseph may have entered him in the local Torah School to learn Hebrew (if there was a Torah School in Nazareth at the time). In synagogues Scripture was first read in Hebrew and then translated into Aramaic. Comments of the reading would have been in Aramaic.

When the scroll was given to Jesus he knew where to find the portion from Isaiah that he read. It seems clear, in Luke's mind at least, that Jesus saw his new ministry as congruent with what God had spoken through the prophet Isaiah. All these actions of Jesus in the synagogue give us clues about Jesus' early formation in the prayer, religious life, and sacred Scriptures of his people. His prayer and life as an adult are rooted in the religious life of his family, his synagogue, and the Scriptures of his people. Jesus' life of prayer had strong roots.

What were the early roots of your life of prayer?

Where are those roots today?

What sustains you in your life of prayer?

BIBLICAL TEXTS FOR STUDY AND REFLECTION:

Luke 4:16–30; Matt 13:54–58; Mark 6:1–6; Isa 42:1–9

DAY 8

Roots produce fruit

> *He unrolled the scroll and found the place where it was written: "The Spirit of the Lord is upon me, because he has anointed me to bring good news to the poor. He has sent me to proclaim release to the captives and recovery of sight to the blind, to let the oppressed go free, to proclaim the year of the Lord's favor." And he rolled up the scroll, gave it back to the attendant, and sat down. The eyes of all in the synagogue were fixed on him. Then he began to say to them, "Today this scripture has been fulfilled in your hearing." All spoke well of him and were amazed at the gracious words that came from his mouth. They said, "Is not this Joseph's son?" (Luke 4:17–22)*

"Is not this Joseph's son?" The little boy and the young adult stand together in the same synagogue. There is little doubt that Jesus heard these same words of Isaiah as a child and perhaps studied them with the synagogue "reader" during his adolescence. A seed had been planted in a young mind and spirit and as Jesus grew and gained life experience he must have begun a process of relating the hard and marginalized lives of his rural, peasant Galilean people with the vision of Isaiah. The vision seemed so distant from small village life dominated by unrelenting work with so little left for family support after paying burdensome taxes levied by oppressive government and religious officials. Each day brought fear that failure of crops, lack of employment, or sickness might lead to loss of family land, debtors' prison, or slavery. Even their culture and religious life were under pressure from spreading Roman influences, disapproval by temple authorities, and suspicion from Herod Antipas. At some point in Jesus' life he realized it was time for Isaiah's words to become a reality and he shared his passion in his village synagogue. *"Today this scripture has been fulfilled in your hearing."* His own people initially *"spoke well of him"* and were amazed that a "local boy" had spoken with such authority. Today we might say, "He really 'gets' what Isaiah was talking about."

Jesus' words and actions in the Nazareth synagogue that day did not just drop down from heaven. They were not some "package deal" that came with being a "son of God." His people were witnessing the result of the gradual development of the seeds of prayer planted in "Joseph's son." The seeds of hearing God's word in sacred Scripture and in the prayers of Mary, Joseph, and Jesus' hometown people were bearing fruit. Jesus had remained rooted in God's word and discerned how he was called to make that word tangible in his life.

An integral part of a life of prayer is speaking and listening to the word of God. But *"Hear, O Israel . . ."* can be risky; there are consequences to becoming involved in the lives of people. Later, Jesus would say to his disciples, *"Remain in my word."* It was not a platitude. He was speaking from experience. When he proclaimed, *"Today this scripture has been fulfilled in your hearing"* he was pointing to the congruency between Isaiah's vision of God's desires for the people of Israel and Jesus' awakening to the consequences of the presence and power of God in his life. The words he had heard as a child and now as an adult were not something from the past that is good to know. It was not about "Bible content." These words were alive, and the presence of God in them was becoming tangible in his life that day in the synagogue.

What passages from the Bible seem most alive in your life right now? Where are they leading?

Biblical texts for study and reflection:

Matt 13:54–58; Mark 6:1–6; Isa 42:1–9; Jer 31:31–34; Mic 4:1–8; 6:6–8

DAY 9

Bearing fruit can be risky

> *All spoke well of him and were amazed at the gracious words that came from his mouth. They said, "Is not this Joseph's son?" He said to them, "Doubtless you will quote me on this proverb, 'Doctor, cure yourself.' And you will say, 'Do here also in your home town the things that we have heard you did in Capernaum.'" And he said, "Truly I tell you, no prophet is accepted in the prophet's hometown. But the truth is, there were many widows in Israel in the time of Elijah, when the heaven was shut up three years and six months, and there was a severe famine over all the land; yet Elijah was sent to none of them except to a widow at Zarephath in Sidon. There were also many lepers in Israel in the time of the prophet Elisha, and none of them were cleansed except Naaman the Syrian." When they heard this, all in the synagogue were filled with rage. They got up, drove him out of the town, and led him to the brow of the hill on which their town was built, so that they might hurl him off the cliff. But he passed through the midst of them and went on his way.* (Luke 4:22–30)

As we have seen, most scholars agree that the first part of Luke's unique account of Jesus reading from Isaiah's vision in the synagogue in Nazareth was scripted by the evangelist. It seems clear that Luke's motive is to show that Jesus was conscious of the congruity between Isaiah's hope for Israel during the birth of his ministry when, in fact, it may have come later in his ministry. Nonetheless, it represents an authentic parallel that Jesus may have shared with his disciples.

But the latter part of Luke's narrative describing the shift from astonishment of those present to rejection of Jesus' preaching is also reported in the Gospels of Matthew and Mark (with Jesus' references to Elijah and Elisha omitted). It seems clear that Jesus did visit the synagogue in Nazareth, taught in that synagogue, that his message caused anger, and that he had to leave his hometown. But why did his visit end with conflict and rejection (in Luke with an attempt to kill him)? Luke gives an explanation by including Jesus' statement that both Elijah and Elisha cured persons who were not Israelites because there was so little faith in Israel. Jesus realized that even though people in his hometown had immense needs and were oppressed, they were still reluctant to embrace change that might bring freedom and justice, especially at the hands of a "local boy." His challenge was interpreted as judgment and their ability to listen was clouded by anger.

We have seen that Jesus' knowledge and earnest reflection on sacred Hebrew Scriptures, especially the Torah and the Prophets, flowed from childhood and adult corporate prayer, coupled with his periods of personal intimacy with God. There is no doubt that the fruit of this listening to God's voice in Scripture and prayer influenced his teaching and ministry. At the same time he accepted the risk that his words and actions would be filled with tension and resistance, even danger. The "answer" to his prayer-filled discernment was not clear sailing. Yet, in the midst of danger *he passed through the midst of them and went on his way.* His prayer led to a difficult situation. It brought courage because he knew the "works" were not his own.

What invitations and challenges have you discerned listening to Scriptures and in your prayer?

When have you experienced tension or conflict in expressing your ideas or your actions?

Biblical texts for study and reflection:

Isa 61:1–4; Matt 4:12–17; Mark 6:1–6

DAY 10

The Hebrew Scriptures provide soil for the seeds of prayer

> *Give ear, O my people, to my teaching; incline your ears to the words of my mouth. I will open my mouth in a parable; I will utter dark sayings from of old, things that we have heard and known, that our ancestors have told us. We will not hide them from their children; we will tell to the coming generation the glorious deeds of the Lord, and of his might, and the wonders that he has done. (Ps 78:1–4)*

> *Praise is due to you, O God, in Zion; and to you shall vows be performed, O you who answer prayer! . . . You visit the earth and water it, you greatly enrich it; the river of God is full of water; you provide the people with grain, for so you have prepared it. You water its furrows abundantly, setting its ridges, softening it with showers, and blessing its growth. You crown the year with your bounty; your wagon tracks overflow with richness. The pastures of the wilderness overflow, the hills gird themselves with joy, the meadows clothe themselves with flocks, the valleys deck themselves with grain, they shout and sing together for joy. (Ps 65:1; 9–13)*

Every Jewish child grew up hearing the Hebrew Scriptures from the mouths of their parents in the home, at synagogue, and for some, at the village Torah School associated with the synagogue. When Mary and Joseph returned from the rite of presenting Jesus in the temple at Jerusalem, Luke comments that they returned to Nazareth where *"The child grew and became strong, filled with wisdom; and the favor of God was upon him"* (Luke 2:40). The Gospels do not give details about Jesus' early growth in wisdom nor do they show specific ways in which there was divine influence on his heart (the Greek word translated *favor* is *"charis,"* often meaning "grace" or interior divine influence). There can be little doubt that Jesus' wisdom and divine influence were steadily and gradually nurtured by his own Hebrew Scriptures, including the wisdom literature.[5] The book of Ecclesiasticus

---

5. Biblical books that form a wisdom tradition and are generally accepted by Jews and Christians are the books of Proverbs, Job, and Ecclesiastes. Roman Catholics add Ecclesiasticus and the Wisdom of Solomon.

personifies God's Wisdom, and she declares that *"Before the ages, in the beginning, he created me, and for all the ages I shall not cease to be. In the holy tent I ministered before him, and so I was established in Zion. Thus, in the beloved city he gave me a resting place, and in Jerusalem was my domain. I took root in an honored people, in the portion of the Lord, his heritage"* (Sir 24:11–12). It is no surprise then, when Mary and Joseph took Jesus to Jerusalem for the Passover celebration, that he stayed behind in the temple *"sitting among the teachers, listening to them, and asking them questions"* (Luke 2:46b). As an Israelite from the Galilean community, he and his parents, having been certified as ritually clean by the Levites at the gate, could enter the Court of Israel. Within the porticoes of the court rabbis taught the people. At twelve years old Jesus could easily have been swept up in the intensity of this teaching and the presence of so many rabbis. In the synagogue, possibly at local synagogue schools, at the temple, and in the presence of his family at home, Jesus demonstrated openness to God's presence in the wisdom of the Hebrew Scriptures. These experiences would influence his relationship to God, his prayer, and would energize his adult ministry.

As Jesus matured he learned through experience that wisdom is neither earned nor limited to an elite group of persons who have leisure or money to attend rabbinic schools in Jerusalem. In his culture wisdom was not abstract. Wisdom, rather, is manifested in behavior that is congruent with what God desires for human life. It becomes tangible through everyday experiences in home and village life.

How does God enter into your prayer through the Bible? What do you experience?

Biblical texts for study and reflection:

Ps 78:1–8; 119:1–16; Luke 2:41–52; 19:47–48; 20:1–8
1 Cor 1:18–25; 2:6–16; Col 2:1–7

DAY 11

Liturgy mentors young people in prayer

> *Now every year his parents went to Jerusalem for the festival of the Passover. And when he was twelve years old, they went up as usual for the festival.* (Luke 2:41–42)

People in rural Galilean villages like Nazareth did not have much time for life in the big cities, especially Jerusalem. They had little contact with the Pharisees, scribes, Sadducees, and temple priests, and their interpretations of the Torah and demands on first-century Jews. Jesus' kin and townsfolk were rural and were relatively conservative in their religious life; their focus was on working long days, paying taxes to Rome and Herod Antipas, and the temple taxes in Jerusalem. Their ancestors had been influenced by several foreign cultures. It was difficult to maintain their faith in God and remain committed to their unique Hebrew religious traditions. Yet they survived, but not without the suspicions of Jewish leaders in Jerusalem. "Can anything good come from Nazareth?" was a phrase used by persons critical of Jesus' teaching and activities.

Galileans remained faithful Jews by retaining personal and familial prayer as well as their local synagogue worship. But they never lost their link to Jerusalem and its temple. *"Now every year his parents went to Jerusalem for the festival of the Passover."* It was a two-to-three day trip, and sometimes dangerous because of robbers. Families traveled together. Passover was a high feast, a gathering to remember their ancestors' exodus from Egypt and God's covenant that gave them identity as a faith community. It was a time of celebration and renewal of friendships. Like all young people from the villages, Jesus must have been caught up in the excitement of recitation of psalms as they approached the holy city. Children had integral parts in both the family and temple Pesah (Passover) liturgy. Families that could not afford to sacrifice their own lamb joined with others to share a lamb. Adults and children would be admitted to the Court of the Israelites and then to area of the Altar of Sacrifice. Levites would be chanting Psalms 113–18 on the steps leading to the altar. They invited children to chant with them so that the high notes would blend with older male voices and the sound of flutes, lyres, and cymbals. Each family or group would slaughter their lamb, give its blood to the priests to be burned at the altar, and return to the place they were staying to roast the lamb and celebrate a family liturgy of Pesah. Rural people could not always get to Jerusalem for the feasts of the New Year (Rosh hashana) in September and then the Day of Atonement (Yom kippur). But they probably celebrated the Feast of the Booths (Sukkoth) at harvest time, when families lived in booths set up in the fields and vineyards and recalled their ancestors' life in the Sinai desert after they escaped from Egypt.

John's Gospel describes Jesus' brothers going up to Jerusalem for the Feast of Booths. Jesus followed later and taught in the temple precincts. From childhood through his adult life Jesus was surrounded by all these festivals, their teaching, and their worship. They mentored him and established a pattern that he maintained until his death. His participation in the festivals in Jerusalem were occasions for some of his most important teaching, and the Passover provided the environment that surrounded events that led to his crucifixion. The liturgies of his faith community were a fundamental part of his life of prayer.

How do your faith community's liturgies form you and complement your personal prayer?

BIBLICAL TEXTS FOR STUDY AND REFLECTION:

John 7:1–52; Luke 2:41–52; 22:1–30; Matt 26:17–30

Desert Day One

Jesus' early personal and spiritual formation

Desert Days are opportunities to *listen,* rather than study. If you take time to listen to God's presence in Holy Scripture, you will be able to recognize that same voice in other aspects of your life.

Desert Days offer conversations rather than a quest for more knowledge. You are invited to go beyond the words of biblical and academic texts toward an inner dialogue, where the Word will enable you to see more clearly. You will experience more than words and discover hidden meanings, because too much emphasis on words and the meaning of words often takes the mind away from the voice of the Spirit.

Saint Benedict, in his Rule for monks, advises them to listen "with the ear of the heart." The result will be delight in the freedom to hear the Spirit speak without your conscious thought determining what the message should be. Rather than searching for meaning you will be able to listen to the meaning *given to you*.

Today is a Sabbath. Rest your mind from reading, studying, and thinking. Being silent and less active will help you listen to the four canonical Gospels in a unique way. When your mind and your heart are integrated you will begin to *experience* Jesus' life of prayer, rather than study about it.

Today let your intellectual discipline be embraced and mentored by contemplative reflection on Jesus' early personal and spiritual formation. Using what you have learned thus far, try to enter into his early life and let it speak to you.

Begin each Desert Day with twenty minutes of silent contemplative prayer. A simple method is described in Appendix E. Find a place that is as quiet as possible. You may prefer to walk to a quiet place and combine a silent walk with sitting once you have arrived.

You may not be able to make Desert Day a full day. But do your best to make it an intentional part of your day. Set aside at least two hours, if possible. During that time let the four Gospels speak to you, rather than deciding what you want to learn from them. A simple prayer may help you, such as "Spirit, reveal what's true. . . . Spirit I bless you." Or "Come, Holy, Holy. . . . Come, Holy Spirit." Try to let go of the outcome of this day.

Toward the end of this day recall what you have heard, learned, and experienced. Ask this question: "What have you to do with me, Jesus of Nazareth?" At the end of the day record your reflections in a journal.

The following questions may help may help your reflection on Jesus' early personal and spiritual formation:

How was Jesus' early life of prayer formed?

What are the implications of Jesus' early spiritual formation for your life of prayer?

What can we learn from Jesus' early life of prayer that will guide the spiritual formation of young persons in our modern faith communities, as well as adults who are embracing Christian living for the first time?

DAY 12

Making room for God

In the morning, while it was still very dark, he got up
and went out to a deserted place, and there he prayed. (Mark 1:35)

As we have seen, there is little doubt that every day in Jesus' home in Nazareth began with recitation of the Shema. *"Hear, O Israel: the LORD is our*
God, the LORD, alone. You shall love the LORD your God with all your heart,
and with all your soul, and with all your might. Keep these words that I am
commanding you today in your heart." This was followed by the eighteen
blessings of God in the *Tephilla*. There were prayers at mid-afternoon and
in the evening before bedtime.

The pattern of beginning the day by making room for God's presence
remained a pattern in Jesus' adult life. Mark does not give the details of
Jesus' early morning prayer. But it was quiet and in a *"deserted place."* Luke
says that *"At daybreak he departed and went into a deserted place"* (Luke
4:42). As a boy Jesus may have played with friends and cousins in the caves
around Nazareth, especially the Qafzeh Cave. There is a cave in the area of
the Mount of Beatitudes where Jesus may have prayed before choosing his
twelve closest disciples and a series of caves on Mount Arbela near Magdala and Ginnosar (Genessaret), where he may have sought solitude. Jesus'
days during his adult life and ministry were filled with preaching, teaching,
healing, controversy, feasts, visits to homes, associating with both religious
leaders and the marginalized, and public worship. Yet his days began in
the quiet presence of God. It was a time for quiet listening and awareness
of God's desires and love. This set the context for the gift and challenge of
each new day.

After hearing about the death of John the Baptist, Matthew narrates,
"Now when Jesus heard this, he withdrew from there in a boat to a deserted
place by himself. But when the crowds heard it, they followed him on foot
from the towns" (Matt 14:13). In the midst of a busy day, after hearing troubling news, Jesus knew his need for personal time with God. The rest of that
day was filled with a feeding of thousands who came to listen to him. After
the great feeding *"he made the disciples get into the boat and go on ahead*
to the other side, while he dismissed the crowds. And after he had dismissed

the crowds, he went up the mountain by himself to pray" (Matt 14:22–23). He prayed there alone for the rest of the afternoon and after joining the disciples in their boat landed at Genessaret on the east side of the sea near the caves of Arbela. *"After the people of that place recognized him, they sent word throughout the region and brought all who were sick to him, and begged him that they might touch even the fringe of his cloak; and all who touched it were healed"* (Matt 14:34–36). Quite a day! Yet he found time for prayer.

How do you begin each day?

In what ways do you make room for God during the day and evening?

Biblical texts for study and reflection:

Mark 1:35–38; 3:13; Matt 5:1; 14:13–36; Luke 4:42–43; 6:12–13; 9:29–30

DAY 13

Prayer and action go hand in hand

As we saw yesterday, when Herod Antipas had John the Baptist executed, some followers of Jesus looked for him and told him what had happened.

> *Now when Jesus heard this, he withdrew from there* [the area east of Nazareth, near the Sea of Galilee] *in a boat to a deserted place by himself. But when the crowds heard it, they followed him on foot from the towns. When he went ashore, he saw a great crowd; and he had compassion for them and cured their sick. When it was evening, the disciples came to him and said, "This is a deserted place, and the hour is now late; send the crowds away so that they may go into the villages and buy food for themselves." Jesus said to them "They need not go away; you give them something to eat." They replied, "We have nothing here but five loaves and two fish." And he said, "Bring them here to me." Then he ordered the crowds to sit down on the grass. Taking the five loaves and the two fish, he looked up to heaven, and blessed and broke the loaves, and gave them to the disciples, and the disciples gave them to the crowds. And all ate and were filled; and they took up what was left over of the broken pieces, twelve baskets full. And those who ate were about five thousand men, besides women and children. Immediately he made the disciples get into the boat and go on ahead to the other side, while he dismissed the crowds. And after he had dismissed the crowds, he went up the mountain by himself to pray.* (Matt 14:13–22)

Jesus received some really troubling news. It wasn't just that his cousin had been murdered. John's ministry had a profound effect on Jesus. John's message outlined vividly how far Israel had strayed from their commitment to God and the destiny given to Abraham. He gave people a unique opportunity to "repent," to begin a new life with God. And to emphasize his message he submerged people in the Jordan River near the place where Joshua led the Israelites from the wilderness to their new life in Canaan. He talked about the need for a "baptism of fire" and a person who will baptize with the Holy Spirit. After John had immersed Jesus in the Jordan, Jesus experienced a palpable awareness of his intimate relationship with God and went directly into a wilderness area to discern what that experience could mean. He felt sure that his passion would be to awaken people to the presence of the realm of God in their midst. Now John was dead. Where did that leave Jesus? How would he continue to pursue what he was now so passionate about?

The first step was very natural for him. He went to a quiet place to listen to God. But people followed him and when he saw them *"he had compassion for them and cured their sick."* Later in the day he made sure they had enough to eat. Jesus' time of prayer resulted in compassionate engagement with the health and hunger of people around him. That was the consequence of his listening to God! That would be his "next step": to be with people who needed tangible evidence of God's love and power in their lives. Jesus' prayer *"in a deserted place"* was not disconnected from his actions. It was not a separate sector of life. And then, after the healings and the feeding of thousands, Jesus returned immediately to quiet listening. Perhaps he was thinking, "Now what was that all about?" or "Is this what baptizing with the Holy Spirit means?" or "Show me what you want next; it's in your hands."

Describe several times in your life when your words or actions flowed from your prayer.

BIBLICAL TEXTS FOR STUDY AND REFLECTION:

Matt 14:1–36; Luke 4:42–44; 6:12–21; 11:1–4

DAY 14

Moments of ecstasy

> *Now when all the people were baptized, and when Jesus had also been baptized and was praying, the heaven was opened, and the Holy Spirit descended upon him in bodily form like a dove. And a voice came from heaven, "You are my Son, the Beloved; with you I am well pleased."* (Luke 3:21–22)

Ecstatic experience takes us beyond where we are at a given moment. It removes us from the status quo. Ecstasy is real, but it is not something we create or conjure—try as we may! Jesus agreed with John that God was doing something new and exciting in the midst of the people of Israel. John's unique form of "washing" in the Jordan River was an opportunity to turn to a new way of living. A new opportunity was being offered to be faithful to the covenant Israel had made with God so long ago. Jesus agreed and was immersed in the Jordan because he too wanted to be part of this renewed presence of God in the life of his people. He wanted to affirm the "turning toward God" (repentance) that John was offering people who came to him. John realized that he was not the center of this new expression of God's presence. There was someone else coming. What did this mean? Who was it? What would this person do?

Luke records that Jesus *"was praying"* as he came out of the water. His heart and mind were turned toward God in the midst of this experience. And then *"the heaven was opened . . . ."* In Jesus' culture, this is an image indicating that the boundary between heaven and earth, between God and human beings, evaporated in that moment of prayer. The appearance of the Spirit in the form of a dove would have been understood as a sign of intimacy. The voice from heaven confirms this: *"You are my Son, the Beloved; with you I am well pleased."* Jesus becomes aware in this outside-of-himself experience that his relationship with God is identical to the unique relationship of a father to a son.[6] And God not only loves Jesus, God delights in him! What did all this mean to Jesus? It is clear that he was not sure. The consequence of his ecstatic experience of prayer during

---

6. For some insights regarding the father/son relationship in Jesus' religious and social culture see Appendix B.

his baptism is record by Matthew. *"Then Jesus was led up by the Spirit into the wilderness to be tempted by the devil"* (Matt 4:1). Jesus needed time to discern the meaning of his experience in the Jordan. This was one of many opportunities in his life of prayer for faithful discernment. It was not easy, but it was necessary.

There will be other ecstatic experiences in Jesus' life of prayer and he will learn that they are not ends in themselves. They are not meant to take him "away" from life. In fact, they bring him closer to his own people and to God's presence in his life. His experience in the Jordan gave him a vivid awareness of the intimate relationship he had with God. This was important, not only for him, but for people around him.

The next three days' reflections will focus on the "practical" results of Jesus' experience in the waters of the Jordan River. He will be tested. Jesus' culture believed in a myriad of spirits that had a direct influence on human lives. In the desert, the dwelling place of malign spirits, Jesus will learn whether or not his relationship with God will benefit other people or only himself. How does a son of God use power? The chief of the spirits, Satan, will be waiting. This, too, is the reality and risk of prayer.

Describe your experiences of God's unique or unusual presence in prayer? What did you learn?

BIBLICAL TEXTS FOR STUDY AND REFLECTION:

Matt 3:13–17; 4:1–11; Mark 9:2–8; Luke 10:21–24

DAY 15

A deeper hunger

> *Then Jesus was led up by the Spirit into the wilderness to be tempted by the devil. He fasted forty days and forty nights, and afterwards he was famished. The tempter came and said to him, "If you are the Son of God, command these stones to become loaves of bread." But he answered, "It is written, 'One does not live by bread alone, but by every word that comes from the mouth of God.'"* (Matt 4:1–4)

Jesus was *"in prayer"* at his baptism when the boundary between heaven and earth became transparent. He heard a voice declare that he was God's Son and now he was being led to the desert to be tested and discern what that meant and how this intimate relationship with God could become tangible in his life. In the Hebrew Scriptures, a "temptation" means a trial or opportunity to prove one's self, rather than a seduction to wrong doing.

Jesus' prayer in the water of the Jordan led to a time apart in the dry and infertile wilderness. It began with a long period of fasting. In Jesus' culture fasting was an act of self-humiliation called *"taanit"* (*"When I humbled my soul with fasting . . ."* Ps 69:10). It was a form of prayerfully approaching God for God's assistance. This is a clear indication that Jesus realized he needed God's help. His prayer of fasting in the desert seems to have been a direct consequence of his prayer during his baptism. He needed help to discern what *"You are my Son"* meant and how that relationship would affect his life. Perhaps he had the words of Ps 70:1 in mind: *"Be pleased, O God to deliver me; O Lord make haste to help me!"*

Jesus reached a point in his fast when *"he was famished."* It seems clear that in his hunger he remembered how God had provided manna in the desert for his ancestors during the time of Moses. Then a demonic thought occurred to Jesus. A demonic thought is one that scatters or disrupts the focus of a person's mind and heart. Why not ask God to do the same for God's Son? With this power he could feed himself and later feed others who are hungry, too. Perhaps images of people in Nazareth and the neighboring villages came to him. After they paid taxes in kind they had so little food left over from their own crops. What's wrong with using God's power to feed them? Feeding the hungry might align people in need to Jesus. They would listen to him. He could change their lives. This demonic thought appeared very convenient. But then it seems Jesus remembered that even though God fed his ancestors manna in the desert, they were only satisfied for a while and did not remain faithful to God. Feeding the hungry might create a following for God's Son, yet fail to feed an additional and deeper need.

Words from Deuteronomy 8:3 helped Jesus decide what he must do. *"He humbled you by letting you hunger, then by feeding you with manna, with which neither you nor your ancestors were acquainted, in order to make you understand that one does not live by bread alone, but by every word that comes from the mouth of the Lord."* Jesus became aware that the power of God flowing into his life was not his and must be used according to God's desires, not his own. Jesus' prayer in the wilderness was forming him, but it was not easy.

God delights in and empowers every person. What has God entrusted to you?

Biblical texts for study and reflection:

Deut 8:1–10; Luke 4:1–13; John 26:36–46; Mark 14:32–42

DAY 16

Prayer is not putting God on the spot

> *Then the devil took him to the holy city and placed him on the pin-*
> *nacle of the temple, saying to him, "If you are the Son of God, throw*
> *yourself down, for it is written, 'He will command his angels con-*
> *cerning you,' and 'On their hands they will bear you up, so that you*
> *will not dash your foot against a stone.'" Jesus said to him, "Again it*
> *is written, 'Do not put the Lord your God to the test.'"* (Matt 4:5–7)

In the Hebrew Scriptures there are two types of "satan." The first is por-
trayed as a colleague of God. In the book of Job this satan questions God
about the integrity of Job's righteousness, not to thwart Job's relationship
with God, but to discern whether it is authentic or not. The second "satan"
is a diabolical figure who tries to scatter a person's desire to be faithful to
God. This satan excels in crafty thinking and demands the center of attention and total loyalty. The second satan can easily be understood as a
person's desire to be in control of her or his life. This *"tempter's"* activity
demands a decision and seems to be the "satan" Jesus encounters in the
wilderness.

In his first temptation Jesus refused to use God's power to satisfy his
hunger. As a prelude to the second temptation the devil repeats, *"If you are*
the Son of God . . . ." It seems clear that Jesus has accepted the declaration of
an intimate relationship that God revealed at his baptism and is struggling
to discern what this identity means. The devil *"took"* Jesus to the temple in
Jerusalem, the center of his people's religious life and the place where God
dwells in a unique way. The temple's pinnacle is the highest point in the wall
that supports the entire temple complex. It is the place where a trumpet was
sounded each day to call people in Jerusalem to prayer.

"Throw yourself down . . . . He will command his angels concerning you
. . . ." This is a struggle, a test, between self-will and letting go of control. In
the midst of his unique relationship with God, Jesus is confronted with the
possibility of claiming God's power as his own. Is he free to summon God's
power and protection at will? The tempter wants Jesus to "turn the tables"
and put *God,* rather than Jesus, "to the test." Will God perform at Jesus'
call? Will Jesus be the one in charge, using God's faithfulness and power

to implement his agenda? Or does a son of God wait for opportunities for God's wisdom and power to flow through his life? Does a son honor the desires of a father?

Once again Jesus remembers what he has learned from his own Scriptures: *"Do not put the Lord your God to the test"* (Deut 6:16). Jesus' prayer in the wilderness demonstrates the importance of self-knowledge that will uncover motives that lead us away from God's desires. When these motives are revealed we have the opportunity to reject what they suggest and remain centered on God's desires. Prayer requires honesty and genuine submission to God.

In what ways are you open to what God desires? Do you reflect on the Bible to assist you?

How do you overcome the desire to be in control of your life and your life with God?

In 1 John 5:11–12 the author proclaims that *"God gave us eternal life, and this life is in his Son."* In Rom 8:15b–17 St. Paul declares *"When we cry 'Abba, Father!' It is that very Spirit bearing witness with our spirit that we are children of God . . . ."* What can it mean to be a child of God, a son or daughter?

BIBLICAL TEXTS FOR STUDY AND REFLECTION:

Matt 4:1–11; John 12:20–26; Deut 6:16–19; Ps 119:1–16

DAY 17

Recognizing and choosing what is fundamental

Again the devil took him to a very high mountain and showed him all the kingdoms of the world and their splendor; and he said to him, "All these I will give you, if you will fall down and worship me." Jesus said to him, "Away with you, Satan! For it is written, 'Worship the Lord your God, and serve only him.'" Then the devil left him, and suddenly angels came and waited on him. (Matt 4:8–11)

Matthew's narrative suggests that Jesus is deep in prayer. It is possible that during prayer his mind was still occupied with discerning what it means to be God's son. Perhaps he was recalling that in his Hebrew Scriptures the people of Israel were collectively called God's son, along with the kings of Israel and Judah. How should he relate to the rest of the world? Will he be "in charge" of a rich and vast empire, like the Roman Emperor, who is also called "son of god"? Perhaps in his mind he had visions of places like Sepphoris in Galilee and the splendor of the holy city of Jerusalem and the temple precincts that he had visited in his youth and as a young adult.

This last desert temptation demanded a fundamental choice. Kingdoms and their splendor are exciting and filled with opportunities for achievement. But what is most fundamental in life? Jesus was rooted in the Torah and the answer already lay in his heart, if he was willing to listen. *"Worship the Lord your God, and serve only him."* Jesus decided to put "worship" into action and his choice to serve God is revealed clearly in his behavior immediately after leaving the wilderness. Matthew reports that Jesus returned to Galilee, left his home in Nazareth, and made a new home in Capernaum. Then Matthew cites the prophet Isaiah to describe how Jesus will serve God: *"Land of Zebulun, land of Naphtali, on the road by the sea, across the Jordan, Galilee of the Gentiles—the people who sat in darkness have seen a great light, and for those who sat in the shadow of death light has dawned"* (Isa 9:1–2). And then Matthew describes the beginning of Jesus' ministry. *"From that time Jesus began to proclaim, 'Repent, for the kingdom of heaven has come near'"* (Matt 4:17).

Jesus' experience of prayer in the wilderness helped him recognize that power over the kingdoms of the world, even at its best, is not an end in itself. In order to be a source of life, power must be linked to what is fundamental in life. Power exists to make the desires of God tangible through justice and righteousness. Jesus, as a Son, accepts the reality that the power is not his. Jesus' passion will be to let God's power flow through him. He will begin at home, in the villages of Galilee, among people who are burdened and have little hope for their future. He will tell people that the reign of God starts like a tiny mustard seed. The discernment and decisions in the wilderness were hard and Jesus had to let go of himself in order to discover himself as God's servant. His physical and psychic energy must have been depleted, but in the midst of all the temptations and trial *"angels came and waited on him."* They were there all the time. He was never alone. More than anything else, Jesus' time in the wilderness displays his genuine humility. He let go of self-reliance, and relied on God to reveal and empower his life.

How does God's power flow through your life?

How do you manifest the reign of God each day?

BIBLICAL TEXTS FOR STUDY AND REFLECTION:

Matt 4:1–11; Isa 61:1–11; 55:1–13; Luke 4:16–19

DAY 18

Action rooted in worship

Reflections for days six through eight described how, according to Matthew, Mark, and Luke, Jesus went immediately from his trials in the wilderness to Galilee, including his home town of Nazareth. (John's chronology of Jesus' early ministry is different. He describes Jesus spending time with John the Baptist at the Jordan where John refers to Jesus' baptism and the descent of the Spirit on him. Then he describes Jesus calling disciples and returning to Galilee for his first miracle at Cana, followed by a visit to Capernaum. From there Jesus travels to Jerusalem for the Passover Feast, where he drives merchants and money changers from the temple, claiming it is a place of prayer, not a marketplace.)

The prayer and discernment in the desert empowered the beginning of Jesus' ministry. He proclaimed that his words and actions were a fulfillment of Isaiah's ancient vision of people being set free from a variety of burdens. He was rejected at Nazareth, but continued on to other towns and villages in Galilee. His message was simple. God was entering the lives of people to restore their dignity and express love for them through Jesus' words and actions. God's reign of justice and righteousness would become directly manifest in people's lives. When John the Baptist sent two disciples to ask Jesus, *"Are you the one who is to come . . . ,"* Jesus replied, *"Go and tell John what you have seen and heard: the blind receive their sight, the lame walk, the lepers are cleansed, the deaf hear, the dead are raised, and the poor have good news brought to them"* (Matt 11:2–5). This really was "good news" for people whose hope and way of life was being crushed by oppressive rulers and the wealthy who held them in low esteem. In Jesus' culture, shame was debilitating and to be avoided at all costs. It is not a coincidence that the first locus of Jesus' teaching and healing is the synagogues of Galilee. Jesus is not a "loner," abandoning his faith community. In fact, Jesus saw the manifestation of God's power in his ministry as a restoration of the integrity of his religious heritage.

"He went down to Capernaum, a city in Galilee, and was teaching them on the Sabbath. They were astounded at his teaching, because he spoke with authority" (Luke 4:31–32). During that Sabbath worship, Jesus healed a man possessed by demons. That evening people brought the sick to Jesus

"and he laid his hands on each of them and cured them." Then, according to Luke, *"At daybreak he departed and went to a deserted place. And the crowds were looking for him; and when they reached him, they wanted to prevent him from leaving them. But he said to them, 'I must proclaim the good news of the kingdom of God to the other cities also; for I was sent for this purpose'"* (Luke 4:42–43). And then, according to Matthew, *"Jesus went throughout Galilee, teaching in their synagogues and proclaiming the good news of the kingdom and curing every disease and every sickness among the people"* (Matt 4:23). All this activity was rooted in Jesus' worship in synagogues and his time alone in prayer. Both corporate prayer with his faith community and his personal prayer nourished and empowered his ministry. His words and actions were an embodiment of his prayer.

Describe words and actions in your life that have their roots in your life of prayer.

BIBLICAL TEXTS FOR STUDY AND REFLECTION:

Matt 11:1–19; Luke 4:14–44; John 1:19–51; 2:1–25

DAY 19

A touching prayer

As soon as they left the synagogue, they entered the house of Simon and Andrew, with James and John. Now Simon's mother-in-law was in bed with a fever, and they told him about her at once. He came and took her by the hand and lifted her up. Then the fever left her, and she began to serve them. (Mark 1:29–31)

Four men left the synagogue in Capernaum with Jesus. They were fishermen. Earlier Jesus had invited them to share in his work as disciples. Just as they knew how to gather fish into nets, Jesus invited them to gather people to participate in the reign of God now breaking forth in Jesus' ministry. Now they joined him for worship in their hometown synagogue in Capernaum. After worship they went to the home of Simon and Andrew. Remnants of that home have been documented recently by archaeologists and biblical scholars. Once inside they tell Jesus that Simon's mother-in-law is sick with a fever. The evangelists Matthew and Mark tell us that Jesus *"touched her hand"* (Matthew) and *"took her by the hand and lifted her up."* Luke says that Jesus *"stood over her and rebuked the fever."* It is clear that by touch, speech, and physical movement she is healed. In Jesus' culture disease was not only a physical dysfunction. A disease could impair a person's ability to fulfill their expected role in society. Simon's mother-in-law, as a woman, was expected to care for the home and provide meals and hospitality. Her fever marginalized her in her own family. Jesus' not only "rebukes" the fever, he restores her place in the family. He literally and figuratively "lifted her up." Jesus' physical contact with a woman was the expression of his unvoiced prayer.

   Here are three manifestations of Jesus' prayer. He does not invoke God's power by name. He touches, and God's energy flows through his desire for the health of Simon's mother-in-law. The Gospel of Mark emphasizes the presence of God's energy in the life and ministry of Jesus. He demonstrates the authenticity of God's presence in Jesus by narrating how often Jesus overcomes the presence of malign "spirits" through his words and actions. Jesus touches people often and many times he touches persons who, according the religious leaders of his day, should be avoided because they are "unclean" and will contaminate anyone who touches them. But Jesus realizes that "holiness" means being compassionate to persons in need, rather than isolating or marginalizing them.

In Jesus' relationships it is clear that prayer, regardless of its intent or form, is a flow of energy. Luke narrates an incident where a woman had suffered from hemorrhages for twelve years. In her mind all she needed was to touch the fringe of Jesus' garment. She touched and was healed. Jesus commented to his disciples, *"Someone touched me; for I noticed that power had gone out of me"* (Luke 8:46). Prayer is rarely about words. When words are involved in prayer they embody genuine desire and compassion that have their origin in intimacy with God. Prayer is the flow of energy between God and human beings.

Describe moments in your life when touch restored your physical or emotional vitality.

When has your touch renewed another person's life?

BIBLICAL TEXTS FOR STUDY AND REFLECTION:

Mark 1:29–34, 40–45; 6:53–56; 7:31–37; 8:22–26; Luke 8:40–56

DAY 20

Prayerful discernment

The four evangelists offer differing details and chronology for Jesus' early ministry in Galilee. They all agree that as word of Jesus' teaching and healing spread, people from the area surrounding Galilee were drawn in to the presence and activity of God in him. He spoke and acted with an authority that was palpable. Luke comments, *"Amazement seized all of them, and they glorified God and were full of awe saying, 'We have seen strange things today'"* (Luke 5:26). Yet, not all were amazed. Some of the Pharisees and teachers of the law (from Jerusalem) took Jesus to task for healing and allowing his disciples to gather grain on the Sabbath, to say nothing about his declaring that a person's sins had been forgiven or that he and his disciples did not need to fast before eating and drinking. Jesus' understanding of the reign of God was becoming controversial. At the same time, his diverse activities were growing and Jesus, like other Jewish rabbis, sages, and teachers in the first century, realized the need to share his wisdom and work with a core of disciples who would follow him constantly and eventually be sent out to share his mission.

> *Now during those days he went out to the mountain to pray; and he spent the night in prayer to God. And when day came, he called his disciples and chose twelve of them, whom he also named apostles: Simon, whom he named Peter, and his brother Andrew, and James, and John, and Philip, and Bartholomew, and Matthew, and Thomas, and James son of Alphaeus, and Simon, who was called the Zealot, and Judas son of James, and Judas Iscariot, who became a traitor.* (Luke 6:12–16)

During *"those days"* of so much activity, receptivity as well as criticism, and teaching in synagogues and in public Jesus obviously sought guidance from God about the direction this movement was taking and how he would describe it to people. During Jesus' temptations in the wilderness he learned that God's kingdom was rushing into people's lives through him. At the same time he knew that the kingdom and the power to make it tangible were from God, not him. And now he sensed the work was moving beyond him. As always, he looked for guidance, and *"he spent the night in prayer to*

God." Two things seemed to have happened within him during that night. He discerned that twelve of his disciples would share more directly in the task God had given him. And he became clearer about the "marks" or patterns of the reign of God. These would be articulated through his preaching on the mountain just after he chose the twelve apostles. (We will look at the Beatitudes in tomorrow's reflection.)

All four canonical Gospels narrate a pattern in Jesus' relationship with the core of disciples he chose. This pattern reflects essential elements common to most Jewish teachers at that time. The primary purpose of the teacher-disciple relationship is to experience the consciousness of the teacher, not simply to learn information. As the Gospels show, Jesus planned for this core to be with him a long time, become close to him, and share his relationship with God. As we shall see, Jesus wanted to transmit his experience of God to them and share the ways God was at work in his life. Jesus' decision about the composition and purpose of this core group was rooted in quiet listening and faithful discernment. Jesus' experience of God in prayer flowed into his decisions about implementing the reality of the realm of God among his people.

When has your prayer and intimacy with God influenced your decisions and actions?

An influential twentieth-century spiritual writer and teacher, Henri Nouwen, taught that all ministry proceeds from intimacy with God. Do you agree? If so, why is this true?

Biblical texts for study and reflection:

Rom 12:1–2; Phil 2:1–13; 2 Tim 1:14

DAY 21

Learning about God and God's desires

What did Jesus learn about God in prayer? What did he sense were God's desires for human beings? Although some scholars have concluded that the Sermon on the Mount is a collection of Jesus' wisdom sayings made at different times throughout his ministry, others are convinced that the Beatitudes represent an authentic teaching incident as recorded in Luke and Matthew. In either case, these wisdom sayings tell us what Jesus learned from God in his quiet listening in prayer.

In Luke's Gospel the context for Jesus' teaching on the mountain is essential for discerning how his experiences in prayer became tangible in his teaching and behavior. *"Now during those days he went out to the mountain to pray; and he spent the night in prayer to God"* (6:12). Jesus chose an isolated place and he had been up all night praying. *"And when day came, he called his disciples and chose twelve of them, whom he also named apostles"* (6:13–16). He calls his disciples and appoints twelve to become the inner core of his followers. (The word "apostle" is a name attached to this group by Luke and means "one who is sent." But this is a later understanding of the purpose of the group Jesus chose. The "disciples" who were following Jesus from place to place were a variety of men and women, some of whom he had specifically called, like Matthew, but most were people who were attracted by his teaching, healing, and charisma. Jesus chose twelve from among this larger group to share his mission in a more intimate way. But they were still called disciples.)

Jesus and his disciples come down to a level place and are met by *"a great crowd"* that had come *"to hear him and to be healed of their diseases"* (6:17–18). Everyone was trying to touch Jesus *"for power came out from him and healed all of them"* (6:19). At this point Jesus looks up at his disciples and speaks. The content of his teaching is not ideological; it is directly related to the experiences in his baptism and temptations in the wilderness (6:20–36). It parallels the vision of Isaiah and the psalms that speak of God's justice and righteousness and God's desire for people to be released from captivity, blindness, poverty, and oppression. Jesus claims this vision as the foundation for his message of *"good news."* That "gospel" speaks of a renewed presence of God among the people. Jesus describes the nature of this reign of God to his disciples so that they will be clear about the mission they will share with him. He is very specific about God's desires for the people whose plight Jesus knows so well. This is where the work will begin. The *"kingdom of God"* (where God reigns) includes the poor, who have been marginalized and neglected (6:20). Those who are hungry *"will be filled"* (6:21). People whose frustrating lives have room only for tears *"will laugh"* (6:21). Jesus tells the disciples that this "renewed beginning" of God's original relationship with the assembly of Hebrews God called at Sinai will not be popular; the messengers of this *"good news"* will be marginalized and discredited by those in power, like the prophets before them (6:22–23). The "powers that be" should take note that justice will prevail (6:24–26). At the same time Jesus says, *"But I say to you that listen, Love your enemies, do good to those who hate you . . ."* (6:27). Jesus has listened to his Abba in prayer and now asks his disciples to listen to him. This *"good news"* describes God's desires for human life and the riches, risks, and change of consciousness it will take to make it a reality. Jesus is sharing what he has heard from his Abba. The "kingdom" begins within each person. In the intimacy of prayer and in the inner chamber of listening to God we learn what the reign of God can be like in daily life.

When you hear the word "gospel" today what does it mean to you?

How does Luke's account of Jesus' gospel about the reign of God compare with the meaning of "gospel" today?

BIBLICAL TEXT FOR STUDY AND REFLECTION:

Read and reflect on Luke's account of the calling of the twelve disciples and Jesus' description of life in the reign of God: Luke 6:12–36

DAY 22

Shepherds in the realm of God

We have seen how the Sermon on the Mount in Luke's Gospel describes Jesus' vision of life in the reign of God. It is a tangible kingdom, here on earth, where justice and righteousness in human relationships prevail. In the Gospel of Matthew Jesus takes his disciples aside and gives specific advice about leadership in God's kingdom. There seems little doubt that Jesus spent time reflecting on the messages of the great Hebrew prophets during his frequent periods of prayer and quiet away from the crowds and his disciples. Perhaps he had these words from Jeremiah on his mind when he began sharing what have become known as the "Beatitudes" or "Blessings."

> *Woe to the shepherds who destroy and scatter the sheep of my pasture! says the* LORD. *Therefore thus says the* LORD, *the God of Israel, concerning the shepherds who shepherd my people. It is you who have scattered my flock, and have driven them away, and you have not attended to them. . . . I will raise up shepherds over them who will shepherd them, and they shall not fear any longer, or be dismayed, nor shall any be missing, says the* LORD. *(Jer 23:1–2a; 4)*

In the Beatitudes Jesus outlines the characteristics of faithful shepherds in the realm of God. He begins each description with *"Blessed are . . . ."* In Hebrew culture a "blessing" is the sharing of power (the life force) from one soul to another. That blessing can make each soul prosper as it fulfills its purpose in the world God has made. The soul of each person will only experience peace (fulfill its purpose) when it is in harmony with all other souls who are committed to the same covenant. The power that makes this possible, the *"berakha"* (blessing), acts within the soul yet cannot be separated from its outward manifestation in the life of a person. One who is blessed will radiate the power of that blessing. Blessing, then, is the source of righteousness, justice, and peace. Happiness is living in the fruits of blessing. *"Tell the innocent how fortunate they are, for they shall eat the fruit of their labors"* (Isa 3:10).

It is with this deeply rooted Hebrew awareness of blessing that Jesus exhorts his disciples in Matthew 5:1–12 to be *"pure in spirit"* (humble), *meek* (not self-serving), to *"hunger and thirst for righteousness"* (work tirelessly for the common good), be *"merciful"* (have patience and solidarity with others), seek *"purity of heart"* (single-minded openness to God and others), become *"peacemakers"* (persons who share a blessing), and trust in the ability to withstand persecution and marginalization for the sake of God's kingdom. These characteristics may be called "prayer-in-action." They make the inner life of the soul tangible in daily life. They were the fruits of Jesus' prayer.

In what ways does Jesus' Hebrew understanding of blessing expand the possibilities for your life of prayer?

How is your life blessed by other people and by your faith community?

What challenges do Jesus' insights in the Beatitudes offer for lay and ordained ministries and the ministry of spiritual direction?

BIBLICAL TEXTS FOR STUDY AND REFLECTION:

Matt 5:1–48; Gen 12:1–3; Ps 29:11; Isa 44:1–8

DAY 23

More than words

Jesus' disciples were on overload. The Sermon on the Mount and the Beatitudes were a tall order. Who could possibly live up to the behavior Jesus was describing? And if that were not enough, he goes on to speak about other aspects of life in the reign of God:

> *You are the salt of the earth; but if salt has lost its taste, how can its saltiness be restored? . . . You are the light of the world . . . let your light shine before others, so that they may see your good works and give glory to your Father in heaven. . . . For I tell you, unless your righteousness exceeds that of the scribes and Pharisees, you will never enter the kingdom of heaven. . . . You have heard that it was said, "An eye for an eye and a tooth for a tooth." But I say to you, Do not resist an evil doer. . . . You have heard that it was said, "You shall love your neighbor and hate your enemy." But I say to you, Love your enemies and pray for those who persecute you.* (Matt 5:13, 14, 16, 20, 38, 43–44)

Talk about impossible dreams! I would have said, "Jesus, get real. Who can possibly do what you are asking?" Jesus was challenging ordinary rural people to share in his remarkable ministry and *"to fulfill"* the Law. It was one thing for *Jesus* to do what he was asking; they could see that his intimate life with God filled him with courage, wisdom, and spiritual energy. The disciples were aware of his quiet times with the Father. They had gone looking for him often and found him deep in prayer. *But now they wanted to share his experience of God.*

> *He was praying in a certain place, and after he had finished, one of his disciples said to him, "Lord, teach us to pray, as John taught his disciples."* (Luke 11:1–2)

Luke places this request further into Jesus' active ministry than Matthew. In Matthew it comes immediately after the Sermon on the Mount and Beatitudes. But in Luke the request comes after an extended pattern of healing the sick, teaching in synagogues and outdoors, calling and sending out the Twelve, cleansing persons possessed with demons, calming a storm on the sea, feeding multitudes, Jesus' transfiguration on the mountain, and the numerous times Jesus went off by himself for personal prayer in the midst of all this activity.

The request was not to learn methods of prayer. They had traveled with him daily and were accustomed to reciting the Shema and the *Tephilla* blessings morning and evening, as well as midday and afternoon prayers. Some of them had been with Jesus to celebrate the Great Feasts. They had been with him long enough to see that Jesus had a distinctive relationship with God, whom he called Abba, that went beyond these fundamental liturgies. Jesus' prayer was more intimate and full of mutual love that overflowed into his words and actions. They saw so many situations where the desires of Jesus and the will of God were not separate. He was different from other teachers. *They wanted to be like him!* The disciples knew they could never fulfill what Jesus was asking in the Beatitudes without sharing his relationship with God. They could easily see the relationship between Jesus' life of prayer and his teaching and actions. They desired his intimate relationship with the Father, rather than words or formulas. The disciples wanted to be transformed by prayer and asked Jesus to be their mentor.

In what ways is your prayer with your faith community different from your personal prayer?

What does your intimacy with God make possible?

BIBLICAL TEXTS FOR STUDY AND REFLECTION:
Luke 11:1–13; Matt 6:5–18; John 14:1–14; 17:1–26

Desert Day Two

Jesus discerns his relationship with God

Desert Days are opportunities to *listen* rather than study. If you take time to listen to God's presence in Holy Scripture, you will be able to recognize that same voice in other aspects of your life.

Desert Days offer conversations rather than a quest for more knowledge. You are invited to go beyond the words of biblical and academic texts toward an inner dialogue where the Word will enable you to see more clearly. You will experience more than words and discover hidden meanings because too much emphasis on words and the meaning of words often takes the mind away from the voice of the Spirit.

Saint Benedict, in his rule for monks, advises them to listen "with the ear of the heart." The result will be delight in the freedom to hear the Spirit speak without your conscious thought determining what the message should be. Rather than searching for meaning you will be able to listen to the meaning *given to you.*

Today is a Sabbath. Rest your mind from reading, studying, and thinking. Being silent and less active will help you listen to the four canonical Gospels in a unique way. When your mind and your heart are integrated you will begin to *experience* Jesus' life of prayer rather than study about it.

Today let your intellectual discipline be embraced and mentored by contemplative reflection on Jesus' early personal and spiritual formation. Using what you have learned thus far, try to enter into his early life and let it speak to you.

Begin this Desert Day with twenty minutes of silent contemplative prayer. A simple method is described in Appendix E. Find a place that is as quiet as possible. You may prefer to walk to a quiet place and combine a silent walk with sitting once you have arrived.

You may not be able to make Desert Day a full day. But do your best to make it an intentional part of your day. Set aside at least two hours, if possible. During that time let the four Gospels speak to you, rather than deciding what you want to learn from them. A simple prayer may help you, such as "Spirit, reveal what's true . . . . Spirit I bless you." Or "Come, Holy, Holy . . . . Come, Holy Spirit." Try to let go of the outcome of this day. Toward the end of this day recall what you have heard, learned, and experienced. Ask this question: "What have you to do with me, Jesus of Nazareth?" At the end of the day record your reflections in a journal.

The following questions may help your reflection on Jesus' early personal and spiritual formation:

How did Jesus' baptism change his life?

What did Jesus discern about his relationship with God during his "temptations" in the wilderness?

What was the relationship between Jesus' "time apart" in prayer at various times of the day and night and his words and actions during his early ministry?

DAY 24

Mutual presence

And whenever you pray, do not be like the hypocrites; for they love to stand and pray in the synagogues and at the street corners, so that they may be seen by others. Truly I tell you, they have received their reward. (Matt 6:5)

But whenever you pray, enter your private chamber and shut your door and offer prayer to the Father in secret; for your Father who sees you in secret will offer a response. (Matt 6:6, author's translation)

In Matthew's Gospel this teaching about personal prayer follows the Beatitudes. In Luke's Gospel, specific teaching about prayer comes later in Jesus' ministry. But the message is the same. In both cases Jesus is sharing his own experience of intimacy with God. We have seen that Jesus balanced prayer with his faith community in synagogues and festivals in Jerusalem with a pattern of going off by himself to be in prayer.

In this teaching about prayer, recorded by Matthew, Jesus is clear that the purpose of the hypocrites' prayer is to be seen praying by other people. Their "reward" is the self-satisfaction of being seen praying as the Torah requires. But their desire to be honored in the eyes of other people deflects the intent of their prayers from God to a self-centered need. In a way, they "answer" their own prayers.

Jesus is saying that prayer is more than words, posture, or spiritual accomplishment. The purpose of prayer, as recommended by Jesus, is to be "seen" by God who will offer a genuine and appropriate response. Matthew uses a play on two Greek words to emphasize this difference. The hypocrites' purpose is μισθὸν (*misthon*, a reward). But Matthew uses ἀποδώσει (*apodōsei*, recompense, or response) to describe the consequence of prayer in a private chamber. It seems clear that Jesus is offering his own experience in prayer as an example for his disciples. The primary purpose is to be present to God in a quiet, secret, and intimate place.

The *"private chamber"* may have both a literal and figurative meaning. It may refer to an inner room in the rear of a typical small Jewish home, separated by a stone wall and away from the normal activities of family life.

(However, few homes among Jesus' Galilean neighbors would be that large.) It may refer, also, to the "inner space" or "heart" of each person where God is present in a unique and personal way. In either case, a person who desires God's presence in this manner will not be disappointed. The listening heart of a person whose focus is on God (without expectations) will be joined by the listening heart of God. It is a flow of energy between a person and God. There is a mutual presence filled with possibilities that are the fruit of intimacy. There is little doubt that Jesus had lots on his mind when he went off to pray by himself. But his intent was simple: to spend time alone with God and to listen. This is the foundation of all contemplative prayer.

Where is your "inner chamber"?

How often do you go there?

What is your experience of God in that inner space?

What supports or inhibits this intimacy with God in your life?

BIBLICAL TEXTS FOR STUDY AND REFLECTION:

Matt 6:1–7; Ps 42:1–3; Isa 55:1–11

DAY 25

Heart to heart

But whenever you pray, enter your private chamber and shut your door and offer prayer to the Father in secret; for your Father who sees you in secret will offer recompense. (Matt 6:6, author's translation)

Where is *"your private chamber"*? Why is this "place" important? It is clear that Jesus recommends entering this chamber because he has found this "placeless place"[7] an essential part of his own life of prayer. All four canonical Gospels describe his pattern of going off to deserted places by himself. *"In the morning, while it was still very dark, he got up and went out to a deserted place, and there he prayed"* (Mark 1:35).

Where was Jesus' *"private chamber"* and what did he experience there? A first clue may be in Ps 119:145–48. The Psalms were the hymns of Jesus' faith community and he quoted them often. Perhaps he had these verses in mind during his quiet listening.

With my whole heart I cry; answer me, O LORD. I will keep your statutes. I cry to you; save me, that I may observe your decrees. I rise before dawn and cry for help; I put my hope in your words. My eyes are awake before each watch of the night, that I may meditate on your promise.

In Jesus' culture, the heart was understood as the essence and character of a person. It was an integral part of the soul containing what the soul values; it was the source of the soul's power manifested in daily life. A pure heart is a heart not influenced or scattered by malign influences. *"With my whole heart . . ."* expresses an undivided desire to be faithful to the covenant Israel made with God at Sinai. As a devout Jew, it is possible that Jesus had the heart in mind when he said, *"But whenever you pray, enter your private chamber."* There is little doubt that Jesus listened with his heart and, like the psalmist, could say, *"I put my hope in your words."* Part of his interior prayer was most likely to *"meditate on your promise."* The *"promise"* is God's part of the covenant: to be close to and care for the people of Israel. *"Truly the eye*

---

7. I am indebted to my colleague, Tilden Edwards, for this phrase.

*of the Lord is on those who fear him; on those who hope in his steadfast love.
. . . Our soul waits for the* LORD; *he is our help and our shield"* (Ps 33:18; 20).

Another clue supporting the heart as the inner or secret chamber is
in statements Jesus makes in John's Gospel about his relationship with the
Father. *"I can do nothing on my own. As I hear, I judge; and my judgment is
just, because I seek to do not my own will but the will of him who sent me"*
(John 5:30). This reflects an intimate relationship between the essence and
character of Jesus (his heart) and the One who sent him. He listens in his
heart to the will of the Father and makes judgments (discernment leading
to action). As a Jew, he understood that justice flows from a heart that is
faithful to the covenant made with God. Justice is behavior that is congruent with what God desires; it is not enforced. It is what the heart desires.
Jesus' passion for what is just had its origin in his prayer where his heart
listened to his Father. In recommending *"whenever you pray, enter your
private chamber"* Jesus is speaking from his own experience of God in the
intimacy of his heart.

In the twenty-first century many people are skeptical of decisions made
from "the heart." We tend to value a more "practical" approach. How do
you make room in your daily life for your "inner room"?

BIBLICAL TEXTS FOR STUDY AND REFLECTION:

Matt 13:10–17; Mark 8:14–21; John 12:37–40

DAY 26

When you pray, say . . .

> *He was praying in a certain place, and after he had finished, one of his disciples said to him, "Lord, teach us to pray, as John taught his disciples." (Luke 11:1–2)*

Jesus' response to his disciples is what is known as "The Lord's Prayer." Although it is probably the most familiar passage in the New Testament, used both in corporate liturgies and personal prayer, it will be helpful to explore its meaning in the context of Jesus' Hebrew culture. If the request, "*Lord, teach us to pray . . .*" expresses the disciples' desire "to be like Jesus," then the prayer can be seen as a self-portrait of Jesus' relationship with his "Father." It reveals how that intimacy relates to his daily life. If this is true, then, the "Lord's Prayer" reveals a lot about the dialogue that took place in Jesus' inner or secret chamber and how that experience guided and energized his ministry. Jesus is sharing the essence and character of his life and not simply an instruction on "how to pray."

The disciples' request did not come "out of the blue." They travelled with him every day. They ate meals with him and slept under the stars or in caves with him. They saw him leave early in the morning or late at night to be alone. They remembered what happened after his solitude. They could see a pattern. He was different from other teachers. He scandalized religious leaders and his own cultural norms by inviting women to be his disciples and travel with him. Although he was a faithful Jewish male who respected the integrity of the Torah, he spoke with an authority all his own and sometimes he challenged traditional interpretations of the Torah. He told people that his words came from "listening to his Abba." He spoke about the "finger of God" being present in his actions, especially his healing the sick. It seems clear that the disciples were beginning to observe that Jesus could see deeper than the surface structures of their religious life. His experience of God went beyond traditional religious practices, as important as they were. The disciples wanted to *experience* Jesus' prayer!

The Lord's Prayer gave the disciples and gives us an experience of Jesus' "consciousness," his inner and authentic self. Jesus' consciousness was formed by his intimacy with God in prayer. After Jesus' resurrection, Saint

Paul urged followers of Jesus to share his consciousness: *"Let the same mind be in you that was in Christ Jesus . . ."* (Phil 2:5). In the Hebrew Scriptures there are many prayers. The language and images used in those prayers express what God is like in the minds of Jesus' ancestors. They tell us a lot, too, about the lives of Jesus' forebears.

During the next week we will explore the meaning of each part of the "Lord's Prayer" in the light of Jesus' first-century culture and religious life. But before we begin, one question remains: if the disciples wanted "to be like Jesus," what was unique about his personal prayer and what does it reveal about his consciousness?

What does having "the mind of Christ" mean to you?

In what ways would you like Jesus to teach you to pray?

How do you experience the deep structure of life?

BIBLICAL TEXTS FOR STUDY AND REFLECTION:

Matt 6:5–15; Luke 11:1–13; John 3:1–21; 1 Cor 2:1–16

DAY 27

Looking for something unique

> *He was praying in a certain place, and after he had finished, one of his disciples said to him, "Lord, teach us to pray, as John taught his disciples." And he said to them, "When you pray, say: Father, hallowed be your name. Your kingdom come. Give us each day our daily bread. And forgive us our sins, for we ourselves forgive everyone indebted to us. And do not bring us to the time of trial."* (Luke 11:1–4)

As we have seen, every faithful Jew in Jesus' time joined others for prayer in the local synagogue and participated in more personal prayer in the family. The *Shema* was recited at the beginning and end of each day. The *Amidah* prayers (also called *Tephilla,* meaning "standing") were recited along with the *Shema* (morning and evening) and in mid-afternoon at the same time the afternoon sacrifice was being made at the temple in Jerusalem. The *Amidah* included eighteen prayers honoring God and God's care for Israel, along with petitions. Some pious Jews would spend an hour in silence before reciting the *Amidah* as a way to prepare their hearts for addressing the Holy One. A *minyan* or gathering of a least ten men was required, when possible, for recitation of the *Amidah*. The *minyan* was a reminder that the *Amidah* is a prayer to be said by the assembly of the descendants of the Hebrews who made the covenant with God at Sinai. It was (and remains) primarily a corporate prayer. But flexibility was permitted. Each male recited the blessings and prayers at his own pace.

There seems little doubt that Jesus and his disciples, as devout Jews, recited these prayers daily wherever they were. Prayer was already an integral part of their lives. It is clear, then, that when the disciples ask, *"Lord, teach us to pray . . ."* they want to share the unique relationship with God that was formed through *Jesus' personal prayer*. There is no reason to believe that their intent was to replace their traditional daily prayers. As we have seen, they were well aware of the relationship between Jesus' intimacy with God and his teaching and activities. Even the Pharisees were aware of his authentic relationship with God. In John's Gospel a learned Pharisee named Nicodemus came to Jesus at night *"and said to him, 'Rabbi, we know that you are a teacher who has come from God; for no one can do these signs that you do apart from the presence of God.' Jesus answered him, 'Very truly, I tell you, no one can see the kingdom of God without being born from above'"* (John 3:1–3).

It is in this context that Jesus responds to his disciples' request with these words, according to Luke: *"When you pray, say: 'Father, hallowed be your name. Your kingdom come. Give us each day our daily bread. And forgive us our sins, for we ourselves forgive everyone indebted to us. And do not bring us to the time of trial'"* (Luke 11:1–4).

In Matthew's Gospel Jesus responds, *"Pray then, in this way: 'Our Father in heaven, hallowed be your name. Your kingdom come. Your will be done, on earth as it is in heaven. Give us this day our daily bread. And forgive us our debts, as we also have forgiven our debtors. And do not bring us to the time of trial, but rescue us from the evil one'"* (Matt 6:9–13).

During the next week we will explore the language of "The Lord's Prayer" from the point of view of a first-century Jew. We will discern, as best we can, what the words and images meant in Jesus' mind.

In what ways are the statement of Nicodemus and the request of the disciples similar?

What do you think Nicodemus and the disciples were looking for?

Biblical texts for study and reflection:

Rom 8:26–27; 1 Thess 5:16–17

DAY 28

"Our Father . . ." (Part One)

In Matthew's Gospel, Jesus exhorts his disciples, *"Pray then, in this way: 'Our Father in heaven . . . .'"* In Luke, Jesus' response is: *"When you pray say, 'Father . . . .'"* In both of these gospels Jesus' use of the name *"Father"* demonstrates a specific relationship with God. In Jesus' experience, prayer begins with an acknowledgment of God's intimate presence as Father. All four canonical Gospels agree that Jesus used the term Father to address God in prayer. In his Hebrew culture a name carries not only an identity, but also the agency or active influence of the person named. To call a person by name is to enter into a relationship or continue an existing relationship. To address God by name is to acknowledge a genuine bond and recall God's prior actions that have formed and sustained that connection. What does Jesus' use of the name Father suggest about the way he felt bonded with God? In what ways did his experience of God form and sustain that relationship? The Hebrew Scriptures and Jesus' first-century Jewish culture can give us some clues.

As we have seen, in Matthew's narrative of Jesus' baptism a voice from heaven declares, *"This is my beloved Son, with whom I am well pleased"* (Matt 3:17, using an alternate translation in margin of NRSV). In Jesus' culture the filial bond between a father and son was deep and powerful. The words "from heaven" confirm that Jesus' relationship with God, although unique and initiated by God, is akin to that shared between a human father and son.[8] Many New Testament scholars conclude that this "consciousness" evolved during Jesus' adult life and was strengthened during his ministry through subsequent experiences of God in both prayer and active ministry. It seems clear that Jesus' distinctive awareness of God as Father was not based on a one-time and rational acceptance of revelation from God during his baptism. The Gospel narratives that follow his baptism attest to a pattern of God's activity in Jesus life that demonstrates God's love, care, and empowerment throughout his ministry. Jesus looked to God for guidance, wisdom, and authentication. He honored God as the source of his life and

---

8. For further background on the filial relationship between a father and a son in Jesus' first-century culture, see Appendix B.

work and constantly expressed his desire to fulfill God's law and be obedient to God's will.

Jesus' understanding of God as Father had its roots in the Hebrew Scriptures where the term "father" is used fifteen times to describe God's relationship with Israel. In other places, God's behavior toward his people is described as being similar to a father's relationship with children, sometimes using both simile and metaphor. Female images are used as well. In these cases it is a corporate relationship rather than an individual affiliation. These images honor God as creator. Moses declares to a wayward people: *"I will proclaim the name of the Lord; ascribe greatness to our God! . . . Is he not your father, who created you, who made you and established you?"* (Deut 32:3, 6). Israel is God's child: *"Israel is my first-born son"* (Exod 4:22). God is a guiding parent: *"The Lord brought us out of Egypt with a mighty hand and an outstretched arm . . ."* (Deut 26:8). The covenant at Sinai affirmed Israel's relationship with God and its responsibilities. Some images describe God's pain when his child disobeys him: *"A son honors his father, and servants their master. If then I am a father, where is the honor due me?* (Mal 1:6). The images also portray God's tenderness and desire for mercy: *"Is Ephraim my dear son? Is he the child I delight in? As often as I speak against him, I still remember him. Therefore I am deeply moved for him; I will surely have mercy on him, says the Lord"* (Jer 31:20). As a Galilean Jew, Jesus learned of God as creator, father, protector, provider, teacher of conduct, merciful, one to be obeyed, and worthy of honor.

As we have seen, Jesus' baptism and wilderness temptations were formative experiences in his life and highlighted by narratives early in Matthew, Mark, and Luke. In addition to their significance in Jesus' life, they may be interpreted as parallels relating Jesus to images in the Hebrew Scriptures that describe the king of Israel as God's son (Ps 2:6–8); the nation of Israel, itself, as a son (Hos 11:1–2); and the servant figure in Isa 42:1–4 that may refer to the nation or an individual in whom God delights. Matthew, in particular, may be relating Jesus' time of testing in the wilderness as parallel to the experience of the Hebrews, who were also tested during their wilderness wanderings. John does not give details of Jesus' baptism, but proclaims that the baptism enables him to see Jesus as the one who is to be sent by God and filled with God's spirit. John declares, *"And I myself have seen and testified that this is the Son of God"* (John 1:34). (See Appendix B.)

In the twenty-first century many persons find the patriarchal language in the Bible, especially the references to God as "Father," offensive and exclusive of women and the feminine dimension of life. Yet this was not the attitude of first-century Jews, who emphatically did *not* intend to suggest that the transcendent God, the LORD, was a male. That would have been considered idolatrous. Putting aside our modern perspectives and preferences, what can we learn from Jesus' unique awareness of God as Father as well as ancient Israel's experience of God as Father?

BIBLICAL TEXTS FOR STUDY AND REFLECTION:

Ps 103:13; Isa 64:7–8; Matt 5:45; Mark 14:36

DAY 29

"Our Father..." (Part Two)

Yesterday we saw that as a devout Jew Jesus undoubtedly knew that his Hebrew Scriptures refer to God as the "father" of the faith community of Israel. There are also references to Israel's king as God's son. In 2 Samuel God makes a covenant with King David and refers to a father-son relationship: *"I shall be a father to him, and he shall be a son to me"* (2 Sam 7:14). These filial images demonstrate God's personal relationship with and activity in the lives of the people of Israel. Their use of the name "father" gives honor and praise to God as the source and protector of their lives. In the Second Temple period (537 BCE to 70 AD) there are liturgical prayers where a person, privately or in the home, addresses God as "father." But the prayers still carry the meaning of God as "father" of Israel. A prayer preceding recitation of the *Shema* reads, *"Our father, our King, for the sake of our fathers, who trusted upon thee and whom thou taughtest the statutes of life–have mercy on us and teach us."*[9] But in first-century Palestinian Judaism there seems to be no record of prayers where an individual addresses God intimately as "father."

Although the image of God as father was common in his religious heritage, Jesus' use of Father as a title describing God's relationship with him is distinctive. Jesus' use of Father in this personal way resulted in efforts to kill him. In the fifth chapter of John's Gospel Jesus heals a man with multiple illnesses on the Sabbath and is sternly criticized: *"But Jesus answered them, 'My Father is still working, and I also am working.' For this reason the Jews were seeking the more to kill him, because he was not only breaking the Sabbath, but was also calling God his own Father, thereby making himself equal to God"* (John 5:17–18).

Jesus begins "The Lord's Prayer" in Luke with the Aramaic word *ab* (Father) and in Matthew with *abba* (our Father). In Middle Eastern languages the root *ab* refers to fecundity and growth and may infer both genders as parents who bring forth life. In Jesus' native Aramaic language, *ab* (also *abwoon*) is the word a child uses for father; it is informal and was generally taught to a child when the child was weaned. In Middle Eastern

---

9. Jeremias, *Prayers of Jesus*, 25.

cultures *ab* or *abba* reflect an intimate, affectionate, and physical relationship. They are also terms of respect, acknowledging and honoring a father as the parent who bears primary responsibility for the welfare, stability, and discipline of the family.

Abba may mean "my father" or "our father" depending on the context. Since the canonical Gospels were written in Greek, the word *pater* (father) is used in place of *abba*, even though *abba* carries a more informal meaning (though not the same as our modern "daddy"). There are three exceptions. Mark uses both the Greek and Aramaic words *"Abba*, Father" together to emphasize the intimacy of Jesus' emotions as he prays: *"Abba, Father, for you all things are possible; remove this cup from me; yet, not what I want, but what you want"* (Mark 14:36). St. Paul recalls Jesus' use of *abba* when he writes *"When we cry, 'Abba, Father', it is that very Spirit bearing witness with our spirit that we are children of God . . ."* (Rom 8:15). Paul understood that the relationship Jesus had with his *abba* can be ours because we are *"heirs with Christ"* (Rom 8:16) and share both his suffering and glory.

To begin a prayer with *"Father"* or *"Our Father"* is to claim the most fundamental relationship in our lives. *"Father"* is very personal. *"Our Father"* is also personal, yet recognizes that we share that relationship with all those who call God *"Father."* Jesus is speaking, within his heritage, about the attitude that makes prayer possible. He is reminding his disciples that humility is the primary foundation for prayer. He exhorts them to begin prayer remembering that God is the One who gives and sustains life; yet, the Creator of heaven and earth may be called "Father" and he will listen. We have confidence that the Lord of life may be approached with honor and intimacy at the same time.

What are you learning about your intimacy with God as you discover Jesus' relationship with God as his Father?

What language and images help you talk about this relationship?

BIBLICAL TEXTS FOR STUDY AND REFLECTION:

John 5:1–18; 10:22–33

DAY 30

. . . in heaven . . .

Matthew's account of the Lord's Prayer begins, *"Pray then, in this way: 'Our Father in heaven . . . .'"* Luke does not include *"in heaven."* In Jesus' culture the earth is at the center of the world. It is a round level plane (not a sphere) and heaven stretches above the earth like the roof of a tent joined to earth with pillars. Under the earth are the waters of the nether world and the oceans. Heaven is the source of light and life and the sun, moon, and stars have their appointed courses across the dome of heaven. The pillars that support heaven are mountains that extend from heaven to earth and continue through the earth into the oceans and become the foundations of the earth. The earth is the environment of life and in Hebrew is called *'adama* and provides fertile land that supports the life of the *'adam*, the human being. When the Israelites refer to "the world" they mean a totality that includes heaven and earth, the places of fertility and life. However, on the earth are also desert areas where nothing grows and there is no water. It is the place of "evil" and inhabited by demons who hurl curses. It is the place of chaos. There is also the place of death and the grave, called *she'ol*, the nether world. The ocean, too, is part of *she'ol* whose waters enclose the dead and is a place of negative power personified by monsters.

The contrasts between heaven and earth and the deserts and nether world demonstrate the struggle between life and death that every human being encounters. Heaven is the place of the Creator, who blesses the physical life of *'adam* with sunlight, rain, and the mystery of fertility and whose breath enables the human to become a living soul (Gen 2:7). *"You have set your glory above the heavens. . . . But the Lord sits enthroned forever, he has established his throne for judgment. He judges the world with righteousness; he judges the people with equity"* (Ps 8:1; 9:7–8). The harmony between the Creator and a human soul and between human souls is called "righteousness"; it is the health (*shalom*) of the soul. Righteousness is the inner character of the soul that becomes tangible in daily life through blessing. Blessing is the sharing of life by acting towards others according to the law of life, taught by God. Happiness is the fruit of living righteously. This is expressed vividly in Psalm 35:27: *"Let those who desire my vindication shout for joy and be glad, and say evermore, 'Great is the Lord who delights in the welfare of his servant.'"* Heaven is the place of and the source of righteousness, the foundation of life: *"In the path of righteousness there is life, in walking its path there is no death"* (Prov 12:28).

When Jesus calls on his Father who is *"in heaven"* he is *naming* the One, the Creator, whose fullness abides above the earth in the place of light and who is the source of life and righteousness. The Father is not limited to any domicile on earth and his care extends to all humanity. *"But I say to you, Love your enemies and pray for those who persecute you, so that you may be children of your Father in heaven; for he makes his sun to rise on the evil and on the good, and sends rain on the righteous and on the unrighteous"* (Matt 5:44–45). To call on the Father *in heaven* is to bond ourselves with the One who is our source of life and whom earth cannot contain. Later in the prayer Jesus will describe the need for congruency between heaven and earth.

Jesus speaks of God as an intimate Father who dwells "in heaven." How do you experience this?

What does the Hebrew "universe" tell us about God and God's relationship with human beings?

BIBLICAL TEXTS FOR STUDY AND REFLECTION:

Ps 19:1–14; 33:1–22; 139:1–16; Isa 66:1–2

DAY 31

. . . hallowed be your name

Jesus' adult life was totally embraced and energized by his intimate relationship with his Abba. This may be why he challenged his culture's patriarchal
perspective on women and children, who were the most vulnerable and
least powerful people in his society. He invited women to be his disciples
and travel with him. Some, like Mary of Magdala and Mary and Martha of
Bethany, he cherished and loved. He rebuked his male disciples when they
tried to keep children away from him. His childlike intimacy and dependence on his Father may explain these firm instructions to his disciples:
*"Let the children come to me, and do not stop them; for it is to such as these
that the kingdom of heaven belongs"* (Matt 19:14). Jesus' unlimited access
to his Father may explain his firm desire to seek company with tax collectors, prostitutes, and other persons who intentionally disregarded the Torah. Jesus, by his behavior, declared that these persons were loved by God,
even though conventional religious practice regarded them as "unclean"
and a danger to the religious community's holiness. Holiness and honor
were regarded as the highest virtues: *"For I am the Lord your God; sanctify
yourselves therefore, and be holy, for I am holy"* (Lev 11:44). Jesus agrees, but
manifests God's holiness through inclusion rather than marginalization.
The holiness of God hallows rather than condemns.

Jesus' metaphor of "father" comes from experience of his faith community and its heritage, his own family, and his experience of God in prayer.
His experience has integrity even though Jesus' society did not esteem
women. From Jesus' point of view, God as a "father" is holy and worthy of
prayerful respect and honor because God has always cared for Israel and
loves every person. A responsible and caring father in Jesus' culture provides food and a dwelling, he teaches and corrects children, and protects
the whole family. A family that loses its father is endangered and if it is
torn apart, widows and children with no male protector become vulnerable
and may be cast off. Jesus teaches the disciples to begin their prayer with a
petition asking that God's name as Father be hallowed in a way that honors
the sacredness of God's name and the ways in which God's presence and
power continually cares for the people of Israel. It should not be confused
as compliance with a patriarchal society that did not value women.

Hallowing God's name helped form Jesus' experience of God. He grew up reciting the eighteen blessings twice a day acclaiming, "O You who are all-good; whose mercies do not fail; You who are all merciful, whose loving-kindnesses never cease, we have hope in You. Because of all this, let Your name, O our King, be blessed and highly exalted continually, forever and ever."[10] The Gospels of Mark and John describe Jesus looking up to heaven as he prayed. The Creator in heaven is also a loving and intimate *abba* and the source of light and life on earth. The whole "world" (heaven and earth) is full of God's presence and nurture. The psalms, the prophets, and the Hebrew wisdom literature are full of references to God's concern for justice, for the care of widows and orphans, the hungry, and the poor. God is the source of wisdom that guides human lives and inspires human consciousness. All these attributes and caring acts of God are manifestations of God's name. We have seen that a "name" is both an identification of a person and the essence, presence, and agency of the person. The petition to hallow God's name recognizes an essential attitude in prayer that reverences God's presence in their lives as holy and worthy of honor. It is never to be abused, forgotten, or (as the Torah instructs) to be used for personal gain or control of others.

"I trust in the steadfast love of God forever and ever. I will thank you forever, because of what you have done. In the presence of the faithful I will proclaim your name, for it is good" (Ps 52:8–9).

How do you hallow God's name?

What causes your heart to be grateful and praise God?

BIBLICAL TEXTS FOR STUDY AND REFLECTION:

2 Sam 7:18–29; Ps 19; 148; 149; 150

---

10. Young, *Meet The Rabbis*, 154. Translation of the Amidah by Brad H. Young.

DAY 32

"Your kingdom come,
Your will be done,
On earth as it is in heaven"

This is Matthew's version. Luke is more concise: *"Your kingdom come."* A literal translation of the Greek text in Matthew is "Let come, your kingdom, let be done, your will, as in heaven, also on earth." The latter translation conveys a more dynamic and urgent intent. The Greek word *thelēma* can mean "design" or "purpose" as well as "will." (Some scholars are convinced that Luke's version is what Jesus probably said and that Matthew added the last two phrases because he was convinced they represent, also, what Jesus taught.) We say these words so often that it is possible to miss seeing how Jesus' ministry and relationships made the fundamental realities of "heaven" tangible in the daily lives of ordinary people.

Jesus is telling his disciples that congruency between life in heaven and on earth is what God desires more than anything else. His people defined the "world" as heaven *and* earth. In heaven the vitality, love, and righteousness of God flow without limitation or boundaries. No person is excluded from this love. Life in heaven demonstrates God's desires for life on earth. But that is not always the way human life is lived on earth: *"How the faithful city has become a whore! She that was full of justice, righteousness lodged in her—but now murderers! . . . Your princes are rebels and companions of thieves. Everyone loves a bribe and runs after gifts. They do not defend the orphan, and the widow's cause does not come before them"* (Isa 1:21, 23). In contrast, the prophet Micah describes what *God* wills: *"He has told you, O mortal, what is good: and what does the* LORD *require of you but to do justice, and to love kindness, and to walk humbly with your God"* (Mic 6:8).

This is not easy. How can God's kingdom become manifest in life on earth? John the Baptist proclaimed that God was about to give his people a new beginning. After John's death, Jesus exhorted people, saying, *"The time is fulfilled, and the kingdom of God has come near; repent, and believe in the good news"* (Mark 1:15). Jesus' passionate message was not about theology or waiting until things "got better." His message was an exhortation for action rooted in prayer; he was conscious that the energy of God in his life was a sign of the coming of the kingdom: *"But if it is by the Spirit of God that I cast out demons, then the kingdom of God has come to you"* (Matt 12:28). The kingdom (or reign of God) "comes" through honoring the worth and integrity of every person and being involved in their needs. But how does this happen and where does the power come from? It is both here and yet to come.

Jesus was clear that the kingdom is not only "outside" in society, it is also within a person's heart. It does not come in great blasts of mega activity or political reform by themselves. The "outside" manifestations are born slowly, mysteriously in each person. The reign of God is like a tiny mustard seed or yeast in the bread dough. "Let come, your kingdom . . ." is not simply asking God to change things in the world and then sit back and wait for it to happen. It is a prayer that we will be open to God's energizing Spirit and desire intimacy with God with the same intensity as we would seek a treasure hidden in a field. Jesus knew that just as a tiny seed eventually becomes a tree, our experience of God in prayer will give birth to justice in society and bond people to each other, one person at a time. "Let come, O Lord!" reminds us of what God desires for the life of the world and exhorts us to collaborate with God in making that tangible. In Jesus' experience it begins with prayer because we do not create the realm of God; we are invited to share it.

In your experience, how can God's kingdom become manifest in modern society?

What are you able to do to fulfill what God desires for the life of the world close to home?

BIBLICAL TEXTS FOR STUDY AND REFLECTION:

Luke 13:20–21; Matt 13:31–32; 13:44–50

DAY 33

"Give us this day our daily bread . . ."

The first three petitions in the Lord's Prayer have parallels in the daily prayers of all Jewish people during the lifetime of Jesus. He grew up with and continued to say prayers honoring God whose dwelling is heaven and whose name is to be revered, although Jesus' use of Father/Abba to call on God directly is most likely unique. In the *Qaddish* prayer and the prophetic tradition there is also mention of the fervent desire for the justice of God's kingdom to become the model for life on earth among the people: "Exalted and sanctified be His great name in the world He has created according to his will . . . . May He hasten the coming of His kingdom in your lifetime and in your days and in the lifetime of the entire house of Israel, speedily and very soon; and say: Amen."[11]

With *"Give us this day our daily bread"* Jesus' prayer makes a transition to petitions for the fundamental needs of people whom God loves. In the Middle East, bread is an essential part of every person's diet as well as a symbol indicating that food is an indispensable part of life. The petition *"give us . . ."* demonstrates Jesus' awareness that food is a gift of God and not something we create or control for ourselves. In Jesus' culture, the agricultural process from the planting of seed to the maturation of a crop at harvest was seen and revered as a mystery. People could see "what" happened, but did not understand "how" seeds were transformed. These mysterious gifts are from God and the petition *"give us"* reminds us that God sustains life. This truth gives birth to gratitude, a fundamental attitude that helps form our relationship with God.

"Give us this day our daily bread . . ." reminds the disciples that they are asking for enough bread for their daily needs, *and no more*. Most peasants in Jesus' day worked all day for enough money to buy one day's food for a family. This petition emphasizes the need for easily satisfied needs for everyone. The phrase *"our daily bread"* is different from asking for "my" daily bread. Bread (basic sustenance) is for everyone and is to be shared. God's gifts are for all.

11. Toledano (ed.), *The Orot Sephardic Weekday Siddur*, 81–82.

The phrase *"our daily bread"* has caused confusion for biblical translators because Matthew used an obscure Greek word usually translated "daily" in place of Jesus' original Aramaic word. The second-century Old Syriac Gospel of Matthew translates this petition "Amen, bread today give to us."[12] This is significant because Syriac is very close to Aramaic and the word "Amen" can mean "lasting or never-ceasing." Perhaps Jesus is saying that the disciples should pray for bread to last today as well as the release from worry about running out of bread for the future. Jesus' petition for bread reveals his awareness that everyone depends totally on God for basic needs and that God's gifts of food are for all. He exhorts his disciples not to ask for more than they need and to remember how hard it is for most people to feed their families day after day.

But there may be another dimension to this petition for "daily bread." It follows immediately after *"your will be done on earth as in heaven."* Jesus' constant desire was to manifest God's kingdom on earth through specific acts of love that would bond people to God. He said, *"My food is to do the will of him who sent me and to complete his work."* (John 4:34). Perhaps Jesus is telling his disciples, and us, to pray for the physical bread we all need to nourish our bodies as well as the passion to do the will of God! He could be exhorting us to ask God to feed our spirits as well as our bodies as we make God's will tangible in our lives.

In a "consumer society" how can a person discern her or his basic needs?

What is the relationship between gratefulness and sharing our resources with persons in need?

BIBLICAL TEXTS FOR STUDY AND REFLECTION:
Matt 6:25–34; 7:7–11; John 6:22–59

---

12. Bailey, *Jesus through Middle Eastern Eyes*, 121. Translation by Kenneth Bailey.

DAY 34

A forgiving heart

"And forgive us our sins, for we ourselves forgive everyone indebted to us" (Luke 11:4). In this petition Jesus continues to emphasize that our life with God cannot be lived in isolation from our neighbors. There are two kinds of daily sustenance to be shared: basic bread that will sustain us physically and forgiveness that will restore our relationships with God and our neighbor. Luke's version of this petition retains the double meaning of the Aramaic word *khoba* (most likely used by Jesus), which means both "sins" and "debts." Matthew chooses to render only the Greek meaning that refers to debts and debtors. *"And forgive us our debts, as we also have forgiven our debtors"* (Matt 6:12). Jesus lived in a culture that was intent on preserving honor and avoiding shame. In Galilean peasant culture, debt was a common source of shame and could endanger a person's or a family's status and well-being. A small land owner might lose his land because of debt and be unable to sustain his income and care for his family. He would be considered "poor." His relationship with neighbors and family was shattered. Gossip and public comments about his situation could intensify his shame and that of his family. In some cases he became an outcast, offering himself for day labor at a wage so small he could barely buy a day's amount of bread. The only way for him to regain his former status and honor was through forgiveness of his debt or receiving generous wages. Jesus used these images in several parables describing God's forgiving heart.

A similar relationship existed between every Jewish person and God. The Torah was the guide for each person's relationship with God. From childhood every Jew learned that God desired each person to be holy, because God is holy: *"Happy are they whose way is blameless, who walk in the way of the Lord! Happy are they who keep his decrees, who seek him with their whole hearts! Who also do no wrong, but walk in his ways"* (Ps 119:1–3). But what if a person's heart falters because of jealousy, greed, or the desire to obtain revenge when another person causes harm to that person or his or her family, especially if that brings dishonor? What if two people are hopelessly engaged in a disagreement that fosters violence? What happens when someone follows "the advice of the wicked?" (Ps 1:1). From the point of view of Jesus' first-century religious conventional wisdom, that person or persons become indebted to God. They are vulnerable to God's response. They often fear punishment and desire mercy.

These relationships of indebtedness to a neighbor and to God form the context for Jesus' petition *"And forgive us our sins, for we ourselves forgive everyone indebted to us."* His religious heritage already knew God as a forgiving God, long-suffering, and eager to forgive: *"Have mercy on me O God, according to your steadfast love; according to your abundant mercy blot out my transgressions. Wash me thoroughly from my iniquity and cleanse me from my sins."* (Ps 51:1–2). Everyone would understand the need for the first part of Jesus' petition. But Jesus goes a step further. He links God's forgiving heart with his awareness that we must have the same kind of heart. This was counter to the conventional wisdom of Jesus' day. The wisdom in Jesus' petition came from his own experience in prayer of God's generous heart and unconditional love. If the forgiveness of God restores a person's relationship with God, a person's forgiveness of another person will restore that relationship as well. And our relationships with other people influence our relationship with God. Experience of God's forgiveness in prayer makes a forgiving heart possible.

In your experience, how has a lack of forgiveness placed barriers in your relationships with other persons?

How does Jesus' awareness of God's desire to forgive sins give you hope in your relationship with God?

BIBLICAL TEXTS FOR STUDY AND REFLECTION:

Sir 28:2–5; Matt 18:21–35; Luke 6:27–42; 7:36–59; 15:1–32

DAY 35

Total dependence on God

"And do not bring us to the time of trial, but rescue us from the evil one."
This is Jesus' last petition according to Matthew. In Luke it reads, *"And do not bring us to the time of trial."* What is *"the time of trial"* and would God put us in such a place intentionally? As we have seen, in Jesus' culture a temptation or trial is a situation in which a person has an opportunity to prove him- or herself rather than being led to doing wrong. All of us, as Jesus found out for himself in the wilderness, are faced with opportunities where personal need, pride, power, or other desires can lure us to behavior that harms our relationship with God and other people. But would God place us in these situations on purpose? Looking again at original texts will help us understand what Jesus is asking in this petition. As we have seen, Matthew wrote in Greek and Greek words do not fully convey the meaning of Semitic thought. This has made it difficult for biblical translators to find accurate meanings in English. The Greek word Matthew used that is translated "bring" in English is *eisphero.* But the Aramaic word *nisyon* that Matthew translates *eisphero,* like so many Aramaic words, has two possible meanings: "cause" or "permit." Which meaning did Jesus intend here? We know from Jesus' preaching and healings that he is telling people around him, emphatically and dramatically, that God is acting through him to demonstrate God's love to people and manifest God's kingdom in their daily lives. In this context, it seems clear that Jesus is exhorting the disciples to pray "Do not *permit* (i.e., 'keep us from') the times of trial." Jesus is affirming the need for total dependence on God. A paraphrase of this intent is: "Lord, we look to you and trust you to lead us on the right path. Let your power help us make right decisions and act according to what you desire." Life brings trials to every person. God's power and wisdom will help us avoid mistakes and sinful behavior.

Jesus' petition infers that these trials are enticements by "the evil one." Mediterranean Semitic cultures believed in a hierarchy of beings with God at the top; then other lower gods and archangels; then non-human persons such as angels, spirits, and demons; then human beings; and finally creatures lower than humans. The higher beings could maintain control of all those below their place on the hierarchy. As we have seen in reflecting on Jesus' temptations in the wilderness, the word "satan" may refer to two beings: the first is a tempter who is a colleague of God who tests a human being's faithfulness to God on God's behalf. The second is a diabolical figure whose aim is to scatter a person's desire to be faithful to God. Jesus' culture also believed in demons and evil spirits who could inhabit a person and cause behavior or health problems that would alienate them from normal responsibilities in society. They would be declared unclean and marginalized. In using the phrase "the evil one" Jesus seems to be referring to the diabolical "satan" whose chief goal is to alienate a person from God. He knows that his followers can be tested by satan and lured toward evil behavior. The petition asks for guidance and strength to avoid situations that will test a person's faithfulness to God and overcome the influence of satan on their lives. Perhaps Jesus had a verse from Psalm 23 in mind as he prayed using the image of being rescued from the evil one: *"Even though I walk through the darkest valley, I fear no evil; for you are with me"* (Ps 23:4). Once I was walking with my wife, Emily Wilmer, through the Wadi Quilt near Jericho. As we walked, our friend Abed El Hawash, pointed out several caves near the path where robbers could hide in the darkness. A traveler's eyes would be adjusted to the bright sun and unable to see the danger lurking in the darkness. Jesus may have had such an image in mind when he calls on his Abba "deliver us from the evil one." There are times in life when the "eyes" of our minds or hearts are unable to see into the "darkness" of options we face; on the surface they may seem both reasonable and good. Evil is adept at masquerading as good! At such times we need to be rescued. Jesus is saying that we need to look to God during these dangers.

At the heart of *"do not bring us to the time of trial, but rescue us from the evil one"* is fidelity to God and what God desires for each person. Temptations and trials can lure us away from this relationship. Jesus reminds us to remain loyal to God at times when we are tempted to betray that relationship. The strength to remain faithful comes from God and nowhere else. That is the intent of this final petition: *"And now, O Lord, what do I wait for? My hope is in you"* (Ps 39:7).

When you are faced with decisions or opportunities that lure you away from what you know God desires, where do you look for strength and discernment?

What strengthens your desire and ability to care for yourself and other people?

Biblical texts for study and reflection:

Matt 7:24–29; Rom 8:18–39; Phil 2:1–13; Jas 1:12–27

DAY 36

Where your heart is . . .

"Lord, teach us to pray." It seems like a simple request, similar to the beginning of a Lenten discipline. But the disciples wanted more than technique, self-help, or wisdom. They had seen Jesus in action and realized how often he was alone in prayer early in the morning and sometimes late into the night. They saw that Jesus himself was changed by what he experienced in prayer. He was *different* because he prayed and the disciples *wanted to be like Jesus.* "The Lord's Prayer" is not a list of things to "pray for." It is a rare opportunity to look into the heart of Jesus and listen to the dialogue of his heart with the heart of God. Jesus' response to the disciples' request is an opportunity to experience his consciousness, the vision and fundamental truth that were the source of his words and passionate engagement with the needs of people around him.

In "The Lord's Prayer" we catch a glimpse of the intimacy that lay behind his realization that *"The Father and I are one."* (John 10:30). He was not making a theological statement about divine status; he was speaking about the location of his heart! This, more than anything else, is what Jesus wanted for all human beings. He lures us toward the intimacy he experienced and the opportunity to change our lives and become a source of life for others. In "The Lord's Prayer" Jesus invites us to a transformed way of seeing life and living.

"Pray, then, in this way . . ."

"Our Father in heaven . . ."
   (Direct your heart and mind to God's presence.)

"hallowed be your name . . ."
   (Honor God's sacred nature and activity in your life.)

"your kingdom come"
   (Open your heart to God's desires for the life of the world.)

"Your will be done, on earth as it is in heaven."

(Let your heart's experience of God be the source of the manifestation of God's righteousness and unconditional love in your personal relationships and care of the earth.)

"And forgive us our debts, as we also have forgiven our debtors."

(When you stray from God and what God desires, ask God to restore you to a right relationship with God, and at the same time let that experience of forgiveness enable you to be reconciled with persons who have harmed you.)

"And do not bring us to the time of trial"

(When situations and self-will challenge your desire to love God with all your heart, soul, mind, and strength, remain rooted in God. God will help you avoid being tested beyond your strength.)

"but rescue us from the evil one."

(Only God can release you from the grip of sinful and self-centered behavior and lead you to repentance and new life.)

Our lives will manifest God's presence when our hearts reside in God's presence: *"For where your treasure is, there your heart will be also"* (Matt 6:21).

How does "The Lord's Prayer" describe what God desires for your life?

How are "The Lord's Prayer" and the "Sermon on the Mountain" similar?

DAY 37

Listening to "The Lord's Prayer" with the ears of your heart (Part One)

We have reflected on "The Lord's Prayer" line by line. Attention was given to Jesus' religious and social cultures, examining his personal patterns of prayer, and the languages he and the evangelists used. In this context, we searched for the meanings of Jesus' response to the disciples when they asked: *"Lord, teach us to pray."* But there is more than cognitive information and ideas in his response. Jesus is speaking about *experience* that transcends words and leads toward a mysterious and grace-filled personal transformation. The disciples could see the transformation that had taken place in Jesus and wanted to experience it themselves. Even though Jesus responds verbally, he invites his disciples into something that transcends words.

When words cannot convey experience, artistic expression, often poetry, is most often the best way to express transcendence without taming its freedom. It is not a coincidence that the translators of the New Revised Standard Version of the Gospels place "The Lord's Prayer" in verse rather than prose. Although we do not know whether it was Jesus' specific intent, "The Lord's Prayer" presents a verbal portrait of his intimacy with God and how that relationship empowered his words and works.

In the first chapter of the Gospel according to John, the evangelist describes two disciples of John the Baptist who follow Jesus as he walks away. When Jesus asks them, *"What are you looking for?"* they reply, teacher *"where are you staying?"* Jesus responds, *"Come and see"* (John 1:35–39). The request *"Lord teach us to pray"* and Jesus' response *"When you pray, say . . ."* is a similar dialogue. Jesus is inviting the disciples to enter where he is "staying" when he prays. The words are specific, but they lead to something that is beyond words. We say *"Lord, teach us to pray."* Jesus replies, *"Come and see."* He invites us to enter his inner life!

Today you begin nine consecutive reflections on the content of "The Lord's Prayer." The format for today and each of the next eight days is the same so that the focus of your attention is directed to a different phrase from "The Lord's Prayer" each day.

Although we have looked at the religious and social contexts that may have influenced this prayer, you are invited to let go of rational analysis and listen with ears of your heart. Let your mind descend into your heart where you can listen to Jesus' words with your whole being. Today a phrase from "The Lord's Prayer" is printed below as it appears in Matthew, Luke, and Q. It is followed by a poetic interpretation, based upon my silent reflection on the phrase. Read the biblical phrase and the poetic interpretation out loud several times and then spend five or ten minutes in silence. Respond in writing to what you hear or discern.

> *"Pray then in this way: Our Father in heaven . . . ."* (Matt 6:9)
>
> *"When you pray, say: Father, ..."* (Luke 11:2)
>
> "When you pray, say: Father, ..." (Q 11:2b)[13]
>
> "When you pray, turn your heart to the One who loves you and delights in you as his child. Heaven and earth call him Lord, yet you may call him Father and he will listen . . . ."

After reflecting in silence, what do you hear or discern in these words?

How would you rephrase these verses?

---

13. All references to Q used in these nine daily reflections have been based on Luke's chapter 11 and verse numeration. The translation of these verses from Q are from Robinson, *The Sayings of Jesus.*

DAY 38

Listening to "The Lord's Prayer" with the ears of your heart (Part Two)

The request *"Lord teach us to pray"* and Jesus' response *"When you pray, say . . ."* exemplifies a dialogue. Jesus is inviting his disciples to enter into his life with God. The words are specific, but they lead to something that is beyond words. If you ask "Lord, teach me to pray," Jesus will reply, "Come and see."

Today is the second of nine days where you will revisit each line of "The Lord's Prayer." Let your mind descend into your heart where you can listen to Jesus' words with your whole being.

Below is a phrase from "The Lord's Prayer" as it appears in Matthew, Luke, and Q. It is followed by a poetic interpretation, based upon my silent reflection on the phrase. Read the biblical phrase and the poetic interpretation out loud several times and then spend five or ten minutes in silence. Then respond in writing to what you hear or discern.

> *". . . may your name be hallowed"* (Matt 6:9)
>
> *". . . may your name be hallowed"* (Luke 11:2)
>
> *". . . may your name be holy!"* (Q 11:2b)
>
> "My heart drops to its knees whenever it hears justice, steadfast love, mercy, and wisdom sing Alleluia to your name. All names have their home in you and long to bless you."

After reflecting in silence, what do you hear or discern in these words? How would you rephrase these verses?

DAY 39

Listening to "The Lord's Prayer" with the ears of your heart (Part Three)

The request *"Lord teach us to pray"* and Jesus' response *"When you pray, say
..."* exemplifies a dialogue. Jesus is inviting his disciples to enter into his life
with God. The words are specific, but they lead to something that is beyond
words. If you ask "Lord, teach me to pray," Jesus will reply, "Come and see."

Today is the third of nine days where you will revisit each line of "The
Lord's Prayer." Let your mind descend into your heart where you can listen
to Jesus' words with your whole being.

Below is a phrase from "The Lord's Prayer" as it appears in Matthew,
Luke, and Q. It is followed by a poetic interpretation, based upon my silent
reflection on the phrase. Read the biblical phrase and the poetic interpretation out loud several times and then spend five or ten minutes in silence.
Then respond in writing to what you hear or discern.

> *"Your kingdom come"* (Matt 6:10)
>
> *"Your kingdom come"* (Luke 11:2)
>
> "let your reign come" (Q 11:2b)
>
> "May the cistern you have formed in every human heart welcome the
> living water of *your divine nature.*"

After reflecting in silence, what do you hear or discern in these words?

How would you rephrase these verses?

DAY 40

Listening to "The Lord's Prayer" with the Ears of your Heart (Part Four)

The request *"Lord teach us to pray"* and Jesus' response *"When you pray, say . . ."* exemplifies a dialogue. Jesus is inviting his disciples to enter into his life with God. The words are specific, but they lead to something that is beyond words. If you ask "Lord, teach me to pray," Jesus will reply, "Come and see."

Today is the fourth of nine days where you will revisit each line of "The Lord's Prayer." Let your mind descend into your heart where you can listen to Jesus' words with your whole being.

Below is a phrase from "The Lord's Prayer" as it appears in Matthew. It is omitted in Luke and Q. The phrase is followed by a poetic interpretation, based upon my silent reflection on the phrase. Read the biblical phrase and the poetic interpretation out loud several times and then spend five or ten minutes in silence. Then respond in writing to what you hear or discern.

> *"Your will be done . . ."* (Matt 6:10)
> [Omitted in Luke]
> [Omitted in Q]
> "Teach our hearts to be fluent in the silent language of your desires for the life of the world."

After reflecting in silence, what do you hear or discern in these words?

How would you rephrase this verse?

DAY 41

Listening to "The Lord's Prayer" with the ears of your heart (Part Five)

The request *"Lord teach us to pray"* and Jesus' response *"When you pray, say . . ."* exemplifies a dialogue. Jesus is inviting his disciples to enter into his life with God. The words are specific, but they lead to something that is beyond words. If you ask "Lord, teach me to pray," Jesus will reply, "Come and see."

Today is the fifth of nine days where you will revisit each line of "The Lord's Prayer." Let your mind descend into your heart where you can listen to Jesus' words with your whole being.

Below is a phrase from "The Lord's Prayer" as it appears in Matthew. It is omitted in Luke and Q. The phrase is followed by a poetic interpretation, based upon my silent reflection on the phrase. Read the biblical phrase and the poetic interpretation out loud several times and then spend five or ten minutes in silence. Then respond in writing to what you hear or discern.

> *". . . on earth as it is in heaven"* (Matt 6:10)
>
> [Omitted in Luke]
>
> [Omitted in Q]
>
> "Father, from the emptiness of your being the waters of righteousness flow through the gates of heaven and water the seeds of your life in us. May the moist and silent soil of your Spirit germinate a harvest of your love that will rise and become the bread of life on earth."

After reflecting in silence, what do you hear or discern in these words?

How would you rephrase these verses?

DAY 42

Listening to "The Lord's Prayer" with the ears of your heart (Part Six)

The request *"Lord teach us to pray"* and Jesus' response *"When you pray, say . . ."* exemplifies a dialogue. Jesus is inviting his disciples to enter into his life with God. The words are specific, but they lead to something that is beyond words. If you ask "Lord, teach me to pray," Jesus will reply, "Come and see."

Today is the sixth of nine days where you will revisit each line of "The Lord's Prayer." Let your mind descend into your heart where you can listen to Jesus' words with your whole being.

Below is a phrase from "The Lord's Prayer" as it appears in Matthew, Luke, and Q. The phrase is followed by a poetic interpretation, based upon my silent reflection on the phrase. Read the biblical phrase and the poetic interpretation out loud several times and then spend five or ten minutes in silence. Then respond in writing to what you hear or discern.

> *"Give us this day our daily bread"* (Matt 6:11)

> *"Give us each day our daily bread"* (Luke 11:3)

> "Our day's bread give us today . . ." (Q 11:3)

> "You are the loaf that feeds our bodies and souls like the lilies of the field. Fill every hand and heart with enough of you to last each day without care for tomorrow."

After reflecting in silence, what do you hear or discern in these words?

How would you rephrase these verses?

DAY 43

Listening to "The Lord's Prayer" with the ears of your heart (Part Seven)

The request *"Lord teach us to pray"* and Jesus' response *"When you pray, say . . ."* exemplifies a dialogue. Jesus is inviting his disciples to enter into his life with God. The words are specific, but they lead to something that is beyond words. If you ask "Lord, teach me to pray," Jesus will reply, "Come and see."

Today is the seventh of nine days where you will revisit each line of "The Lord's Prayer." Let your mind descend into your heart where you can listen to Jesus' words with your whole being.

Below is a phrase from "The Lord's Prayer" as it appears in Matthew, Luke, and Q. The phrase is followed by a poetic interpretation, based upon my silent reflection on the phrase. Read the biblical phrase and the poetic interpretation out loud several times and then spend five or ten minutes in silence. Then respond in writing to what you hear or discern.

> *". . . and forgive us our debts, as we also have forgiven our debtors"* (Matt 6:12)

> *". . . and forgive us our sins, as we ourselves forgive everyone indebted to us"* (Luke 11:4)

> *". . . and cancel our debts for us, as we too have cancelled for those in debt to us"* (Q 11:4)

> "Take the stones we use to build a wall that separates us from you and our neighbor and turn them into gates that bring our lives together again."

After reflecting in silence, what do you hear or discern in these words?

How would you rephrase these verses?

DAY 44

Listening to "The Lord's Prayer" with the ears of your heart (Part Eight)

The request *"Lord teach us to pray"* and Jesus' response *"When you pray, say . . ."* exemplifies a dialogue. Jesus is inviting his disciples to enter into his life with God. The words are specific, but they lead to something that is beyond words. If you ask "Lord, teach me to pray," Jesus will reply, "Come and see."

Today is the eighth of nine days where you will revisit each line of "The Lord's Prayer." Let your mind descend into your heart where you can listen to Jesus' words with your whole being.

Below is a phrase from "The Lord's Prayer" as it appears in Matthew, Luke, and Q. The phrase is followed by a poetic interpretation, based upon my silent reflection on the phrase. Read the biblical phrase and the poetic interpretation out loud several times and then spend five or ten minutes in silence. Then respond in writing to what you hear or discern.

> *". . . and do not bring us to the time of trial, but rescue us from the evil one"* (Matt 6:13)

> *". . . and do not bring us to the time of trial"* (Luke 11:4)

> *". . . and do not put us to the test"* (Q 11:4)

> "In the midst of life's storms that blind and tempt us to rely on our own sense of direction, give us patience to wait for you and follow your footsteps toward what is real."

After reflecting in silence, what do you hear or discern in these words? How

would you rephrase these verses?

DAY 45

Listening to "The Lord's Prayer" with the ears of your heart (Part Nine: praise above all)

Today is the last of nine days where you will revisit each line of "The Lord's Prayer." Although we have looked at the religious and social contexts that may have influenced this prayer, you are invited to let go of rational analysis and listen with ears of your heart. Let your mind descend into your heart where you can listen to Jesus' words with your whole being.

In the canonical Gospels the Lord's Prayer does not include this familiar doxology: *"For the kingdom, the power, and the glory are yours, now and forever. Amen."* The earliest followers of Jesus were Jews and the first community of "the followers of the Way" was in Jerusalem with James, the brother of Jesus, as spiritual leader. Most scholars agree that this doxology was added after Jesus' death and resurrection by these early faith communities because most Jewish daily prayers, especially the *Kaddish* and *Amidah*, included and ended with praise and blessings to God.

> May His great Name be blessed forever, and for all eternity. Blessed, lauded, glorified, exalted, extolled, honored, and praised be the Name of the Holy One. Blessed is He, above all blessings, songs, praises, and words of consolation that may be uttered in the world; and say, Amen.[14]

Eventually the doxology became part of the Lord's Prayer in many, if not most, Christian faith communities and denominations. Although it was added to the end of Jesus' original prayer, it is congruent with its beginning. Our days and our prayers begin and end with praise to the Holy One.

Read the doxology out loud several times and then spend five or ten minutes in silence. Then respond in writing to what you hear or discern.

> "For the kingdom, the power, and the glory are yours, now and forever. Amen"

---

14. Toledan (ed.), *The Orot Sephardic Weekday Siddur.* "Kaddish Al Yisrael: Morning Prayer," 82.

Using all the verses you have rephrased, record "The Lord's Prayer" in your own words.

How has your paraphrase clarified or changed your understanding of the prayer?

DAY 46

A Poetic Interpretation of the Lord's Prayer

This paraphrase by David Keller is based on the meaning and spirit of Jesus' words as a devout first-century Jew and his enlightened experience of his Abba in his contemplative prayer.[15]

> The disciples asked Jesus, "Lord, how can we share your relationship with God?"
>
> Jesus responded, "When you pray, turn your heart to the One who loves you and delights in you as his child.
>
> Heaven and earth call him Lord, yet you may call him Father and he will listen.
>
> Say to him:
>
> My heart falls to its knees and sings Alleluia when
>> I hear justice, steadfast love, mercy, and wisdom pronounce your name.
>
> Every name has its home in you and longs to bless you.
>
> May the inner room you have formed in every human heart welcome
>> the living water of your divine nature.
>
> Teach every person's heart to learn and respond to the silent language
>> of your desires for the life of the world,
>
> so that waters of righteousness will flow from your dwelling place
>> and water the seeds of your life in us.
>
> Father, you are the loaf that feeds our bodies and souls like the lilies of the field.
>
> Fill every hand and heart with enough of you to last each day
>> without care for tomorrow.

15. This paraphrase was completed in 2010 after study and meditation on texts from Matthew 6:9–13 and Luke 11:1–4 (NRSV) and the original Greek texts from The Greek New Testament (UBS 4th ed.; Nestle-Aland 27th ed.) and some early Syriac texts. I have attempted to convey the meaning and spirit of Jesus' words recorded in the Greek text from the point of view of a devout first-century Jew as well as Jesus' unique experience of his Abba that led him to proclaim that the realm of God was becoming tangible in his words and actions. I am convinced that the "Lord's Prayer" gives us a window into the consciousness of Jesus and an authentic look at his experience of God's desires for human life.

And take the stones we have used to build walls that separate us from you and our neighbor and help us turn them into firm pathways leading toward healing and reconciliation.

When we are in the midst of blinding storms that tempt us to rely on what is false, give us patience to wait for you and follow you toward what is real."

In what ways does "The Lord's Prayer" describe what it means "to be like Jesus"?

Desert Day Three

The heart and center of Jesus' life

Today is a Sabbath. Rest your mind from reading, studying, writing, and thinking. Being silent and less active will help you listen to the four Gospels in a unique way. When your mind and your heart are integrated you will begin to *experience* Jesus' life of prayer rather than study about it.

Today let your intellectual discipline be embraced and mentored by contemplative reflection on Jesus' intimacy with God and his teaching about prayer. Using what you have learned thus far, try to enter into his early ministry and let it speak to you.

Begin this day with twenty minutes of silent contemplative prayer. A simple method is described in Appendix E. Find a place that is as quiet as possible. You may prefer to walk to a quiet place and combine a silent walk with sitting once you have arrived.

You may not be able to make this Desert Day a full day. But do your best to make it an intentional part of your day. Set aside at least two hours, if possible. During that time let the four gospels speak to you, rather than deciding what you want to learn from them. A simple prayer may help you, such as "Spirit, reveal what's true . . . . Spirit I bless you." Or "Come, Holy, Holy. . . . Come, Holy Spirit." Try to let go of the outcome of this day. Toward the end of this day recall what you have heard, learned, and experienced. Keep your reflections in a journal.

The following questions may help your reflection on Jesus' intimacy with God and his teaching about prayer:

What does Jesus' intimacy with God reveal about his Abba?

What does the "Lord's Prayer" reveal about Jesus' inner consciousness—what Paul called "the mind of Christ" in Phil 2:5–11?

What does the "Lord's Prayer" reveal about God's desires for human life?

DAY 47

Jesus participated in the liturgical life at the temple in Jerusalem: *Sukkot*

The Gospel of John narrates Jesus' participation in *Sukkot*, the Feast of Booths, in the same year as his death and resurrection. The intensity of efforts by religious authorities in Jerusalem to discredit Jesus has escalated and he is in danger of being stoned to death as a heretic. Jesus knows the feast of *Sukkot* intimately and his words and actions at this particular feast show how he relates the significance of the feast to his consciousness of God's unique presence in his life and ministry. He responds with passion to its solemn liturgies.

Sukkot was an ancient feast with roots going back to the early settlement of the Hebrew tribes in the land. It began as a local feast for each tribal group as they celebrated the harvests of grapes and corn. When Israel became a nation and Solomon built the temple in Jerusalem *Sukkot* became a feast that brought people from the villages and towns together to celebrate the harvest of crops as a sign of God's continuing goodness and to remember how the Israelites had once had to live in booths in the Sinai wilderness on their way to the land promised by God.

Eventually *Sukkot* became a harvest feast, a feast celebrating their redemption, and a reminder of the *continued need* for redemption from sin. This was symbolized liturgically through the sacrifice of animals throughout the seven solemn days of the feast. The Torah required that every family live in simple booths made of boughs of trees and palm branches. The Water Pouring Ceremony took place during the morning of the seventh day. This solemn ceremony thanked God for the rain that produced healthy crops during the previous year and asked God for plentiful rain for the next harvest. Priests went in solemn procession to the Pool of Siloam and filled sacred vessels with water and returned to the temple, where they poured water and wine on the sacred altar.

The Gospel of John (chapter 7:37–39) describes a bold statement by Jesus during the seventh day of *Sukkot*. During the Water Pouring Ceremony Jesus cried out in a loud voice: *"Let anyone who is thirsty come to me, and let the one who believes in me drink. As a scripture has said, 'Out of the believer's heart shall flow rivers of living water.*" Perhaps Jesus had these words of the prophet Isaiah in mind: "*With joy you will draw water from the wells of salvation*" (Isa 12:3). Jesus' relates the *Sukkot* water ceremony to the activity of God's Spirit in and through his own life. Just as crops depend on God's gift of rain, the activity of God's Spirit in Jesus' life will restore the dignity and well-being of people whose lives have been diminished. The realm of God is breaking in through God's powerful healing presence in Jesus. Jesus is convinced that every person who places her or his trust in the presence of God in his life will be renewed with living water flowing from their hearts. This was his offer to the woman at the well in Samaria recorded in John 4:1–42. The wealthy and religious leaders had taken most of the harvests of crops away from the ordinary people through taxes. Jesus realizes that God's presence in his life will restore and redeem people—just like *Sukkot*—through the living water of God's care and justice. Jesus is talking about the transformation of society through the transformation of people. His life of prayer is flowing into his desire for the basic needs of the people.

The Feast of Lights takes place during the last evening of *Sukkot.* Early in the morning of the next day—according to an addition to John's original narrative—Jesus returns to the temple and is confronted by scribes and Pharisees who have cast judgment on a woman caught committing adultery. He resists their effort to test his adherence to the law of Moses by challenging any one of them who is without sin to cast the first stone. Everyone except the woman walks away and Jesus exhorts her to go her way and sin no more. Then Jesus speaks again to the scribes and Pharisees and proclaims, "*I am the light of the world. Whoever follows me will never walk in darkness but will have the light of life.*"

How do Jesus' actions at *Sukkot* demonstrate the influence of the liturgical life of first-century Judaism on his life of prayer and ministry?

How did the water and light ceremonies of *Sukkot* provide symbols for Jesus to use as he taught in the temple about his role in the reign of God?

DAY 48

Jesus Participated in the Feasts of Passover and Unleavened Bread

The Gospel of Luke records that Mary and Joseph went up to Jerusalem *every year* for the Feast of the Passover. This was a pattern in Jesus' life as a child and Luke describes a visit for the Passover when Jesus was twelve years old.[16] He remained in Jerusalem after his parents left for Nazareth listening to the teachers of the Torah in the temple and asking them questions. All four Gospels confirm that Jesus continued to participate in these feasts as an adult either in Galilee or Jerusalem. (The Passover could be celebrated away from the temple, but without a sacrificed lamb at the meal.) Passover and Unleavened Bread became the focus of the religious life of his people and yearly reminders of the covenant Israel had made with God, of their calling to be a people rooted in God's law, of their reliance on God's constant care, and on the need for God's forgiveness of sin and redemption for new life, year after year.

The *Pesah* (Passover) was, and continues to be, a major festival commemorating the escape of the Hebrews from their bondage to the Pharaoh of Egypt. It is celebrated in the month of Abib, usually April. God led the Hebrews out of slavery into the wilderness of Sinai and at Mount Sinai they made a covenant with God. This established both a relationship with God and a unique identity as a people called to be a blessing to all people (fulfilling God's promise to Abraham). The Law given at Sinai was the guide for faithful commitment to the covenant. *Pesah* is an ancient liturgical feast originally practiced in the homes of families all over Israel. When Jerusalem became the national and religious center of Israel, *Pesah* was observed in Jerusalem. All Jewish males were required to participate, and the feast was a sign of the unity of God's people. Although liturgical sacrifices were at the temple, *Peash* remained a family liturgy for the families that had gathered for the feast in and around Jerusalem. By the time of Jesus, *Pesah* remained

---

16. Some scholars are convinced this narrative is not part of oral tradition and was added by Luke to emphasize Jesus' wisdom and passion for his Jewish heritage. In either case, it underlines the conviction of the earliest communities' awareness of Jesus commitment to his Jewish heritage. See: Schröter, *Jesus of Nazareth,* 47.

a family celebration, usually in Jerusalem, and included a liturgical meal that recounted the exodus from Egypt. At the center of the meal in Jerusalem was a roasted lamb that had been sacrificed at the temple. The shedding of the lamb's blood on the altar in the temple recounted the placing of the blood of lamb on the lintel of the doors of the Hebrew homes in Egypt so that the angel of death would pass over these homes while striking the firstborn in Egyptian homes. Bitter herbs used at the meal represented the hard life of the Hebrews in the Sinai wilderness. *Pesah* was the first of a seven day feast. The final six days formed the Feast of Unleavened Bread, commemorating the need for haste in escaping the army of Pharaoh. There was no time for bread to rise, yet even with so little provisions God delivered them. No leavened bread could be eaten during the seven day commemoration.

There is no doubt that Jesus knew and valued this major feast. It helped form his understanding of God's caring relationship with his fellow Jews and their responsibilities to fulfill the covenant. It must have influenced his awareness, also, of how far his faith community—especially its leaders—had strayed from their responsibilities to fulfill the Torah. This lack of fidelity was at the heart of Jesus' awareness that God was "breaking into" the lives of the Jewish people to renew their lives through his teaching and activities. *Pesah* was also associated with the coming of the Messiah. It symbolized the "heavenly meal" when all God's faithful would be gathered by the "Anointed One" to celebrate freedom from oppression. Each yearly celebration was held with this anticipation. All this tradition and anticipation was present when Jesus arranged to celebrate the *Pesah* with his disciples on the night before he was crucified

What does Jesus' faithful participation in the corporate worship of his faith tradition tell you about his spiritual formation?

How have the major festivals and liturgies of your faith tradition helped form your life of prayer?

How do these liturgies continue to form and nourish you?

DAY 49

"You judge by human standards; I judge no one" (John 8:15)

Day before yesterday we reflected on Jesus' participation in the Feast of Booths, *Sukkot*, and the way in which he related the solemn Water Ceremony to his ministry of bringing the life-giving presence of God to ordinary people, *"Let anyone who is thirsty come to me . . ."* (John 7:37b). The blessing and libation of water on the temple altar was a prayer for adequate rain for the crops during the coming year. As we have seen, crops were everything for peasants. If there was not a good harvest their lives were at risk and they could go into debt, lose their land, and become destitute. Jesus relates the essential need for rain to the need for *"rivers of living waters"* that will flow from a believer's heart. He was speaking of the Spirit of God and a person's fundamental need for a source of inner vitality. This is an unconditional source of water that will always produce a harvest. Jesus wants to share *what he has already experienced.*

When Jesus spoke about "rivers of water" on the last day of *Sukkot* it produced a division in the crowds that had come to the feast. Some doubted that a man from backwater Galilee could have such prophetic wisdom. The chief priests and Pharisees saw him as a dangerous heretic. They continued to look for a way to discredit him and force him to say or do something that warranted arrest. As we have seen, the next day Jesus went back to the temple early in the morning. Some scribes and the Pharisees brought a woman to him who had been caught in adultery and asked for Jesus' judgment, hoping he would say something contrary to the Law. Jesus turned their accusation around, inferring that no human person can judge because no one is without sin. He exhorted the woman to *"Go your way, and from now on do not sin again"* (John 8:11b).

Then Jesus turned to the crowds and said, *"I am the light of the world. Whoever follows me will never walk in darkness but will have the light of life"* (John 8:12). (There is little doubt that Jesus is speaking in the context of the Feast of Lights from the previous night.) He had just shown compassion for a woman who had been grasped in the darkness of adultery. He saw through the darkness of the narrow mindedness and arrogance of the scribes and Pharisees. He offers light to all of them. But the religious leaders continue to accuse him of being the judge of his own words and actions. They confront him about what they interpret as personal authority without divine testimony. It is in this context that Jesus says, *"Even if I testify on my own behalf, my testimony is valid because I know where I have come from and where I am going, but you do not know where I come from or where I am going. You judge by human standards. I judge no one. Yet even if I do judge, my judgment is valid; for it is not I alone who judge, but I and the Father who sent me"* (John 8:14–16).

Here, at the end of a major Jewish feast at the temple in Jerusalem, Jesus is aware of his experience of God in prayer. He links this personal experience of God with the liturgies of *Sukkot*. But the scribes and the Pharisees he encounters rely on their minds to assess what is acceptable according to the Law. They rely on *human standards*. Jesus points to the discernment he experiences through his relationship with "the Father." The Greek word translated "judge" here means to discern between two or more things. The time Jesus spends in prayer bears fruit in both wisdom to discern what God desires and to act with compassion in the face of sin and narrow-mindedness. In the midst of a major liturgical feast, the fruits of Jesus quiet time with his Abba become tangible. Wisdom is consummated through compassion.

Describe one or more situations in your life when a decision to speak out or act on someone else's behalf came from your discernment of what God desires rather than a rational "solution."

How does your personal prayer influence your relationships and actions in daily life?

When has your prayer shown you that you acted in haste or without compassion?

DAY 50

"You know neither me nor my Father. If you knew me, you would know my Father" (John 8:19)

Yesterday we reflected on Jesus' encounter with some of the scribes and Pharisees at the temple in Jerusalem. The Feast of Booths, *Sukkot*, had just ended. These scribes and Pharisees accused Jesus' of testifying on his own behalf when he said, *"I am the light of the world."* Jesus realized that their inability to trust him was based on their reliance on "human standards." Their reliance on intellectual interpretations of the Torah was incomplete. Jesus explains that his testimony about himself is not his own, but comes from *"the Father who sent me."* Jesus is aware that his wisdom, *"the light of the world,"* is not his own, but has been discerned through his relationship with his Father in prayer. The scribes and Pharisees still cannot see beyond Jesus, whose teaching they consider a challenge to their authority. They ask, *"Where is your Father,"* not realizing he is speaking about God. Jesus answers, *"You know neither me nor my Father. If you knew me, you would know my Father"* (John 8:19).

Unlike Jesus' disciples, the scribes and Pharisees present in the temple that day could not discern the presence of God in Jesus. They chose to look at everything through the lens of "orthodox" teaching. Their mental, and often literal, oral interpretations of the Torah blinded them from first-hand experience of God. Even though many Pharisees were concerned to preserve Jewish identity and faithfulness to the Torah in the midst of alien Roman and Greek influences, some scribes and Pharisees saw Jesus' teaching as a similar threat. Their personal control of what may be said and done in God's name restricted their freedom to trust the authenticity and authority of Jesus. They emphasized external practice. Jesus was concerned with internal motivation.

What Jesus experienced in prayer became tangible in his teaching and actions. His life was congruent with his intimacy with God. The disciples could see the consequences of that harmony and, as we have seen in earlier reflections about the "Lord's Prayer," wanted to be like him. That is why they asked, *"Lord, teach us to pray."* Not all scribes and Pharisees were as narrow-minded and villainous as those who wanted to discredit and silence Jesus.

They were all devout Jews and Jesus never ceased to share his wisdom and experience of God with them. But the scribes and Pharisees who confronted Jesus the day after the feast of *Sukkot* seem to have disconnected their study and teaching of the Torah from their prayer. Jesus tells them that if they had experienced God in prayer they would have recognized that same presence of the Holy One in Jesus. If they had been willing to enter into a relationship of trust with Jesus, they would have trusted God's presence in him. (*"If you knew me . . ."*).

Jesus' life of prayer demonstrates that all words and actions, all talk about God, and all compassionate behavior have their roots in experience of God in prayer. As we continue to reflect on Jesus' life of prayer, with mind and heart, we will have the opportunity to learn more of what God is like and enter into Jesus' experience of God. As we experience God in prayer we will see that same presence in Jesus. The authority and authenticity of Jesus' life and teaching will be revealed through our own experience of God.

When have you experienced the presence of God?

How does your experience of God in personal prayer enable you to recognize God's presence in other aspects of your life?

BIBLICAL TEXTS FOR STUDY AND REFLECTION:

John 8:12–20; 16:1–15; Luke 11:33–54; Matt 13:10–17

DAY 51

"I declare what I have seen in the Father's presence; as for you, you should do what you have heard from the Father" (John 8:38)

For the past two days we have reflected on Jesus' encounters with scribes and Pharisees during and just after the Feast of Booths, *Sukkot*. These religious leaders have been unable to discern God's presence in Jesus because their perception seems limited to their oral interpretations of the Torah. As we have seen, the scribes and Pharisees were pious, scholarly, and devout Jews who followed the *Halakhah*, an oral interpretation of commonly accepted rules that guide a person's behavior for every situation in daily life. It was their "way" or "path" to being faithful to the intent of Israel's covenant with God. At the time of Jesus they had a political agenda as well. They were intent in protecting the integrity of Israel's religious life from assimilation into Roman culture. Their political agenda was to keep their "way" intact and to avoid any change or conflict that might cause a serious Roman intervention into Israel's religious culture. They honestly believed that because they were "the children of Abraham," God was "on their side." Thus, Jesus' unique teaching and new interpretations of parts of the Torah, his healing ministry in the name of God, and his growing popularity with more and more people were seen by the Pharisees as a danger to the status quo as well as a challenge to their authority.

But not everyone was repelled by Jesus teaching and activity. After his confrontations with the scribes and Pharisees at *Sukkot*, the evangelist John comments that *"many believed in him"* (John 8:30). They were willing to entrust their lives to the presence of God in his life and teaching. Jesus' encouraged them saying, *"If you continue in my word, you are truly my disciples; and you will know the truth and the truth will make you free"* (John 8:31b–32). This puzzled some of them because, like the Pharisees, they considered themselves descendants of Abraham and had never been slaves to anyone. They were still ambivalent about Jesus. Jesus reminded them that they were still "slaves to sin." They were "missing the mark" in their devotion to God and their behavior was harmful to themselves and to other people. Jesus was convinced that the "word" he heard from his Abba in prayer was the truth that would restore people's fidelity to what God desires for human life. This will free them from false lives that "miss the mark." God is the source of truth.

Then Jesus exhorts the people who were open to his teaching to *"continue in my word."* But Jesus' word is not his own word; it is what he has *"seen in the Father's presence"* (John 8:38a). Jesus is urging those present to listen to God, in prayer, in the same way he listens to his Abba. He declares, *"as for you, you should do what you have heard from the Father"* (John 8:38b). The truth that brings freedom will be experienced in prayer. Prayer requires faithful listening. "Remain in my word." But it is more than listening! *"[Y]ou should do what you have heard from the Father."*

It is exciting to see how Jesus' quiet listening to his Abba when he is alone bursts into teaching and action. His faithfulness to participate in the feasts of his faith community, in this case *Sukkot*, is part of his attention to *Halakhah*. Yet this provides a venue for him to share what he experiences in his prayer. He connects what he hears in prayer with the lives of the people who have come to celebrate *Sukkot*. He realizes that the intent of *Halakhah* will be fulfilled by responding to *"what you have heard from the Father."* God makes following "the way" possible.

How do you listen to God? What do you hear and experience?

In what ways do you "do" what you hear from God?

BIBLICAL TEXTS FOR STUDY AND REFLECTION:

Isa 55:1–13; Jer 31:31–34; John 14:15–31

DAY 52

"I have not come to abolish, but to fulfill [the Law]*"* *(*Matt 5:17b)

As we have seen in the past two days' reflections, it would not be accurate to demonize all Pharisees as narrow minded, ultra conservative Jews obsessed with a literal, unchanging view of observance of the Torah. Actually, Pharisees were lay persons devoted to an oral interpretation of the Torah that would enable Jews to remain faithful observers in the midst of societal change without losing the "heart" of their Jewish path and identity. They, in fact, took a more liberal view to integrating the Torah into daily life than the Sadducees. The presence and influence of the Pharisees extended beyond Jerusalem into the villages of Galilee and applied the intent of the Torah to almost every aspect of daily life. Their aim was to extend the practice of religious life beyond the temple to the homes and families of faithful Jews. Pharisees gathered in local groups, as scholars, to debate and discuss the Torah. These gatherings were in homes, usually in the context of a meal and were called *haveroth*, "the table-fellowship of friends." The Gospels narrate several times when Jesus, while not a Pharisee, was invited to *haveroth*. This may indicate that some Pharisees saw common ground with Jesus. Luke's Gospel narrates certain Pharisees warning Jesus about Herod and after his crucifixion that a "member of the council" offered his tomb for the body of Jesus. John's Gospel narrates that the Pharisee Nicodemus, who early in Jesus' ministry visited him privately to learn more about his activities, brought spices to anoint the body of Jesus. It is only when Jesus speaks, teaches, or acts in contradiction to their protocols that some Pharisees take issue with him. One example is when Jesus ate with tax collectors and sinners.

Although Jesus and some of the Pharisees had strong disagreements they shared dedication to the Torah and the heart of what it meant to be a faithful Jew. At the same time, Jesus had strong words of condemnation for some Pharisees when their outward practices were obvious sources of personal pride and when they used their prominent position as religious leaders to take advantage of people who looked to them for leadership. They often laid unnecessary burdens on people to ensure their compliance with oral interpretations of the Torah. It would not be wise to ignore these conflicts, but they should be placed in context.

It is clear that Jesus' life of prayer was lived in the context of the Torah. *"Do not think that I have come to abolish the law or the prophets; I have come not to abolish but to fulfill. For truly I tell you, until heaven and earth pass away* [that is the world], *not one stroke of a letter, will pass from the law until it is accomplished. . . . For I tell you, unless your righteousness exceeds that of the scribes and the Pharisees, you will never enter the kingdom of heaven"* (Matt 5:17–18; 20).

Jesus was clear about his call from God to "accomplish" what God intended in the Torah. It was a path and guide to righteous living. Jesus' life made the Torah tangible and he was passionate to share that life with all who would listen and follow. Jesus' life is what life "in the kingdom" looks like. His reference to exceeding the righteousness of the scribes and Pharisees is not criticism. He is saying that their example, even though dedicated, does not yet demonstrate the fullness of what is possible with God. Jesus was not an angry revolutionary trying to start something new. He saw how his faith community was "missing the mark" in their desire to accomplish what the Torah intended. He reinterpreted aspects of the Torah so that they would be congruent with God's unconditional love. Jesus prayer enabled him to see how the Torah could be fulfilled.

In the first century, Pharisees were trying to minimize the influence of secular Roman society on their faith tradition. How have modern Christian denominations taken on aspects of modern society?

How can "being like Jesus" be fulfilled in your life?

DAY 53

Written on your heart

What do you treasure? What is most fundamental in your life? As Jesus was beginning a journey, a wealthy young man asked Jesus, *"Teacher, what good deed must I do to inherit eternal life?"* Jesus responded by referring the young man to the commandments Moses received on Mount Sinai. The young man replied, *"I have kept all these; what do I still lack?"* Jesus declared," *If you wish to be perfect, go, sell all your possessions, and give the money to the poor, and you will have treasure in heaven; then come, follow me."* When the young man heard this, *"he went away grieving, for he had many possessions"* (Matt 19:16, 20–22). Jesus discerned that the young man was more committed to his wealth than Torah. He challenged the young man to see that the Torah is fulfilled through loving God and neighbor *with our entire being*. Torah is a verb, not a noun. Torah is a way of life, not an end in itself.

Perhaps Jesus had an extraordinary passage from the prophet Jeremiah in mind when he responded to the wealthy young man:

> *The days are surely coming, says the Lord, when I will make a new covenant with the house of Israel and the house of Judah. It will not be like the covenant that I made with their ancestors when I took them by the hand to bring them out of the land of Egypt—a covenant they broke, though I was their husband, says the Lord. But this is the covenant I will make with the house of Israel after those days, says the Lord: I will put my law within them, and I will write it on their hearts; and I will be their God, and they will be my people.* (Jer 31:31–33)

Both John the Baptist and Jesus saw their ministries as testimony that God was acting to establish a new covenant with God's people. But it was not simply a renewal of commitment to the Torah as an external demand or authority. Jesus' experience of God was rooted in his heart, both in quiet listening and active engagement with the needs of people around him. His fulfillment of the Torah was to embody its wisdom in the way he lived. The Torah was not an external expectation. It was a passionate desire to love God and neighbor flowing from his heart. Jesus' life of prayer made the

Torah transparent, and he invited those close to him to live the Torah in the same way.

> *If you love me, you will keep my commandments. And I will ask the Father, and he will give you another Advocate, to be with you forever. This is the Spirit of truth, whom the world cannot receive, because it neither sees him nor knows him. You know him, because he abides with you, and he will be in you.* (John 14:15–16)

"If you love me, you will keep my commandments" is not a challenge or a prerequisite for God's love. Jesus is telling us that the source of fulfilling his commands (including the Torah, summarized in the Great Commandment and the *Shema*) is a relationship of love. Living compassionately is the fruit of love, not coercion or the need to please God. Although the commands are not easy to live, the *"Spirit of truth"* will provide guidance and strength. But this is not an external "Advocate." The Spirit abides within us. Jesus is speaking again of experience of God (who is love) in prayer. Our intimacy with God will give us both the desire and the power to love God and our neighbor. The prophet Isaiah describes the fruit of this kind of love:

> *If you remove the yoke from among you, the pointing of the finger, the speaking of evil, if you offer your food to the hungry and satisfy the needs of the afflicted, then your light shall rise in the darkness and your gloom be like the noonday. The LORD will guide you continually, and satisfy your needs in parched places, and make your bones strong; you shall be like a watered garden, like a spring of water, whose waters never fail.* (Isa 58:9b–11)

The fruit of listening to God in prayer is that *"the Lord will guide you continually"* and the waters of love will flow from us like *"a spring of water, whose waters never fail."*

In the context of our current consumer society, what can you learn from the narrative about Jesus and the wealthy young man regarding balancing what you desire with what you need?

What is the relationship between wealth and loving God and our neighbor?

BIBLICAL TEXTS FOR STUDY AND REFLECTION:

Mark 10:17–31; Matt 6:19–21; 13:44–45

DAY 54

Prayer is tangible

We usually think of prayer as "a time of prayer." It is intentional communication with God. You could say it is a noun describing a "space," either within us, in a group, or in public worship. In these contexts, prayer is something amorphous, yet has its own discreet sector in life. Jesus' prayer, rather his life of prayer, demonstrates that prayer is a verb as well as a noun. As we have seen in earlier reflections, Jesus went off to quiet places, intentionally, at different times of day to be in God's presence. He worshiped regularly with his family as a child and with his disciples and villagers as an adult. It was his custom to worship on the Sabbath in synagogues and participate in the great feasts of his faith community in the temple in Jerusalem. At the same time, all these aspects of prayer had direct influences on Jesus' life. They extended beyond his "times of prayer" into his "life of prayer." His prayer became decisions, wise teaching, acts of healing, discernment of the needs of people around him, and specific acts of compassion. Prayer became *tangible and practical*. It was experience of God embodied in specific behavior as well as "a time."

Today we begin a series of reflections on Jesus' "times of prayer" that preceded specific incidents in his life. While it is not appropriate to assume there was a direct causal relationship in Jesus' mind, it seems clear from the Gospel narratives that his prayer, in its variety of forms and venues, empowered his discernment, words, and actions. When we look at all four canonical Gospels, a threefold pattern becomes clear: (a) quiet listening and experience of God's presence, (b) faithful discernment of God's desires, and (c) compassionate engagement in the lives of people.

The first incidents for reflection are Jesus' baptism and temptation in the wilderness:

> Now when all the people were baptized, and when Jesus also had been baptized and was praying, the heaven was opened, and the Holy Spirit descended upon him in bodily form like a dove. And a voice came from heaven, "You are my Son, the Beloved, with you I am well pleased." (Luke 3:21–22)

Jesus' consciousness was turned toward God when this experience took place. Then, *"Jesus, full of the Holy Spirit, returned from the Jordan and was led by the Spirit in the wilderness, where for forty days he was tempted by the devil"* (Luke 4:1–2). Jesus was praying when the Spirit came upon him. His "time of prayer" was a relationship of personal openness with the Spirit's response. While *"full of the Spirit"* he was *"led"* into the wilderness to discern the meaning of *"You are my Son, the Beloved . . . ."* This mutual presence in the Jordan led to an extended period of discernment in the wilderness. Jesus' openness was filled with the Spirit. He *listened* to the Spirit and *followed* the Spirit's path.

The incidents in the Jordan and the wilderness show that Jesus learned a great deal about himself and God in his prayer. His sense of being a beloved son came from his *experience of God* rather than the formation of an idea in his mind. His awareness of how this filial relationship would be lived began to be shaped in the "temptations" in the wilderness. He began to discern how he should act as a son by experiencing what God is like in his prayer; the son will be like the father. At the same time, his prayer in the wilderness and the "temptations" enabled him to relate the Hebrew Scriptures to his relationship with God in specific ways.

When has your experience of God in prayer become manifest in your words or actions?

How would you respond to a person who says, "Prayer is personal and has nothing to do with the workplace or politics."

BIBLICAL TEXTS FOR STUDY AND REFLECTION:

Matt 3:13–17; 4:1–11; Luke 3:21–22; 4:1–13

DAY 55

Listening to Scriptures

It is tempting to think of Jesus' time in the desert primarily as an encounter with the "devil." It is true that Jesus is confronted with the dark side of being "God's Beloved" and the possibilities of misusing God's power. But along with these possibilities, Jesus' inner ear is still hearing the voice of the One whose Spirit led him into the wilderness. This time God's voice is not audible as it was at his baptism (according to the Gospel narratives). In the silence and austerity of the desert, the place where his people believed "evil" prevailed, Jesus hears again the wisdom he learned in synagogue school and the synagogue readings and oral commentary about his ancestors' trials and covenant with God in the wilderness of Sinai.

> It is written, "One does not live by bread alone, but by every word that comes from the mouth of God." (Matt 4:4, quoting Deut 8:3)

> Again it is written, "Do not put the Lord your God to the test." (Matt 4:7; quoting Deut 6:16)

> Away with you Satan! For it is written "Worship the Lord your God, and serve only him." (Matt 4:10b; quoting Deut 6:13)

"It is written," "it is written," "it is written." In the silence of the desert Jesus' listens to ancient words from the sacred Scriptures that formed him and were inscribed on his heart.

We know nothing of Jesus' formal education in Hebrew Scriptures. We can assume, like other Galilean boys, he most likely studied Hebrew and listened regularly to interpretations (in Aramaic) in the synagogue in Nazareth (which may have been in a home or a simple building similar to a home). Lacking documentation does not rule out the possibility that he was well educated in Scriptures. The canonical Gospels narrate Jesus' fluency in Scriptures and describe occasions where he teaches in synagogues and comments on them. The best indication of his familiarity with the Hebrew Scriptures is the way his teaching and ministry mirror so much of the writings from the Psalms and the Prophets. Although in some instances the evangelists may be using Scripture to authenticate aspects of Jesus' ministry (such as Luke 4:16–20), there can be little doubt that Jesus carried the Scriptures within and they were part of his prayer, teaching, and actions. It is possible that they "taught" him who he was and gave guidance for his life.

The Spanish New Testament scholar José Pagola cites these examples from the Psalms that are congruent with Jesus' teaching and understanding of God's activity in his life:

> The LORD is merciful and gracious, slow to anger and abounding in steadfast love. He will not always accuse, nor will he keep his anger forever. He does not deal with us according to our sins. . . . As a father he has compassion for his children, so the LORD has compassion for those who fear him." (Ps 103:8–10, 13)

> Do not forget the life of your poor forever. Have regard for your covenant, for the dark places of the land are full of the haunts of violence. Do not let the downtrodden be put to shame; let the poor and the needy praise your name. (Ps 74:19b–21)

It seems clear that the kind of listening Jesus did in the wilderness after his baptism was a natural part of his life of prayer. But listening was not an end in itself. During long days and nights in the wilderness, Jesus decided that *"God's Beloved"* will depend on and serve only God. That awareness empowered the beginning of Jesus' ministry. *Listening became action:*

> Then Jesus, filled with the power of the Spirit, returned to Galilee, and a report about him spread through all the country. He began to teach in their synagogues and was praised by everyone. (Luke 4:14–15)

How have the Hebrew Scriptures (the Old Testament) and the New Testament influenced your life?

What opportunities does your local congregation offer for substantive study of the Bible?

DAY 56

Guidance for important decisions

The Synoptic Gospels (Matthew, Mark, and Luke) tell us that immediately after Jesus' testing in the wilderness, the Spirit of God led him to Galilee to begin his ministry. We have seen how Luke sets Jesus' new work in the context of the prophet Isaiah's vision of bringing good news to the poor, release to captives, recovery of sight to the blind, letting the oppressed go free, and proclaiming the year of the Lord's favor. In other words, Jesus' preaching and work would meet specific needs of people and demonstrate God's presence and care. The reign of God begins with those whose needs are the greatest. We saw that this included preaching in synagogues, preaching outdoors, healing a variety of diseases, freeing persons from unclean spirits, and dialogue about his words and actions with some of the scribes and Pharisees. (Jesus' words and actions almost immediately began to encounter resistance.) His innovative ministry challenged the status quo.

> *Now during those days he went out to the mountain to pray; and he spent the night in prayer to God. And when day came he called his disciples and chose twelve of them, whom he named apostles.* (Luke 6:12–13)

Jesus spent the night on a "mountain"—actually a high hill. Early tradition locates this hill south of Capernaum, on the west side of the Sea of Galilee. Half way up the hill is a cave in an area where a slope forms a natural amphitheater. It is possible that Jesus spent the night in the cave *"in prayer to God."* Once again he sought God's presence in solitude. Early tradition calls this place the "The Cave of Solitude." In that temporary seclusion it is likely that, as Jesus reflected on the myriad of events taking place in his life, he discerned the need to include others in his work, because first thing in the morning he *"called his disciples and chose twelve of them, whom he named apostles."* It is easy to let Luke's short reference to his night of prayer slip by in the midst of his very active life. But it was crucial. It is clear that prayer informed and empowered his decisions.

In the wilderness, following his baptism, Jesus realized that his filial relationship with God should not direct attention only to himself, personally. He realized that any response to his words and actions should be based on the recognition that God is speaking and acting through him. Later in his ministry he would declare, *"But if it is by the finger of I cast out demons, then the kingdom of God has come to you"* (Luke 11:20). It was the tangible presence of God in his life that drew people to him and motivated them to fall to their knees before him, rise, and follow him. Falling to your knees was a Semitic practice honoring the presence of a person who has authority over you or whose presence manifests the presence and Spirit of God. As this calling began to unfold Jesus realized that his words and actions had their source in his Abba; he was not acting on his own from a reservoir of his original thoughts and unique power. And now, Jesus realizes it is time to share the manifestation of God's presence with others. In Jesus' eastern Mediterranean culture there were very few "schools," and most of them were in the cities and most students were the sons of wealthy landowners, political figures, and religious leaders. Education outside the home ended at twelve years for girls, whose "place" was in the home. In the towns and villages young men usually became apprentices to their fathers.

Another common form of teaching was the "master and disciple" relationship. Some Jewish "sages" chose disciples and they shared property and lived a common life. As David Flusser and Brad H. Young, scholars of first-century rabbinic teachers, point out,[17] the role of the disciple was not simply "listening" to the sage, but developing intimacy and sharing the life of the "master." Other "masters" lived with their disciples outside a local center, wandering from place to place and teaching outdoors, in synagogues, in orchards, near vineyards, and in market places. They ate meals together as they traveled and attracted local people to the "master's" teaching. Does this sound familiar?

What did Jesus mean when he said, *"Follow me"*?

How do you follow Jesus?

BIBLICAL TEXTS FOR STUDY AND REFLECTION:
Luke 4:14–29; Isa 42:1–9

17. See Flusser, *The Sage from Galilee,* 12–17, and Young, *Meet the Rabbis,* 30–33.

DAY 57

Discerning God's kingdom

Psalm 89 was composed centuries before the life of Jesus. Yet two of its verses express the longing of Israel in the first century for the restoration of God's rule in the midst of the dominant influence of foreign power. *"How long, O LORD? Will you hide yourself forever? . . . LORD where is your stead-fast love of old, which by your faithfulness you swore to David?"* (Ps 89:46, 49). Both John the Baptist and Jesus believed God was acting to re-establish God's covenant with Israel; that was the "good news" Jesus proclaimed. John's message was more austere, with images of judgment, calling for people to renounce their sinful lives and turn toward God's renewed activity in the life of Israel. Jesus' message was more focused on God's desire to bring abundant life to people who are suffering, hungry, and deprived of their livelihood and dignity. Both Jesus and John exhorted people to embrace God's immanent activity by "turning toward God." In the first century there was great expectation that the prophet Elijah would return as a sign that God was restoring the House of David. Jesus was convinced that God was acting in his life to restore the lives of people who had been oppressed, not only by the Romans, but by many of their own people. People were drawn to Jesus and his influence for change was growing. But there was also serious doubt, confusion, and resistance to his teaching and works. Who was he?

Luke describes a dialogue between Jesus and his closest disciples that took place shortly after the feeding of a crowd of five thousand people who had come to listen to Jesus near Bethsaida at the north-west corner of the Sea of Galilee. *"Once when Jesus was praying alone, with only the disciples near him, he asked them, 'Who do the crowds say that I am?' They answered, 'John the Baptist; but others, Elijah; and still others, that one of the ancient prophets has arisen.' He said to them, 'But who do you say that I am?' Peter answered, 'The Messiah of God'"* (Luke 9:18–20). In the midst of his personal prayer, Jesus turns to the disciples and asks how the "crowds" identify him. He is not interested in "titles," but in people's awareness of the significance of his life and work in their midst. In his culture a "name" carries the agency and presence of the person named. It is clear from the variety of responses that many people sense the presence of God in Jesus as a prophet, perhaps the prophet Elijah, who will be a sign of the restoration of the House of David. Then Jesus asks the disciples how they perceive him as a result of witnessing his teaching and works. We can never know what took place in Jesus prayer at that moment, yet his question arises in the context of his time with his Abba. Peter responds: *"The Messiah of God."* Luke uses the Greek word *Christos*, a transliteration the Hebrew word *Mâshiyach*, meaning "one smeared with oil" or "the anointed one." Israel's chiefs, kings, priests, and some prophets were anointed with olive oil, to signify the indwelling of God's Spirit upon them. Israel's kings, especially David, their ideal king, became "a different person" when they were anointed and were "given a different heart" by God (1 Sam 10:1–10). They were now to act on behalf of God. The foundation of their throne and authority was to ensure that the people would be governed with justice, righteousness, steadfast love, and faithfulness (Ps 89:14). Peter senses that Jesus has been anointed by God's Spirit and is the one who will restore God's kingdom. He sees the presence of the Spirit in Jesus' teaching and works. He sees "a changed man." But he does not yet discern the fullness of God's presence and work in Jesus. He will learn more on the Mount of Transfiguration and in the events leading toward Jesus' suffering and crucifixion.

Who do *you* say Jesus is?

Who are persons today who, from your point of view, have been anointed with God's Spirit? How do their words and actions embody God's Spirit?

DAY 58

Seeing beyond the surface

> *Now about eight days after these sayings Jesus took with him Peter
> and John and James, and went up on the mountain to pray. And
> while he was praying, the appearance of his face changed, and his
> clothes became dazzling white . . . . (Luke 9:28–29)*

Jesus takes three disciples, whom he knows well, up on a mountain to pray.
(Two great Hebrew prophets, Moses and Elijah, had experienced God's
presence on mountains in the forms of a burning bush and a whisper.) Perhaps Jesus thought Peter, John, and James were now ready to share what he
experienced in the solitary presence of his Abba. In Luke's Gospel the original Greek says that Jesus was "in prayer." He was in his "inner chamber"
(Matt 6:6) when his countenance is transformed and his clothes shine with
penetrating light. Enclosed in the canopy of light the disciples see Moses
and Elijah speaking with Jesus. Peter wants to preserve the experience by
building booths and remaining on the mountain. But as he expresses his
desire, a dark cloud overshadows them and their delight and awe become
terror as they hear a voice declare, *"This is my Son, the Beloved, with him I
am well pleased; listen to him!"* (Luke 9:35b). Then, according to Matthew's
Gospel, *"Jesus came and touched them, saying, 'Get up and do not be afraid.'
And when they looked up, they saw no one except Jesus himself alone"* (Matt
17:7–8).

At his baptism Jesus heard a voice from heaven say, *"You are my Son,
my Beloved."* Now Peter, John, and James hear the same message with the
exhortation, *"Listen to him!"* Following this incident Jesus continues his
healing and teaching ministry and sends out seventy disciples to share that
work. He begins to speak about the personal cost of following him and how
kings and prophets yearned to see and hear what the disciples are witnessing. It is then that the disciples ask Jesus, *"Lord, teach us to pray."* Jesus
responds with the "Lord's Prayer" and urges them to persevere in prayer.
*"Ask and it will be given you; search and you will find; knock and the door will
be opened to you"* (Matt 7:7).

Prayer is the threshold that will guide the disciples as they try to make
sense of this new intensity in Jesus' ministry. And yet Jesus knows it will

take time for them to grasp what took place on the mountain as well as the events that will lead to his crucifixion. He will not force a change in consciousness. He knows and loves them too much for that. *"I still have many things to say to you, but you cannot bear them now. When the Spirit comes, he will guide you into all the truth . . ."* (John 16:12–13).

Yet, questions remain. What really happened on the mountain? What does it tell us about Jesus? Whose experience is Luke portraying? Are we witnessing an event in Jesus' life as it actually happened or are we looking at the event through the faith of the post-resurrection followers of Jesus? James Dunn, a respected New Testament scholar, is convinced that narratives like this can demonstrate authentic aspects of Jesus' personal experience of God as well as post-resurrection experiences of the risen Christ that formed the faith of the followers of the Way. Both Jesus and members of the early Christian communities experienced God at the deepest level of their being. They were led by the Spirit, as Jesus promised, to see beyond the surface of what they experienced. In the same way that Jesus' experience of God formed and empowered his teaching and ministry, the early Christians experienced the presence of the risen Christ in ways that empowered their lives, teaching, and ministries. The Transfiguration tells us that Jesus experienced God on the mountain with such clarity that it confirmed his filial identity with God and the authority of his message. The voice told the disciples, *"Listen to him!"*

In modern society there are many voices competing for our attention. How do you listen to Christ Jesus? What distracts you? What supports you?

BIBLICAL TEXTS FOR STUDY AND REFLECTION:

John 8:31–38; Luke 10:21–24; 11:5–13

DAY 59

Practicing what you pray

The consequences of prayer are totally in God's hands, yet are usually manifested in many ways, some so mysterious that they escape our awareness. We have seen that Jesus' words and actions were influenced by his solitary prayer, corporate prayer in family and synagogue, and in his participation in the great feasts of his faith community at the temple in Jerusalem. Jesus' heart bonded with his Abba in prayer and led to the tangible presence of his Abba in the words and behavior of his daily life. Would Jesus' have known what to say or to do without his prayerful experience of God? We cannot say, except that it seems clear from several unexpected incidents that followed his prayer that Jesus, like us, left things in God's hands. Perhaps the most dramatic example is the relationship between his intense prayer in the Garden of Gethsemane and what happened in the Garden immediately after his disciple, Judas, betrays him with a kiss.

> *Then Jesus went with* [his disciples after eating the Passover Meal] *to a place called Gethsemane; and he said to his disciples, "Sit here while I go over there and pray." He took with him Peter and the two sons of Zebedee* [the same three that he took with him to the Mount of Transfiguration] *and began to be grieved and agitated. Then he said to them, "I am deeply grieved, even to death; remain here and stay awake with me." And going a little farther, he threw himself on the ground and prayed, "Father, if it is possible, let this cup pass from me; yet not what I want but what you want."* (Matt 26:36–39)

During Jesus' prayer he had to awaken the disciples three times. Finally, he says, *"Get up, let us be going. See my betrayer is at hand."* Then Judas arrives with a large crowd *"with swords and clubs, from the chief priests and the elders of the people."* Judas identifies Jesus with a kiss. *"Then they came and laid hands on Jesus and arrested him. Suddenly, one of those with Jesus put his hand on his sword, drew it, and struck the slave of the high priest, cutting off his ear. Then Jesus said to him, 'Put your sword back into its place; for all who take the sword perish by the sword'"* (Matt 26:46, 47, 50b–52).

As we have seen, many people believed Jesus was the one who would re-establish the House of David. Luke's Gospel reports that temple police, armed with swords and clubs were among the crowd. The high priest was appointed by and with the support of Roman authority. This confrontation was filled with possibilities for violence and revolution. According to Luke, Jesus' followers said to him, *"Lord, should we strike with the sword?"* and Jesus replies, *"No more of this!"* Then Jesus touched the high priest's slave and healed him (Luke 22:49b, 51a).

Jesus prays to his Abba *". . . yet not what I want but what you want."* Soon after this, in the midst of violence, he declares *"No more of this!"* Jesus was aware of the risks of the "cup" he accepted. His love for all those around him, including those who came to arrest him, was too powerful to allow false values to prevail over his personal experience of God's desires for human life. He was aware that death might be the cost of standing firm for authentic life. His non-violent response to those who came to arrest and execute him was a powerful statement of the difference between his consciousness and theirs. He knew that they had no idea of the emptiness of their values and power. After his arrest Jesus would say to Pontius Pilate, *"My kingdom is not from this world"* (John 18:36a). He was practicing what he prayed.

Describe a situation, decision, or encounter that, in retrospect, was influenced by your personal prayer.

Describe changes in your life, the way you have changed your mind on an issue, or the direction your life has taken. How are any of these changes related to your life of prayer?

DAY 60

Prayer transcends all barriers

Yesterday we reflected on Jesus' prayer in the Garden of Gethsemane, followed by his refusal to permit a violent response to his arrest. His healing of the High Priest's slave shattered both conventional wisdom and the hopes some people had placed in him as a messianic figure. Jesus' behavior demonstrated congruence between his action and his teaching about loving one's "enemy." By healing the slave Jesus removed the label of "enemy" and replaced it with "one who is worthy of healing." Jesus manifests the forgiving nature of his Abba as a threshold for an alternative to violence. Throughout his ministry Jesus repeatedly claimed that he learned this forgiving attitude from his Abba and in this incident is able to make it tangible.

When Jesus is arrested his followers desert him and at his religious and political trials he refuses to claim his authority or invoke God's power on his behalf. During his ministry many unsuccessful attempts were made to shame him. In Jesus' culture shame is to be avoided at all costs. Now he will suffer humiliation and his society's most shameful death, crucifixion. His shame is confirmed by suffering physical pain, taunting, and torture. What the world sees as shame will be transformed into honor. This is the context for Jesus' three prayers from the cross.

In the presence of crowds, soldiers, and temple leaders who are mocking him, Jesus prays aloud, *"Father, forgive them; for they do not know what they are doing"* (Luke 23:34). Jesus speaks from a form of human consciousness that is entirely different from those who taunt him. He knows the will of his Abba, whose "ways" are not the "ways" of the earth, yet are possible if we desire them. Jesus is living the words of the prayer he taught his disciples: "Your will be done on earth as in heaven."

The evangelists place Jesus' last two prayers at three in the afternoon, the time of daily evening prayer when the afternoon sacrifice was taking place in the temple. Although weak and near death, Jesus must have heard the trumpets from the temple proclaim the beginning of evening prayers at that hour. Jesus' second prayer is a loud cry: *"My God, my God, why have you forsaken me?"* This is the first verse of Psalm 22, a psalm of passion and suffering associated with messianic hope recited as part of the evening prayers. Although the evangelists record Jesus reciting only the first verse, he may have continued with verses describing a servant who suffers, yet will praise the Lord and turn the hearts of many to remember God. We have no way of knowing what Jesus' was feeling. Yet he begins with *"My God, my God . . . ."* Even though he shares the emptiness felt by the psalmist, he still is not disconnected from his Abba. He is praying, and his prayer expresses tension between what he is experiencing and the trusting relationship with God that has been the source of his wisdom and works throughout his life.

All devout Jews in Jerusalem and throughout Israel would have begun evening prayers with the *Tephilla*: "Blessed be thou (our God and the God of our fathers), the God of Abraham, the God of Isaac and the God of Jacob (God, great, mighty, and fearful), most high God . . . ."[18] Jesus' third prayer—*"Into your hand I commit my spirit; you have redeemed me, O LORD, faithful God"*—is the fifth verse of Psalm 31, also part of evening prayer. Jesus learned these words as a child and his life ends with the same words on his lips.

His mother, Mary, was close enough to the cross to hear Jesus' prayer, perhaps reciting the words of evening prayer, herself. Jesus' life of prayer was rooted in the prayers of his family and his religious tradition. This foundation never left him and was the ground that led him to the unique intimacy with God that was the source of his wisdom and works. Prayer never left him, regardless of the circumstances.

Sometimes we lose our desire to pray. When has that happened to you?

What helps you restore your life of prayer when it gets hard or seems fruitless?

18. Quoted in Jeremias, *Prayers of Jesus*, 74.

DAY 61

Body prayer

The next series of reflections will focus on the relationship between healing and Jesus' life of prayer. The first example comes early in Matthew's Gospel and provides some important insights into Jesus' culture that will explain his attitude and behavior in the midst of illness.

> *When Jesus had come down from the mountain,* [immediately after the Sermon on the Mount] *great crowds followed him; and there was a leper who came to him and knelt down before him, saying, "Lord, if you choose, you can make me clean." He stretched out his hand and touched him, saying, "I do choose. Be made clean." Immediately the leprosy was cleansed. Then Jesus said to him, "See that you say nothing to anyone; but go, show yourself to the priest, and offer the gift* [of thanksgiving] *that Moses commanded, as a testimony to them."* (Matt 8:1–4)

As we have seen, in Jesus' culture shame was to be avoided at all costs. Honor was the primary value. The well-being of each individual and the community was based on full participation in the life of the Torah, the center of life's meaning and purpose. There were many boundaries that ensured the purity of Israel's religious community and each individual's life within the community. An individual's impurity could endanger the purity of another person and, through them, the purity of the community. Religious purity was a source of honor. Along with the need to conform to religious purity was the requirement to fulfill one's responsibilities within a system of patronage. Persons of political or religious authority and persons of wealth provided physical, spiritual, and economic well-being and protection for persons of lower status in society. "Ordinary" persons and the "poor" worked for their patrons and were required to pay their patrons taxes or "in kind" contributions in return for their patrons' protection and employment opportunities. God was the supreme patron, followed by religious and political leaders, and the wealthy. Unless the patronage system was abused, it provided stability and well-being in society. Ideally, it was based on justice and righteousness.

Illness separated a person from others and the community because contact with them would make others unclean and profane sacred places and rites. In like manner, a person who sinned against another or did not fulfill the requirements of the Torah or Oral Law was considered unclean and an object of shame. Depending on the nature of their illness or sins, their participation in community life would be limited in various ways. In severe cases, such as leprosy, they were excluded and placed outside the margins of society with little hope for survival. They were to be avoided and became helpless. Such persons could not fulfill the duties required by their patrons or the Torah and, therefore, disrupted the well-being of others.

Jesus' encounter with a leper in Matthew 8 demonstrates a living example of the "breaking-in" of the reign of God into Galilean society through the ministry of Jesus. The leper recognizes the authority of God's presence in Jesus (a patron) and kneels before him and pleads, *"Lord, if you choose, you can make me clean."* The leper is asking for healing of the illness that has taken away his well-being, dignity, and separated him from his community. Jesus *"stretched out his hand and touched him"* and the leprosy was cleansed. Jesus' prayer is *a healing touch* that according to conventional norms will make him unclean also. It seems clear that Jesus' "prayer" in this situation is the presence and power of his Abba within him. He needs no words. He knows what his Abba desires, even if it contradicts oral interpretations of the Torah. Restoring a person to fullness of life is more faithful to the Torah than maintaining the status of purity.

Who are the "persons to avoid" in our society?

How can followers of Jesus welcome them and help restore their place in society?

DAY 62

Prayer without words, touch, or boundaries

Yesterday we reflected on God's presence through Jesus' healing touch of a leper. God is the healer. Jesus says, *"Be made clean."* He does not say, "I make you clean." Once the leper's body is healed, Jesus says, *"go and show yourself to the priest, and offer the gift that Moses commanded . . . ."* This will demonstrate to the priest that the leper is no longer impure and can be restored to his proper place in society. His well-being is healed as well as his body. God is, indeed, at work in Jesus *"to let the oppressed go free."* God's kingdom is present through the restoration of the dignity and health of a leper. The flow of God's energy is tangible.

After Jesus healed the leper, Matthew reports that he enters Capernaum and is approached by a Roman Centurion, a commanding officer of one hundred soldiers stationed near the town. When the Centurion asks Jesus to heal a servant in his home, Jesus replies, *"I will come and cure him"* (see Matt 8:5–13). But the Centurion insists that he is not worthy to have Jesus enter his home; Jesus' word is all that is necessary. This is an amazing conversation because the Centurion has authority over the people of Galilee and he, himself, is under and represents the authority of Rome. He is the patron who Jesus should look to for protection and whose authority he should obey. Yet the Centurion considers Jesus more worthy than he and is willing to place his reputation and the well-being of his slave in the hands of Jesus. Jesus replies to all who are present, *"Truly I tell you, in no one in Israel have I found such faith."* The "faith" is the Centurion's willingness to place himself in the hands of Jesus. A foreigner, who is outside the authority of the Torah, stakes his reputation and the health of his servant on his recognition of the power of God in Jesus, a Galilean. The Centurion is willing to enter into the presence of God's power in Jesus' life. This is one of the few examples of Jesus' willingness to extend his ministry beyond his own people.

The narrative ends with Jesus saying, *"Go; let it be done for you according to your faith."* And the evangelist, Matthew, adds, *"And the servant was healed in that hour."* Jesus seems completely present to his Abba in this situation. He knows from his own experience that God's power is changing lives through him and all around him. He realizes that this power does not originate from his words and presence. The "prayer" of Jesus is his aware-ness that *God* will be fully present to restore the health of the Centurion's slave. He places everything in God's hands. So did the Centurion. *"Truly I tell you, in no one in Israel have I found such faith."*

Jesus' life of prayer includes "room for God." In this incident God is "front and center." It seems clear that Jesus "knows" God is present and will act. This is not intellectual knowledge. It is awareness, based on a mu-tual presence that opens the opportunity for God to act in Jesus' life. This knowledge is the foundation of all prayer because prayer is a relationship made possible by mutual presence. This means, as in the incident with the Centurion, there will be times and places where words and personal inter-vention are not necessary. God's presence is enough. We are not "left out." We are present with God. That is not unimportant.

How is this narrative about Jesus and the Roman Centurion related to per-sonal intercessory prayer for healing today?

What can we learn about healing from this narrative?

Biblical texts for study and reflection:

Matthew 8:1–13; 2 Kings 5:1–19; Luke 7:1–10

DAY 63

Being aware of God's desires

As we have seen, in Jesus' culture the written Torah and the oral interpretations of the Torah by the scribes and Pharisees determined the way to ensure the religious and social well-being of society. In this context, a sinner was a person whose behavior was unfaithful to the Torah and therefore delinquent in his or her responsibilities to other persons and to society. Sin brought stress and sometimes disintegration to relationships between people, with social as well as religious consequences. It brought shame and alienation to the sinner and his or her family. Illness had a similar effect because it was perceived as a consequence of personal failure, rather than biological dysfunction. In Jesus' culture illness and sinful behavior were directly related. When someone became ill a common question would be, "What has this person done to warrant this?" *"As he walked along, he saw a man blind from birth. His disciples asked him, 'Rabbi, who sinned, this man or his parents, that he was born blind'"* (John 9:1–2). This attitude toward the relatedness of illness and sin was not hard-heartedness. Its origin may lie during the time of Moses just after the Hebrews had escaped from Egypt. In the wilderness they found only bitter springs and God instructed Moses to cast wood into the water to make it sweet. This was the occasion for a statute exhorting the people to *"give heed to* [God's] *commandments"* so that God would not *"bring upon you any of the diseases that I brought upon the Egyptians"* (Exod 15:25b–26). The Hebrews perceived God as the source of both blessing and curses. Therefore, as Jesus traveled throughout the Galilean villages, the sick, blind, leprous, lame, and demon-possessed he encountered were considered by the people to be under punishment from God as sinners. But Jesus saw them as persons whom God loves and who should be restored to abundant life and reconciliation with their community. God wants to relieve their suffering. This was Jesus' message and most likely the reason why so many came to him to be cured.

The evangelist Matthew describes Jesus returning to Capernaum where he meets some people carrying a paralyzed man on a bed hoping Jesus will cure him (Matt 9:1–8). He is moved by their strong desire to bring the man to him. It is obvious to Jesus that they are aware of God's power in his life and want to entrust their friend's life to him. *"When Jesus saw their faith, he said to the paralytic, 'Take heart, your sins are forgiven.'"* Jesus' first words acknowledge both the paralytic's discouragement about his physical limitation and the effect it has had on those who are close to him. *"Take heart, . . ."* offers the man—whose heart is dimmed by his disability and the limitation and shame it brings—assurance that God will restore his well-being. Then Jesus declares boldly that the man's sins are forgiven and the source of his shame is removed. He is certain that God will restore the paralytic to fullness of life. Knowing that God's healing power is present, Jesus turns to the man for the third time and exhorts the paralytic, *"Stand up, take your bed, and go home."* Jesus seems so vividly aware of God's desire to heal the man that he tells him to go home and resume his normal role in his family. Although Jesus' words are not intercessory prayers in the conventional sense, they convey his strong desire for the paralytic's healing and his complete trust in God's presence and intention to transform the man's life. Jesus' openness to God and willingness to respond to God's initiative tell us that prayer can be more than words.

How do you understand the relationship between a person's health and sinful behavior?

What does the incident described above tell us about our need for healing of both body and spirit?

BIBLICAL TEXTS FOR STUDY AND REFLECTION:

John 9:1–41

DAY 64

Liberating prayer

Yesterday we reflected on Jesus' awareness of God's intent to heal a paralyzed man, his declaration that the man's sins were forgiven, and his exhortation *"Stand up, take your bed, and go home."* Matthew reports that *"When the crowds saw it, they were filled with awe, and they glorified God, who had given such authority to human beings"* (Matt 9:8). Jesus' experience of God through his life of prayer enabled him to discern God's presence and desires in this and other situations and willingly become a channel for God's Spirit to act. His trust in the movement of God through his words and presence made God's will tangible. When the crowd witnessed God's Spirit acting through Jesus *"they were filled with awe, and they glorified God, who had given such authority to human beings"* (Matt 9:8). The crowds were awestruck as they saw the power of God forgive and heal through Jesus' prayer. Jesus was completely aware of God's desires in that situation and his prayer made that desire tangible. Jesus was sharing the fullness of his experience of God with an oppressed and alienated person; he believed that this was the nature of God's kingdom. His goal was not to establish a "sign" of his authority and power. His desire was to demonstrate the caring mercy of God.

Jesus' healing prayer is filled with trust. Sometimes the words are not directed toward his Abba because, as his intimacy with God continues throughout each day, he seems to know what God will do in a specific situation. There is no separation and no need for words. A good example is in Luke's Gospel (Luke 13:10–16).

> Now he was teaching in one of the synagogues on the Sabbath. And just then there appeared a woman with a spirit that had crippled her for eighteen years. She was bent over and was quite unable to stand up straight. When Jesus saw her, he called her over and said, "Woman, you are set free from your ailment."

The woman appears suddenly in the midst of Jesus' commentary on a portion of the Sabbath reading. She does not seem to interrupt Jesus intentionally, yet he stops and calls her over to him. (Luke comments that an unknown spirit had crippled her. Peasant women in Galilee were under great pressure and subject to abuse, especially widows. All we know about this woman is that the source of her disability is external.) Without any further dialogue, or an invocation to God, Jesus declares, "*Woman, you are set free from your ailment.*" As we have seen, there is no question in Jesus' mind that God has "been set loose" in Galilee to liberate people from disease and oppression. Jesus' "prayer" is to declare what God is doing for the woman because he knows that in God's kingdom God will show mercy on those who are afflicted. It is what the realm of God is like. It's who God is.

"*When he laid his hands on her, immediately she stood up straight and began praising God.*" The consequences of the healing are set in motion by Jesus' touch and the woman's praise. Although in her culture her disability made her the object of shame and marginalization, her healing is a bold statement that God's favor and mercy have restored her dignity and ability to function normally. She is filled with gratitude and joy and that is the capstone of her healing process.

Yet the leader of the synagogue is upset with Jesus because by healing the woman Jesus has performed "work" on the Sabbath (at least, in the eyes of some Jewish interpretations of the Torah's general prohibition of work). Jesus is quick to point out that since animals are untied in order to feed and drink on the Sabbath, there is no reason why this woman, also, should not be "*set free from this bondage on the Sabbath day.*" Jesus' prayer and action are always focused on the desire of God for the well-being of every person. This provides both the motive and confidence for Jesus' prayers of healing.

The bent-over woman's posture and therefore her dignity were disfigured. Who are the "bent over" in our society?

How can their spirits as well as their bodies be restored? Who will help them?

DAY 65

Prayerful power over demons

Word about Jesus as a healer was spreading throughout Galilee and beyond. The sick, the lame, the blind, the deaf, the mute, and persons possessed by demons were healed. It was clear to Jesus that the power of his Abba manifest in these remarkable transformations was a sign that the reign of God was coming and, indeed, here. But liberating persons with demons got him into the most trouble. Religious leaders were concerned that the people he freed would form a movement in society and challenge their authority and control.

> *Now he was casting out a demon that was mute; when the demon had gone out, the one who had been mute spoke; and the crowds were amazed. But some of them said, "He casts out demons by Beelzebul, the ruler of the demons." Others, to test him, kept demanding a sign from heaven. But he knew what they were thinking . . . .* (Luke 11:14–17a)

In Jesus' culture people believed that clean and unclean spirits (demons) were part of a hierarchy of beings. Demons had less power than God, but were able to control humans. Demons attacked the goodness in people and could alienate them from God and their normal relationships in family and community. This produced shame on the person and their family and often a person who had a demon was pushed to the margin of social and religious community life. Although demons are present in a variety of narratives in the Hebrew Scriptures and the New Testament, it is difficult for twenty-first-century readers, scholars, and medical professionals to discover and explain how people in the first-century would have experienced, understood, and responded to demons and demonization. We can do our best to analyze these biblical accounts and their social settings, but should be cautious of making assumptions from our point of view.

At the same time, New Testament scholars and historians have identified conditions that may have contributed to the behaviors of persons who were described as having a demon. First-century peasants in Judea and Galilee lived under intense fear and stress because of the Roman occupation. Peasant village and family life was very unstable, even though family loyalty was strong. Women, especially widows and children, were especially vulnerable to abuse in a patriarchal society and men, under heavy levels of taxation by Rome and graft by local tax collectors, could easily lose their property and ability to care for their families. Life spans were short (rarely past forty years) and work was intense. These conditions may have contributed to dysfunctional behavior that could be directed toward the persons or circumstances that were crushing and intimidating them. In conscious or unconscious desperation, some persons may have displayed unusual behavior to defend themselves from the people or situations that oppressed them and removed their dignity and place in society. Sometimes they were violent and had to be restrained or banished to caves. At other times they, like the mute man in this narrative, remained in villages. Regardless of the causes of their behavior those afflicted in these ways were cut off from their normal place in society and some were described in biblical narratives as having a demon.

When Jesus "cast out" the demon from the mute man there was amazement and anxiety in the crowd. The power of God or the power of demons was the only plausible explanation for Jesus' behavior. Those who were unsure of Jesus' identity accused him of being demon-inspired himself, using the power of the ruler of demons, *Beelzebul*. But Jesus' response is clear and unequivocal: you cannot use demonic power against demonic power. Then he declares, "*But if it is by the finger of God that I cast out the demons, then the kingdom of God has come to you*" (Luke 11:20). It is the work of God who cast out the demon from the mute man and restored him to his rightful place in society. In this context, once again, Jesus' "prayer" is making the power of God manifest through his actions, but it is *God* who acts through him. The New Testament scholar James Dunn is convinced that Jesus' personal prayer enabled his life to become an agent for God's activity. Jesus' experience of God in prayer confirmed his awareness of a filial relationship with God and this bonding was demonstrated by Jesus' emphatic conviction that the Spirit of God acted directly through him during his ministry of healing. Jesus identified this power as evidence that God was acting through him to establish the long-awaited kingdom where God would overcome evil with goodness.

We live in a different scientific world than Jesus. Yet the human dysfunctions he faced were real, regardless of their causes. His response was always to rely on God's power. What are the "demons" of modern society?

How can they be "cast out"?

Where is "the finger of God" today?

BIBLICAL TEXTS FOR STUDY AND REFLECTION:

Luke 11:14–28

DAY 66

Prayer and faith

Matthew narrates Jesus' cure of a boy with a demon. (Matt 17:14–21).
Although the NRSV translates the boy's illness as epilepsy, the Greek text
uses a word that accurately describes how Galilean peasants would have
described him: "a lunatic" (literally, "moon-struck"). Demoniacs were often
described as being out of their minds. Jesus was accused of being "out of his
mind" because he associated with demoniacs and challenged the demons
to leave their lives. The boy in this narrative could have been epileptic, but
we should not assume this diagnosis is accurate by looking at the narrative
with twenty-first century eyes. Galilean peasants, as we have seen, lived
under tremendous political and personal pressure. In some cases, when
that oppression became unbearable a person could be driven out of their
mind or could consciously or unconsciously take on another identity. The
new behavior, such as this boy's falling into the fire or water, or screaming,
or acting in anti-social ways became a means of getting attention and ex-
ercising power. A helpless person could now control others. Yet their need
for attention and inclusion still alienated them from their authentic place in
family and society. It was a tragic situation.

> "Lord, have mercy on my son, for he is a [lunatic] and he suffers
> terribly; he often falls into the fire and often into the water. And I
> brought him to your disciples, but they could not cure him." . . . And
> he rebuked the demon, and it came out of him, and the boy was
> cured instantly. Then the disciples came to Jesus privately and said,
> "Why could we not cast it out?" He said to them, "Because of your
> little faith."

What is the "little faith"? It seems clear from earlier incidents that in
Jesus' mind *faith is entrusting one's life or a situation to the presence and
power of God.* It is not "faith" that a disciple's prayer or action will be effec-
tive. It is not certainty about ensuring an outcome. It is entrusting everything to God. Jesus is very clear that God is always the healer. This is not the
first time Jesus has been frustrated with his disciples. They do not yet seem
able to open their lives to God with the depth of intimacy that melts away
separation and fills a person with God's energy. The healings that take place

with Jesus spring forth from his constant intimacy with his Abba. There is no time when he is "away from" God. He and his Abba are united in such a way that Jesus knows when the healing energy of God will flow through him to another person. The "prayer" in this instance is his trust in God's presence and power. *"But if it is by the finger of God that I cast out demons, then the kingdom of God has come to you."* In other words, God is acting! Jesus' "casting out" of the demon is the fruit of his intimacy with the Holy One. He places the boy's healing completely in God's hands. Jesus' faith is his willingness to accept what God desires.

In the Gospels Jesus uses a variety of images to describe what God desires for human life. It is like a mustard seed that grows into a bush where birds make their nests to bring forth new life and like a woman who needs a judge's help and will not let him sleep until he responds. Faith opens the flow of energy between God and a person. It is like knocking at a door, knowing it will be opened. Jesus' prayer for the young lunatic was his awareness of the palpable presence of God waiting to release the boy from the malign influences that controlled his life. Jesus knew that the boy's healing would proclaim the presence of the reign of God.

Jesus' life reveals that prayer will open the flow of God's desires and energy in our lives as well. It is not something we accomplish; *it is who we become in God.* As Jesus learned in the wilderness, we do not "show up" so God can act through us on demand. It is not up to us. The initiative is *God's.* The intimacy of prayer is the womb of God's work through us.

Perhaps the disciples' "little faith" was their determination to ensure an outcome. Perhaps they could not trust that God's healing power would flow through them. Perhaps this incident—and others like it—prompted one of the disciples to ask, "Lord teach us to pray."

What is your response to this incident in Jesus' life?

Describe your experiences of prayer for healing, either your prayer for another person or times when other persons have prayed for you. How did they care for you?

BIBLICAL TEXTS FOR STUDY AND REFLECTION:

Matt 7:7–11; 13:31–32; Luke 11:5–13; Luke 18:1–8

DAY 67

Prayer's purpose is compassion not proof

We know very little about Jesus' posture during his prayer, whether by himself or in public. Mark's Gospel narrates a healing incident where Jesus' body is an integral part of his prayer for a deaf man who also has an impediment in his speech. These two limitations make him unable to have a normal relationship with people in his village and make him vulnerable to shame, gossip, and ridicule. Since he cannot work, he will most likely have to beg to survive. Yet this man has some friends who care enough about him to bring him to Jesus as he is returning from the region of Tyre to Galilee (Mark 7:31–37).

> . . . and they begged him to lay his hands on him. He took him aside in private, away from the crowd, and put his fingers into his ears, and he spat and touched his tongue. Then looking up to heaven, he sighed and said to him, "Ephphatha," that is, "Be opened." And immediately his ears were opened, his tongue was released, and he spoke plainly. Then Jesus told them to tell no one; but the more he ordered them, the more zealously they proclaimed it.

"Ephphatha." The man's ears and tongue were opened; he could hear and speak plainly. But equally important, his former life was re-opened. He could re-enter society from its fringes. This kind of opening gave Jesus great delight because, as his bodily actions in this healing show, he cared for the man in the same way his Abba cared about him. At the same time, the focus was on the man, not Jesus: *"tell no one."*

Jesus' body language with the man is a profound sign that he, and his Abba, whose life is woven so completely in his life, are *literally* connected to this man. In Jesus' culture, heaven is above the earth, the abode of God. Yet Jesus body language shows that God is not far away from this man. Jesus physically *"took him aside," "put his finger into his ears,"* and *"spat and touched his tongue."*

First, Jesus takes him aside so that they are alone. Perhaps he has words of the prophet Isaiah in mind, *"Because their shame was double, and dishonor was proclaimed as their lot, therefore they shall possess a double portion; everlasting joy shall be theirs"* (Isa 61:7). Then, like all the Hebrew prophets before him who articulated the pathos or sympathy of God for his people, Jesus looks up to heaven and he sighed. Although we have no way of knowing what Jesus was thinking (other than his body language), Jesus' compassion for this man is giving him a new birth. His life in his community is being re-created. In this instance Jesus prays with touch, words, a sigh, a gesture toward heaven, his spittle, and his fingers. The intimacy with the man embodies Jesus' intimacy with his Abba.

Shortly after this healing some Pharisees argue with Jesus asking him for a "sign" to verify the authority of his teaching and activities. Jesus' response is another sigh "deep in his spirit." This is different from the sigh for the man he recently healed. This is a sigh of exasperation that seems to be saying, "If you can't see God's compassionate presence in my actions you are the blind ones." His exasperation is not judgment. He truly wants these Pharisees to see God at work, but they suffer from their self-imposed blindness. His response in unequivocal: *"Why does this generation ask for a sign? Truly I tell you, no sign will be given to this generation"* (Mark 8:11–12). Jesus' prayer enabled him to see beyond such self-imposed efforts to define what life should be like. The authority for Jesus' vision is his experience of God in prayer and the embodiment of that experience in the restoration of the man's hearing and speech.

Facebook, Twitter, smart phones, and the internet seem to dominate most lives today. They have positive and negative influences on us. In what ways do electronic devices inhibit our desire for and comfort with face-to-face encounters where our lives can—physically and spiritually—*touch* each other?

The canonical Gospels show us that Jesus prayed with his whole being: body, mind, and spirit. In what ways are you able to integrate mind, body, and spirit in your prayer?

DAY 68

Renewing life when everything seems lost

Although there are many other incidents where Jesus prays for persons who are ill, disabled, or demon-possessed, we will end our reflections on Jesus' healing prayer with his encounter with a woman from the village of Nain in Galilee. After Jesus healed a Centurion's servant in Capernaum he travels southwest.

> Soon afterwards he went to a town called Nain, and his disciples and a large crowd went with him. As he approached the gate of the town, a man who had died was being carried out. He was his mother's only son, and she was a widow; and with her was a large crowd from the town. When the Lord saw her, he had compassion for her and said to her, "Do not weep." Then he came forward and touched the bier, and the bearers stood still. And he said, "Young man, I say to you, rise!" The dead man sat up and began to speak, and Jesus gave him to his mother. (Luke 7:11–15)

As we have seen, in Jesus' culture women were vulnerable and under the control of men. They were the property of their fathers, then of husbands, and, if widowed, became the property of sons, brothers, or fathers once again. If there was no male to give them security, widows could be cast out with no home or livelihood. Often they chose prostitution as their only option and, therefore, all widows were held in suspicion. Since women were not permitted to move about villages without a male, the life of a widow without a male protector was bleak. They had little, if any, future. They had no identity and were vulnerable to male assault.

The widow of Nain was weeping for her only son, as only a mother grieves for her flesh and blood. She had given her husband a male heir and now both of them were dead. Her family and her security were gone. (Luke does not mention any daughters.) Her grief was heavy, compounded by her awareness of a bleak, perhaps terrifying future.

Although Jesus' calling her son back to life could easily be the focus of this incident, Luke begins the action with Jesus' attention to the mother: "When the Lord saw her, he had compassion for her and said to her, 'Do not weep.'" His compassion extended beyond a mother's grief at the death of an only son to awareness that *her life* could be ending as well. Jesus' "prayer" is manifested, once again, in both touch and compassion. Two persons are given new life and the crowd understands fully what has taken place: *"Astonishment seized all of them; and they glorified God, saying, 'A great prophet has risen among us!' and 'God has looked favorably on his people'"* (Luke 7:16).

These two exclamations are rooted in Hebrew belief. As we have seen, ancient Hebrew prophets were recognized because God's Spirit "rested on them." They were chosen; they did not apply for the position! The presence of the Spirit gave the prophet authenticity and authority as a messenger and servant of God. The prophet was a "changed" person and exhibited God's presence in a variety of ways. Jesus' actions and charisma caused the enthusiastic response, *"A great prophet has risen among us!"* There was great expectation in Jesus' day that God would send a prophet (or that the prophet Elijah would return) as the sign that God would restore the kingdom of Israel. The second response reflects the belief that God is the only source of all good things. Those present see God's presence and power in Jesus' action. The focus is on what God has made possible. This confirms Jesus' personal awareness that his experience of God in prayer is the source of the Spirit's movement in his life.

The widow of Nain could have become a refugee from her own home. Describe persons in your own community who have become refugees because of conditions or circumstances beyond their control.

How can their lives be renewed? Who is responsible?

DAY 69

Prayer is a journey into life with God

For the past sixty-eight days we have reflected on specific incidents in Jesus' life that provide a portrait of his life of prayer: quiet prayer in solitude, prayer in his family and local synagogue, participation in the great liturgical feasts in the temple in Jerusalem, discerning prayer at his baptism and transfiguration, prayer for guidance in choosing disciples, quiet reflection on the meaning of being "God's Son," and his role in making God's kingdom tangible in people's lives. We have explored his healing prayer, casting out demons, spontaneous prayers of thanksgiving, prayers for courage in the Garden of Gethsemane, prayers at his crucifixion, and more. It is quite a list! It is clear that prayer was the foundation of Jesus' life with his Abba and the source of his energy, wisdom, teaching, and action in society. We have seen that Jesus did not have to use words for prayer; he used touch often. But most of all we have seen that Jesus' most powerful "prayer" was his constant awareness that he was in the Father and the Father was in him. Prayer was a state of "being with" his Abba all the time. His life was in and entrusted to God; this "faith" opened the flow of energy between Jesus and his Abba that became his "prayer."

For the next thirty-two days we will reflect on *what we can learn about prayer from Jesus' life of prayer*. We will begin with an incident from the first chapter of John's Gospel that takes place just after Jesus appears at the place where John is baptizing in the Jordan River. John sees the Spirit descend on Jesus and proclaims that Jesus is the "Lamb of God" who is to come after him.

Read the passage below and let it speak. Try not to analyze it. Imagine that you are present to what is going on. As best you can, develop a relationship with the passage. This means letting go of your need to "find out what it means." This type of quest usually brings personal needs, assumptions, and often bias with it. That is our part of the relationship. The mind usually takes over and works overtime. There is nothing wrong with this, except that most often it prevents the passage from having its part in the relationship. Let the passage speak on its own terms. You may want to speak to the persons in the passage and listen in silence for a reply. Another way of listening is simply to read it three times out loud and then be completely silent for twenty minutes. Or you can write it down and take it with you throughout the day. Whatever method you choose, the point is to listen, not search. Submit yourself to the passage.

Tomorrow we will take a closer look at its inner message. The Gospel of John always has an inner message written between the lines.

> *The next day John again was standing with two of his disciples, and as he watched Jesus walk by, he exclaimed, "Look, here is the Lamb of God!" The two disciples heard him say this, and they followed Jesus. When Jesus turned and saw them following, he said to them, "What are you looking for?" They said to him, "Rabbi, (which translated means Teacher), where are you staying?" He said to them, "Come and see." (John 1:35–39)*

Let this passage be your companion for the next twenty-four hours.

DAY 70

The journey of prayer begins with dialogue

> *The next day John again was standing with two of his disciples, and as he watched Jesus walk by, he exclaimed, "Look, here is the Lamb of God!" The two disciples heard him say this, and they followed Jesus. When Jesus turned and saw them following, he said to them, "What are you looking for?" They said to him, "Rabbi, (which translated means Teacher), where are you staying?" He said to them, "Come and see."* (John 1:35–39)

This encounter of two of John's disciples with Jesus is not, itself, an example of prayer. Yet the dialogue between Jesus and the two men demonstrates some fundamental aspects of the way God responds to persons who seek God for the first time or want to go deeper in their life with God.

As we have seen during Jesus' baptism and his early ministry, he is a person chosen by God and filled with the Spirit of God to have a unique role in the manifestation of God's kingdom. God's presence is incarnate in Jesus' life and Jesus is very clear that his words and actions have their source in God (John 5:19–20; 7:16–18). With this in mind, Jesus' responses to John's disciples reveal that God responds to persons who seek his presence by listening and inviting them deeper and deeper into a journey of discovery. It is a dialogue that demonstrates the dynamics of prayer. Seeking God or desiring a more mature relationship with God—with or without words—is genuine prayer.

Prayer (the journey) begins by *hearing*. John's two disciples heard him proclaim: *"Look, here is the Lamb of God!"* John was not the center of his proclamation; he was pointing beyond himself to Jesus. His role was to "watch" and make the two disciples aware of what he saw. The disciples heard John's voice and message and *"they followed Jesus."* Listening to John's proclamation awakened their desire to *follow* Jesus. They are looking for something and are drawn to Jesus. *They demonstrate that the first steps in the journey of prayer are awareness of God's presence and responding to that presence.* But that is just the beginning.

"When Jesus turned and saw them following, he said to them, 'What are you looking for?'" Jesus was aware of the disciples' desire to follow him

and his response is to begin a dialogue with a question, not requirements, promises, or answers. The journey of prayer continues with *God's response to our desire*. God's response is to initiate a conversation. God does not describe conditions for the journey or determine its destination. God does not coerce or impose. God, too, is listening. God's wants to know more about our desires, "*What are you looking for?*"

This encounter of Jesus and the two disciples of John is congruent with the way ancient Hebrews experienced God. God was not a concept shrouded in theology or conceived as an unchanging, remote being. God was known by the ways God entered into their lives. God offered a relationship made through a covenant at Sinai. God was known by what God said and did. The Hebrew Bible is a record of God's word and actions and of the Hebrew's responses.

Tomorrow we will reflect on the next steps in the journey of prayer. Reread the suggestions for reflection from Day 69 and then spend time with the next part of the passage from John's Gospel.

> *They said to him, "Rabbi, (which translated means Teacher), where are you staying?" He said to them, "Come and see."*

Let this passage be your companion for the next twenty-four hours.

DAY 71

The journey of prayer creates a relationship

The next day John again was standing with two of his disciples, and as he watched Jesus walk by, he exclaimed, "Look, here is the Lamb of God!" The two disciples heard him say this, and they followed Jesus. When Jesus turned and saw them following, he said to them, "What are you looking for?" They said to him, "Rabbi, (which translated means Teacher), where are you staying?" He said to them, "Come and see." (John 1:35–39)

Yesterday we reflected on two actions of John's disciples: They "heard" John's proclamation about Jesus and they "followed." These actions may be seen as the beginning of the journey of prayer: awareness of God's presence and responding to that presence. But that is only the beginning.

What were these two disciples looking for? It is clear that they were not sure. But it was something compelling and mysterious about Jesus and they wanted to find out more. So they follow Jesus as he walks by. Some New Testament scholars are convinced that Jesus spent time with John the Baptist and was influenced by him. John's message was that God was about to enter into the life of Israel again and renew their life; he called people to repent and turn away from their unfaithfulness. He saw Jesus as one who would begin to implement a "baptism of Spirit and fire." Perhaps this is what prompted the two men to follow Jesus.

Jesus responds to their movement toward him. *"What are you looking for?"* He continues the conversation with *an invitation for the men to say more and enter further into a relationship with him.* They call him "teacher" and ask *"where are you staying?"* The men are hungry for what Jesus can share as rabbi, but they want to know where his knowledge comes from. They want to be with him and experience the mystery they have unconsciously sensed lies within his consciousness.

But again, Jesus does not give them information. He does not say, "Well, let me tell you." He invites them further into the journey, *"Come and see."* The relationship is still open and the dialogue will continue as he leads them toward what they seek.

This encounter manifests the journey of prayer and demonstrates Jesus' understanding that *prayer is fundamentally a relationship that bonds a person with the mystery of God's presence*. There was energy flowing between the men and Jesus. That flow of energy was prayer. The two disciples sensed something about Jesus' consciousness and they wanted to dwell in that same place even though they were not sure "where" it was. As a flow of energy, prayer is a sharing of consciousness. It is a process of co-inherence. This is what bonds a person's life to God.

What did you hear from this passage?

What did you learn about prayer?

What personal invitation or challenge did you sense?

Desert Day Four

The integration of Jesus' prayer with his daily life and ministry

Today is a Sabbath. Rest your mind from reading, studying, writing, and thinking. Being silent and less active will help you listen to the four Gospels in a unique way. When your mind and your heart are integrated you will begin to *experience* Jesus' life of prayer, rather than study about it.

Today let your intellectual discipline be embraced and mentored by contemplative reflection on the integration of Jesus' prayer with his daily life and ministry. Using what you have learned thus far, try to enter into his ministry and let it speak to you.

Begin this day with twenty minutes of silent contemplative prayer. A simple method is described in Appendix E. Find a place that is as quiet as possible. You may prefer to walk to a quiet place and combine a silent walk with sitting once you have arrived.

You may not be able to make this Desert Day a full day. But do your best to make it an intentional part of your day. Set aside at least two hours, if possible. During that time let the four Gospels speak to you, rather than deciding what you want to learn from them. A simple prayer may help you, such as "Spirit, reveal what's true. . . . Spirit, I bless you." Or "Come, Holy, Holy. . . . Come, Holy Spirit." Try to let go of the outcome of this day. Toward the end of this day recall what you have heard, learned, and experienced. Keep your reflections in a journal.

The following questions may help your reflection on the integration of Jesus' prayer and his daily life and ministry:

How did Jesus manifest his relationship with God in his teaching, healing, his faith community, the Torah, the lives of people in his society, and his personal relationships?

How did Jesus' prayer form the context for his vision of "the reign of God"?

How did Jesus' relationship with God affect the people around him?

How did people respond to Jesus' words and actions?

Describe the variety of ways Jesus prayed for and with people.

DAY 72

A Life of prayer demands single-heartedness

Prayer is a journey into a relationship with God and Jesus is our mentor. He spoke often about the need to desire only God as the path to abundant life—a life of fullness.

Both Matthew and Luke describe Jesus' emphasis on single-hearted desire for God. He uses the image of sight and light to describe the path toward fullness of life; life that shares in the fullness of God. He spoke from his own experience of his Abba.

> *The eye is the lamp of the body. So, if your eye is healthy, your whole body will be full of light; but if your eye is unhealthy, your whole body will be filled of darkness. If then the light in you is darkness, how great is the darkness!* (Matt 6:22–23)

> *No one after lighting a lamp puts it in a cellar, but on the lampstand so that those who enter may see the light. And your eye is the lamp of your body. If your eye is healthy, your whole body is full of light; but if it is not healthy, your body is full of darkness. Therefore, consider whether the light in you is not darkness. If then your whole body is full of light, with no part of it in darkness, it will be as full of light as when a lamp gives you light with its rays.* (Luke 11:33–36)

In Jesus' Hebrew culture light was associated with joy, blessing, and life itself. Light was a sign of God's presence among God's people and signified God's favor: *"The Lord is my light and my salvation; whom shall I fear?"* (Ps 27:1). When Jesus began his ministry of making God's kingdom tangible in the lives of people around him he must have remembered these words of the prophet Isaiah: *"The people who walked in darkness have seen a great light; those who lived in a land of deep darkness have seen a great light; those who lived in a land of deep darkness—on them light has shined"* (Isa 9:2).

The word used by Matthew and Luke for "body" may also be translated "being." Jesus wanted everyone around him to have their whole *being* full of God's presence and favor. He wanted them to know God's love and experience fullness of life. This is what he meant when he said: *"turn and entrust yourself to the good news!"* (Mark 1:15; author's translation). Single-hearted desire for God will bring light into each person's being. Prayer is turning with one's whole being to the One who loves each person without condition. God will not coerce; therefore, we must turn and accept the fullness of life God offers.

How do you describe "single-hearted desire for God"? What difference does it make in your life?

Where have you experienced "a great light" in our world that is often shrouded in "deep darkness"?

DAY 73

A Life of prayer demands reliance on God

Jesus' life of prayer radiates his single-hearted desire for God. This was the source of his reliance on God as the source of his words and actions. Reliance eliminates the need for worry.

> He said to his disciples, "Therefore I tell you, do not worry about your life, what you will eat, or about your body, what you will wear. For life is more than food, and the body more than clothing. Consider the ravens: they neither sow nor reap, they have neither storehouse nor barn, and yet God feeds them. Of how much more value are you than the birds. And can any of you by worrying add a single hour to your span of life? . . . And do not keep striving for what you are to eat and what you are to drink, and do not keep worrying. For it is the nations of the world that strive after all these things, and your Father knows that you need them. Instead, strive for his kingdom, and all these things will be given to you as well."

> Do not be afraid, little flock, for it is your Father's good pleasure to give you the kingdom. Sell your possessions, and give alms. Make purses for yourselves that do not wear out, an unfailing treasure in heaven, where no thief comes near and no moth destroys. For where your treasure is, there your heart will be also. (Luke 12:22–25, 29–31, 32–35)

Jesus is not suggesting that our busy and responsible lives are irrelevant. Nor is he suggesting that each person sell everything, give the proceeds to the poor, and enter a monastery—although some persons have an authentic call to that way of life. Jesus is pointing to two essential qualities of human life: grateful recognition that God is the source of everything we have and that we can rely on God to sustain our needs. When we rely on ourselves we are setting ourselves up for worry and fear—worry that we will "run out" of what we need and fear about our survival when we are no longer in control.

Jesus was speaking to Galileans who had very little and whose lives were uncertain. Religious and political leaders extracted excessive amounts of their produce and income. Loss of income or poor crops could mean

debt, loss of land, prison, or slavery. They were often terrified of offend-
ing the Roman authorities; they had seen or heard of massive crucifixions.
Their life spans were short, under forty years, and they had little access to
healing of diseases, deformities, and mental stress. Jesus' words were meant
to give genuine hope, not a patronizing message of "just have faith and
all will be well." What Jesus learned from his Abba in prayer is that the
uncertainty of people's lives will not be solved simply by changing physical and social conditions. If people remain rooted in God's care for them,
spiritually, they will not be overcome by the stresses of life, even if those
stresses continue. He saw his teaching and healing as signs that God's reign
was entering into the lives of his people; that kingdom is a place where each
person is valued and is a gift of the Father. That is a treasure.

Perhaps all this does not make "sense" in conventional thinking. But
reliance on God brings change. It may not solve every problem right away.
Yet, turning our hearts toward God will make the kingdom close at hand in
the way we live and relate to each other. It makes us see ourselves and others
in a different way. We face our needs with a difference perspective, even if
we have to wait for society to change. Reliance on God will make it happen!

In a world where a "culture of fear" is often manufactured to control people,
what will help us move from fear to reliance on God?

What are you grateful for? How do you discern the difference between what
you *want* to do and what you are *able* to do?

DAY 74

Prayer is a flow of life, a persistent pattern, and way of being

> Jesus said, "*Ask, and it will be given you; search, and you will find; knock, and the door will be opened for you. For everyone who asks receives, and everyone who searches finds, and for everyone who knocks, the door will be opened. Is there anyone among you who, if your child asks for bread, will give a stone? Or if the child asks for a fish, will give a snake? If you then, who are evil, know how to give good gifts to your children, how much more will your Father in heaven give good things to those who ask him?*" (Matt 7:7–11)

In Jesus' society "sin" or "evil" was a violation or infringement of interpersonal relationships as well as intentional abandonment of the Torah. The power of Jesus' teaching in Matthew 7 lies in the shame-honor foundation of Galilean life. Jesus was aware of how often adults let each other down and at the same time how they care for their own children. Unlike the fragile and unpredictable relations between local people, God's loyalty and care can be trusted. So we can be free to ask, knock, and seek. God will respond. This can be a pattern in our life with God.

> *Very truly I tell you, the one who believes in me will also do the works that I do and, in fact, will do greater than these, because I am going to the Father. I will do whatever you ask in my name so that the Father may be glorified in the Son. If in my name you ask me for anything, I will do it.* (John 14:12–14)

Jesus can be trusted because he and the Father are completely united: "*I will do whatever you ask in my name.*" When we ask "in Jesus' name" we ask on the basis of our relationship with him. It is not just the "invocation" of Jesus by name. It is calling on his presence, character, and agency as one who is filled with the presence of his Abba. We, in fact, are praying in Jesus, as he prayed in the Father.[19]

---

19. I am grateful to Rowan Williams for his emphasis on this insight. Christians pray *in* Jesus, as well as *to* Jesus. See Williams, *Being Christian*, 64–65.

"Very truly I tell you, the one who believes in me will also do the works that I do and, in fact, will do greater than these, because I am going to the Father." This statement contradicts some modern doctrine and theology that emphasizes the exclusive power of Jesus, as God's Son. It declares that we cannot do what Jesus did. Yet Jesus could not be clearer. If we entrust our lives to the presence of the Father in him we, like him, will be able to do what the Father wills. The life of God in Jesus will continue to be made tangible in *our* lives. That is the power of a life of prayer. It is a constant flow of energy between us and God. It forms a way of being.

What "good things" do you desire for your life and the lives of other people?

How is doing greater works than Jesus did possible in your life and your faith community?

DAY 75

A life of prayer requires being
aware, open, and watchful

A clear and persistent pattern in Jesus' life of prayer was his awareness that he was never "away from" his Abba. The Father was present in his consciousness every moment and became tangible in his desires, words, and behavior. This was possible because Jesus was not the center of his own life. The more he let go of himself, the more he was watchful and aware of God's presence. A life with God requires letting go of one's self and being open to God's life in us.

> *Those who find their life will lose it, and those who lose their life for my sake will find it.* (Matt 10:39)

> *He called the crowd with his disciples, and said to them, "If any want to become my followers, let them deny themselves and take up their cross and follow me. For those who want to save their life will lose it, and those who lose their life for my sake, and for the sake of the gospel, will save it."* (Mark 8:31–33)

Jesus is calling people to a change of consciousness. It is a radical exhortation. They must "deny" control over their own lives and die. (Taking up the cross was a vivid image, because many, if not most Galileans, had seen hundreds of their countrymen executed by the Romans on crosses.) Jesus' gospel involved showing people they are held in high esteem by God. He exhorted people not to hoard possessions, but share them. He declared that God was entering into ordinary peoples' lives through his teaching, healing, feeding, and acts of compassion. To "follow" Jesus was to become *like* him—to enter into his life. But this required total commitment and a break from conventional relationships and norms. He called the crowds and his disciples to "lose" their lives so that they could find themselves as participants in the kingdom or reign of God. This "finding of self" was seeing one's self and life in a totally new way.

The new life Jesus invites people to share with him requires being aware of God's presence with faithful watchfulness. *"Be dressed for action and have your lamps lit; be like those who are waiting for their master to return from the wedding banquet, so that they may open the door for him as soon as he comes and knocks"* (Luke 12:35–36. Cf. Matt 25:1–13 and Luke 17:26–36).

In Jesus' culture, social responsibilities were taken very seriously. This example of servants having lamps lit and being available for their master's return would strike a vivid chord in the minds of his listeners. Failure to fulfill a master's expectations would result in shame on a servant's family and possibly loss of their occupation. The consequences were serious. Therefore, any person who wants to be a faithful servant of God's active presence in society should be "ready for action" and watchful.

Watchfulness, openness, and awareness are integral parts of a life of prayer.

Twenty-first-century culture sustains itself through manufacturing and acquiring material possessions. How is it possible to "let go of control" and "deny one's self."

How will this make a difference? Where do we begin? Where can you begin?

What is the relationship between prayer and having easily satisfied needs?

DAY 76

Prayer is a way of life

Jesus' life of prayer was centered on his relationship with his Abba. This relationship was based on constant mutual presence: Jesus' presence to his Father and the Father's presence to him. This enabled him to see life through God's "eyes" and desire what God desires. *"May your will be done on earth as in heaven."* Prayer was Jesus' way of life, not a part of his life reserved for certain times and circumstances, such as the Sabbath or feasts or crises. Jesus is our mentor in prayerful living. He shows us that prayer is a way to live and the challenge of prayer is to know and travel that way. This is never easy. The good news is that Jesus is not only our mentor and example. If we pray in him we share in his relationship with his Abba. How do we begin? The first steps are desire and humility—in other words, our attitude.

> *At that time Jesus said, "I thank you, Father, Lord of heaven and earth, because you have hidden these things from the wise and intelligent and have revealed them to infants. Yes, Father, for such was your gracious will."* (Matt 11:25–26)

Before his ascension Jesus told the disciples that he was leaving and that they would know both how to follow him and where he was going. *"'And you know the way to the place where I am going.' Thomas said to him, 'Lord, we do not know where you are going. How can we know the way?' Jesus said to him, 'I am the way; and the truth and the life'"* (John 14:4–6).

The best way to know prayer as a way of life is to meditate on the way Jesus embodied prayer in his life. As we have seen, the canonical Gospels are invaluable for this search and that has been the purpose of these daily reflections. There are other sources that can help us discern the wisdom of Jesus, especially The Sayings Gospel Q and the Thomas Codex (that includes 114 sayings of Jesus). They should not be ignored. But Matthew, Mark, Luke, and John provide the narratives of Jesus' experience that were *the sources of the wisdom* that flowed from his life of prayer. The wisdom of his sayings came forth from the crucible of his life experience and the intimacy of his prayer.

Describe the ways Jesus embodied prayer in his daily life.

What was the relationship between Jesus' prayer and his active involvement in society?

How would you describe the distinction between saying prayers and living a life of prayer?

DAY 77

Discernment is an integral part of prayer

As we have seen, Jesus' quiet reflection provided opportunities for him to discern his Abba's desires for his life. He was clear to those around him that his words and actions were not his own, but came from his Father. Many of his most important decisions and activities were preceded by early morning, afternoon, evening, and sometimes all night solitude with God. Jesus spoke often about "seeing" and being aware.

> *The eye is the lamp of the body. So, if your eye is healthy, your whole body will be full of light; but if your eye is unhealthy, your whole body will be filled with darkness. If then the light in you is darkness, how great is the darkness!* (Matt 6:22–23)

Jesus was clear that God had called him to help people live in light rather than darkness. The lives of Galileans were dark in so many ways. Jesus discerned that he would help fulfill God's intent expressed by the prophet Isaiah. A leader will come and *"in the latter time he will make glorious the way of the sea, the land beyond the Jordan, Galilee of the nations. The people who walked in darkness have seen a great light; those who lived in a land of deep darkness–on them light has shined"* (Isa 9:1b–2).

When Jesus chose disciples to share his message and ministry he knew they would face the same criticism and challenges he faced. He exhorted them to discern, in prayer, how they would proceed without being dragged down by discouragement.

> *Be on guard so that your hearts are not weighed down with dissipation and drunkenness and the worries of this life, and that day catch you unexpectedly, like a trap. For it will come upon all who live on the face of the earth. Be alert, at all times, praying that you may have the strength to escape all these things that will take place, and to stand before the Son of Man.* (Luke 21:34–36)

Discernment in prayer is not only about making decisions. It enables a person to see into what is taking place in society and find courage rather than discouragement. Discernment in prayer is being with and "standing before" Jesus, and the One who sent him. But this confidence does not come "out of the blue." Jesus shows that it is the consequence of being in the presence of God and trusting that God's wisdom and power is present in every situation.

In the next several days we will continue to reflect on discernment as a rich fruit of commitment to prayer.

What do you "see" during your personal prayer?

What do you "hear"?

Where does prayer lead you?

What place does prayer have in social issues and politics?

DAY 78

Discernment is an internal way of seeing life

Jesus spoke about seeing with the heart, but seeing with the heart is not possible if we do not take time to be present to what takes place in the heart. The heart is the place where the Spirit of God and each person's spirit can live together. This mutual presence enlightens a heart with the desires and vision of God. Inability to see into the heart (or be present to the heart's vision) creates barriers between us and God and prevents us from experiencing fullness of life.

> After Jesus has told the parable of the Sower, the disciples ask, "Why do you speak to them in parables?" He answered, "To you it has been given to know the secrets of the kingdom of heaven. For to those who have, more will be given, and they will have an abundance; but from those who have nothing, even what they have will be taken away. The reason I speak to them in parables is that 'seeing they do not perceive, and hearing they do not listen, nor do they understand.' With them is indeed fulfilled the prophecy of Isaiah, 'You will listen, indeed, but never understand, and you will indeed look, but never perceive. For this people's heart has grown dull, and their ears are hard of hearing, and they have shut their eyes; so that they might not look with their eyes, and listen with their ears, and understand with their heart and turn—and I would heal them.' But blessed are your eyes, for they see, and your ears, for they hear. Truly I tell you, many prophets and righteous people longed to see what you see, but did not see it, and to hear what you hear, but did not hear it." (Matt 13:10–17)

Prayer is spending time with God in the inner chamber of the heart so that we will see and hear God's presence and activity in the rest of life. It is possible for a person to live every detail of the Torah and listen for God's voice and be blind and deaf if he or she has a heart that has "grown dull." Discernment in prayer is releasing control of our heart so that it can be filled with the brightness of God's presence. That will enable us to "turn" toward the light and embrace healing of the inability to see, hear, and understand. Prayer is a path toward enlightenment. The "secrets of the kingdom" are not kept for a select few, but without a desire to let go of control of what we want to see or hear, we will miss the "secrets" that are right before our eyes and being spoken within our hearing.

Saint Benedict taught that our hearts will "expand with delight" if we spend time in God's presence regularly. What do you think he meant?

How will listening with the ear of your heart influence your reading, studying, writing, and your quest for what is most fundamental in your life?

DAY 79

Prayerful discernment will help us see what is real and avoid what is not real

We have already seen that Jesus' solitude in the desert following his baptism was an opportunity to discern his unique relationship with God and how he would fulfill that relationship in society. It boiled down to use or misuse of power based on discernment of God's desires. But this need for clarity continued throughout his adult life and ministry, and he exhorted his followers to choose between what is real (life-giving) and unreal (life-denying).

> *Then if anyone says to you, "Look! Here is the Messiah!" or "There he is!"—do not believe it. For false messiahs and false prophets will appear and produce great signs and omens, to lead astray, if possible, even the elect. Take note, I have told you beforehand."* (Matt 24:23–25)

> *The Pharisees and Sadducees came, and to test Jesus they asked him to show a sign from heaven. He answered them, "When it is evening, you say, 'It will be fair weather, for the sky is red.' And in the morning, 'It will be stormy today for the sky is red and threatening.' You know how to interpret the appearance of the sky, but you cannot interpret the signs of the times."* (Matt 16:1–3)

In Jesus' culture people believed it was natural for God to act directly in people's lives and in society. But how could God's authentic presence be verified? Traditionally, God's presence in a leader was authenticated through anointing by a prophet or by the Spirit. The issue behind the "test" of Jesus demanded by the Pharisees was authority. They wanted a distinctive "sign," a major proof. Jesus' response is simple. The "signs" of God's presence in his life are in acts of healing, restoration of sight, expulsion of demons, feeding of the hungry, and teaching that is recognized as authentic without reference to "the authorities." Jesus is not calling attention to himself, but the power of God being manifested in his life. The power in his life is life-giving.

"*But if it is by the finger of God that I cast out demons, then the kingdom of God has come to you*" (Matt 12:28). The earthy and human image of "the finger of God" acknowledges that God has acted; his presence is there for all to see, if they are able and willing.

Discernment takes place in the context of ordinary, daily life and is related to living in God's presence. If a person discerns God's presence in the intimacy of prayer, then God's presence can be recognized everywhere. Its hallmark is life-giving power. It is real whenever and wherever it is experienced. Experience of what is real will unmask what is not real. Jesus calls us to discern what is real and entrust ourselves to the One who is real.

Modern society pressures everyone to "get real." What is real in your life?

How can a person encounter more than the surface structure of life?

What is the relationship between the inner dimension of life and its outer characteristics and demands?

DAY 80

A life of prayer manifests God's presence and power

Jesus was very clear that God's life was present in his life. *"I and the Father are one."* As we have seen, this was not a theological statement; it was a description of the depth of his intimacy with God. His openness to his Abba in prayer extended to every word and action in his daily life. He did not need to invoke God's presence to "make" his teaching and behavior filled with God's Spirit. He lived each day in God, surrounded and filled with his Abba. *"Very truly, I tell you, the Son can do nothing on his own, but only what he sees the Father doing, for whatever the Father does, the Son does likewise"* (John 5:19).

Where did Jesus "see" his Father at work? Jesus spoke often about the need for vision in a person's life: *"If your eye is single, your whole being will be filled with light"* (Matt 6:22b, author's translation). In Jesus' culture light is a primary symbol of God's presence. Jesus must have "seen" his Abba in his times of quiet reflection, in his faith community's Scriptures, in public worship, in the world of nature, and wherever justice and righteousness were present in the lives of people around him. But it seems clear that Jesus *made room* for this "seeing" by letting go of control of his own life through prayer and discernment of God's desires. "Jesus said, 'Images are visible to people, but the light within them is hidden in the image of the Father's light. He will be disclosed, but his image is hidden in the light'" (Gospel of Thomas, logia 83).[20]

"For those who want to save their life will lose it, and those who lose their life for my sake will find it" (Matt 16:25). Living in the realm of God requires a denial (submission) of the self we have fabricated (our false self): *"For all who exalt themselves will be humbled, and those who humble themselves will be exalted"* (Luke 14:11; Q). Jesus was very clear that this denial of self, in prayer, must issue forth in (be congruent with) the way we live. *"Not everyone who says, 'Lord, Lord,' will enter the realm of God, but only the one who does the will of my Father in heaven"* (Matt 7:21).

Jesus became frustrated with his followers when they showed reluctance or inability to accept the challenges he offered. *"Why do you call me*

20. Meyer (ed.), *The Nag Hammadi Scriptures, 150.*

Lord, Lord, and do not do what I tell you?" (Luke 6:46). Jesus was not asking for blind obedience. He was explaining the cost of following him; to be his disciple meant bearing the fruit of what God desires.

> *No good tree bears bad fruit, nor again does a bad tree bear good fruit; for each tree is known by its fruit. Figs are not gathered from thorns, nor are grapes picked from a bramble bush. The good person out of the good treasure of the heart produces good, and the evil person out of evil treasure produces evil; for it is out of the abundance of the heart that the mouth speaks.* (Luke 6:43–45)

Prayer reaches into the good treasure of the heart and becomes the flow of God's life into our words and actions. This is the invitation and challenge Jesus offers a person who desires to follow him.

How does your prayer influence what you say or refrain from saying?

In what ways are you aware that your prayer gives birth to fruitfulness, insight, and confidence in your actions?

What is the difference between "results" and fruitfulness?

DAY 81

Prayer combines listening and acting

How does a follower of Jesus manifest the presence of God in her or his words and behavior? What is that person like? Jesus, as always, responds in language that was familiar to his Galilean listeners.

> *Why do you call me, "Lord, Lord" and do not do what I tell you? I will show you what someone is like who comes to me, hears my words, and acts on them. That one is like a man building a house, who dug deeply and laid the foundation on rock; when a flood arose, the river burst against that house but could not shake it, because it had been well built. But the one who hears and does not act is like a man who built a house on the ground with no foundation. When the river burst against it, immediately it fell, and great was the ruin of that house.* (Luke 6:46–49)

Jesus' response does not give a list of acceptable behaviors, but he is clear about the source of our ability to do what he "says." Our ability to live according to God's commandments (God's desires for life in God's kingdom) is directly related to our relationship to God in prayer and our personal experience of God's love. He puts it this way in another image:

> *I am the true vine, and my Father is the vinegrower. He removes every branch in me that bears no fruit. Every branch that bears fruit he prunes to make it bear more fruit. You have already been cleansed by the word that I have spoken to you. Abide in me as I abide in you. As the branch cannot bear fruit by itself unless it abides in the vine, neither can you unless you abide in me.* (John 15:1–4)

Pruning is a powerful image in the Bible, used to demonstrate God's desire to cut away influences that sap a person's life with God. Removing what keeps us from doing what Jesus "says" may be painful, but it leads to spiritual health and fruitfulness. The key is *abiding* in Jesus throughout each day in the same way he embodied his Abba day and night. *"A disciple is not above the teacher, but everyone who is fully qualified will be like the teacher"* (Luke 6:40; Q). Whether it is a "firm foundation on bed rock" or "abiding in the vine," doing what Jesus asks depends not only on listening to wise words, but depending totally on God and *acting accordingly*. It is nothing less than entrusting our lives to God. It is a three-fold pattern: listening, trusting God, and taking action. Discernment is one of the fruits of prayer.

How has prayer invited or challenged you to do things that are difficult or that you would prefer to avoid?

What has prayer revealed about aspects of your life that God desires to prune, change, or strengthen?

DAY 82

Prayer makes an intimate relationship with God possible

We have seen, in many ways, how Jesus' relationship with his Abba was intimate and was not limited to "times of prayer." What is surprising to many people today is that in some respects Jesus did not think his relationship with God was unique. He was unique and, in the words of Saint Paul, *"He is the image of the invisible God, . . . For in him all the fullness of God was pleased to dwell, . . . "* Col 1:15; 19). Yet Jesus was very clear that we share his relationship with God and what that relationship will make possible in our lives.

> *Very truly, I tell you, the one who believes in me* [who entrusts her or his life to me] *will also do the works that I do and, in fact, will do greater works than these, because I am going to the Father.* (John 14:12)

In the same way that Jesus' words and works flowed from his relationship with his Abba, it was his intent that, through prayer, we be enlightened and entrusted to make God's desires for the world tangible. We are invited to share God's wisdom and power. One of the earliest followers of the Way expressed it clearly in 2 Peter by saying that Jesus has given us his promise that we *"may become partakers of the divine nature"* (see 2 Pet 1:3–7). *"For His divine power has given us everything needed for life and godliness, through the power of him who called us by his own glory and goodness"* (2 Pet 2:3).

Jesus expressed this himself in the most audacious, yet powerfully true, terms.

> *I do not call you servants any longer, because the servant does not know what the master is doing; but I have called you friends, because I have made known to you everything that I have heard from my Father. You did not choose me but I chose you. And I appointed you to go and bear fruit, fruit that will last, so that my Father will give you whatever you ask him in my name. I am giving you these commands so that you may love one another"* (John 15:15–17)

In the same way that Jesus listened to his Father in prayer, God will speak to us in prayer.

> His disciples said, "Show us the place where you are, for we must seek it." He said to them, "Whoever has ears should hear. There is light within a person of light, and it shines on the whole world. If it does not shine it is dark."
> Jesus said, "Love your sibling like your soul; protect that person like the pupil of your eye." (Gospel of Thomas, logia 24; 25) [21]

In the same way that what Jesus experienced in his prayer became tangible in his words and actions, our intimacy with God in prayer will guide and empower our lives. We are called to listen and bear fruit.

Describe your awareness of God's presence when you are praying?

How do you respond when God seems absent or not responding?

What has Jesus' formation in prayer taught you about entrusting your life to God?

How does your intimacy with God influence other aspects of your life?

21. Meyer (ed.), *The Nag Hammadi Scriptures,* 143.

DAY 83

Prayer is experience of, and union with, God for the life of the world

Jesus' identity and life were formed and empowered by his prayer-filled experience of his Abba. He came to know his true identity (his true self) because he saw himself reflected in his experience of the One who sent him. In other words, Jesus found himself through intimacy with God. He made this clear when some Pharisees questioned his authority to teach at the Feast of the Tabernacles in Jerusalem.

> "I am the light of the world. Whoever follows me will never walk in darkness but will have the light of life." Then the Pharisees said to him, "You are testifying on your own behalf; your testimony is not valid." Jesus answered, "Even if I testify on my own behalf, my testimony is valid because I know where I have come from and where I am going, but you do not know where I have come from or where I am going. You judge by human standards; I judge no one." (John 8:12–15)

Later in the same day people around Jesus asked him,

> "Who are you?" Jesus said to them, "Why do I speak to you at all? I have much to say about you and much to condemn; but the one who sent me is true, and I declare to the world what I have heard from him" They did not understand that he was speaking to them about the Father. So Jesus said, "When you have lifted up the Son of Man, then you will realize that I am he, and that I do nothing on my own, but I speak these things as the Father has instructed me. And the one who sent me is with me; he has not left me alone, for I always do what is pleasing to him." As he was saying these things, many believed in him. (John 8:25–30)

Jesus knows the source of his being and sees his purpose clearly: "I know where I come from and where I am going." These fundamental insights about identity and purpose must have come from experience of his Abba in quiet solitude. Jesus declares that any truth he speaks is not his own, but from the One who is truth, itself. It seems clear that Jesus listens to his Abba in prayer. He declares that his words and actions come from the Father.

Although Jesus makes claims about himself, the focus is not on him, but on God who has not left him alone. The experience of God Jesus has in prayer is carried with him; he is never apart from that intimate presence. The purpose of this intimacy is to bring light and life to the world. Yes, he always does what is pleasing to the Father because his desires are congruent with God's desires for the world. This is not arrogance. He is practicing what he taught his disciples: pray that God's will be done on earth as in heaven.

In the days ahead we will reflect on Jesus' insistence that this is true, also, for all who entrust their lives to his experience of the Father: *"All things have been handed over to me by my Father; and no one knows who the Son is except the Father, or who the Father is except the Son and anyone to whom the Son chooses to reveal him"* (Luke 10:22; Q).

How does your intimacy with God shape your speech and behavior?

What does your silent presence with God teach you about yourself?

How does your prayer help you discover God's desires for people and situations around you, including both close personal relationships and persons you do not know?

DAY 84

Jesus' life of prayer is a path leading others to union with God

We have seen that Jesus' disciples were aware of the power of God in his life. They noticed that his daily life was filled with times of solitude and prayer. They could not help but notice, also, that after his "going apart" on mountains or in wilderness areas he made decisions, taught with wisdom that possessed internal authority, and healed and fed many people. This must have prompted them to ask, *"Lord, teach us to pray."* As we have seen, "The Lord's Prayer" gives a vivid insight into Jesus' relationship with his Abba and what God desires for the life of the world.

Later in his ministry, not long before his crucifixion, he said he was going to prepare a place for his disciples and that they would know the way. It is significant that Jesus says,

> And if I go and prepare a place for you, I will come again and will
> take you to myself, so that where I am, there you may be also. And
> you know the way to the place I am going. (John 14:3–4)

Where does Jesus want to take the disciples? And what is that place like? The most important place in his life is his relationship with his Abba. That is the "place" that constitutes his life, fills it with meaning, and empowers all he says and does. It seems clear that Jesus is offering that same place to the disciples (and to us). But Thomas, perhaps like most of us, has little idea of what Jesus is talking about. *"Lord we do not know where you are going. How can we know the way?"* (John 14:5). Jesus' response to Thomas reveals what is most important in Jesus' life:

> I am the way, and the truth, and the life. No one comes to the Father
> except through me. If you know me you will know my Father also.
> From now on you do know him and have seen him. (John 14:6–7)

Jesus makes it clear that Thomas and the disciples who are with him can rely on his relationship with the Father as the way that will lead them to the "place" where Jesus dwells—union with God. By entrusting their lives to Jesus' relationship of complete union they will share that same *"truth and life."* Jesus continues. *"If you know me you will know my Father also."* Jesus is speaking as a Jew. "Knowing" the Father means *experiencing God*, rather than gaining information about God. Those who are intimate with Jesus will experience intimacy with his Abba.

"No one comes to the Father except through me." Jesus' response to Thomas emphasizes that the only "way" to God is authentic experience of God and that in his life that "way" to the Father is embodied right before their eyes![22]

But Thomas—perhaps, again, like most of us—still has trouble seeing the Father "through" the life of Jesus. Perhaps he was unable to recognize, and therefore experience, the power of God in Jesus' life. Philip is uncertain, as well. *"Philip said to him, 'Lord, show us the Father, and we will be satisfied'"* (John 14:8). With great pastoral sensitivity Jesus realizes Philip's lack of vision and says, *"Have I been with you all this time, Philip, and you still do not know me? Whoever has seen me has seen the Father. How can you say, 'Show us the Father?'"* (John 14:9). This is Jesus' boldest and clearest statement yet about *the living presence* of his Father in his life. It is not a theological statement about his identity! It is not a claim to divine status! It is a simple and profound awareness of God's abiding presence in his life. Jesus is speaking about the completeness of his union with God. His purpose is not to draw attention to himself but to the fullness of God's presence in him.[23]

God's presence in Jesus' life animates every aspect of his life and this is what he wants to share with us. He wants to "take us to himself." He desires with all his passion that we will see God's presence in him and embody that same presence in our lives. That is why Jesus' understood himself to be (at that time and with the disciples who were present) the way, and the truth, and the life. Later he will declare in his prayer to the Father that it is his

22. Jesus' reply to Thomas is congruent with John the Evangelist's understanding that Jesus is the Word of God (John 1:1–18). This Word of God brought all creation into being and is the source of all life. The Word became flesh and lived among human beings as Jesus of Nazareth. Therefore, according to John's theological perspective, Jesus is indeed the One who reveals the Father and through whom, in human form, a person experiences the Father in a unique way. *"Whoever has seen me has seen the Father."* At the same time Jesus' unique manifestation of the Father is not exclusive because he passionately desired that persons who entrusted their lives to him would share his union with God and *through them* other persons would be drawn to the Father. (See John 14:12–14; 17:1–26; Eph 3:14–21; Phil 2:1–12; Col 1:9–20; 2:6–6; 2 Pet 1:3–8). Ultimately this is a mystery, yet John's perspective is based on his personal experience of Jesus before and after his resurrection (1 John 1:1–4).

23. See Col 1:15–20; 2:6.

wish for everyone to *"be where I am"* (John 17:24).[24] That place is in union with God. It is where we belong and where we will find fullness of life and compassion for others.

What is your reaction to Jesus' desire to share his experience of God with you?

In what way do you share the Thomas' desire to "know the way" and Philip's desire to "see the Father"?

Where is Jesus leading you?

24. See John 17:1–26.

DAY 85

Prayer embodies unconditional love

Jesus' life of prayer was the primary relationship in his life. All other relationships flowed from experience of his Abba. At his baptism Jesus learned how close this relationship would be as well as the extent and quality of God's love for him. *"This is my Son, the Beloved, with whom I am well pleased"* (Matt 3:17). Jesus experienced a relationship with God that was as intimate and cherished as that between a father and a son. But there was more. God "delights in him." Jesus did not have to worry that this relationship would end because he had neither earned nor deserved it. It was a relationship sought and sustained by God. We have seen that Jesus, as the "Beloved," incarnated the desires, words, and presence of God in his daily life. His passionate love for the oppressed, disdained, and abused people in Galilee came from his Abba. This love, as the Father's love for Jesus, was unconditional.

Jesus' relationship with God, although unique, was not exclusive. It was meant to incarnate the relationship God desires with every human being. Jesus is showing what human life really is. On the Mountain of Transfiguration God declares once more that *"This is my Son, the Beloved."* But this time the voice adds, *"listen to him!"* (Mark 9:7) Listening is an essential part of the relationship between disciple and master. "If you become my disciples and listen to my sayings, these stones will serve you" (Gospel of Thomas, logia 19:2).[25] Jesus' sayings are not meant to increase a person's knowledge or wisdom. His sayings and parables are meant to change a person's consciousness and experience of life. The Beloved's words and example will draw others to the relationship he has with his Abba. Jesus' mission was not to make people wise; wisdom is not an end in itself. We have seen that the love Jesus experienced with God in prayer was the source of his compassionate engagement with the people and situations around him. Jesus wanted his disciples to share his intimacy with God and at the same time to make the love present in that relationship tangible in their lives. *The reason for listening to Jesus is to learn to love as God loves.*

25. Meyer (ed.), *The Nag Hammadi Scriptures*, 142.

"If you love me, you will keep my commandments" (John 14:15). This statement is related to Jesus' claim that he had not come to abolish the Torah, but to fulfill it. The Torah, when it was not abused or used by religious authorities to control people, was the path to the life God desires for the world. It was an expression of how God's will "in heaven" can be present on earth. It was summed up in the *Shema* that was spoken in every Galilean home morning and night. Jesus is proclaiming that "keeping the commandments" flows from love. The Torah is love in action. Jesus' actions had their origin in the love he shared with his Abba. In like manner, he exhorts his disciples, *"If you love me, you will keep my commandments."* Loving God and neighbor flow from love, not obligation or self-serving duty. Loving Jesus means doing the "works" that he did . . . and more: to teach, heal, live justly, not to be troubled or afraid, and love without condition.

> *If you keep my commandments, you will abide in my love, just as I have kept my Father's commandments and abide in his love. I have said these things to you so that my joy may be in you, and that your joy may be complete.* (John 15:10–11)

Love is the source of joy. In the twenty-first century this seems counter-cultural, but it is true!

When have you experienced unconditional love?

Describe your response to the fact that God loves and delights in you?

Jesus realized that love gives birth to ethical behavior. What does this mean?

How does keeping God's commandments relate to decisions and legislation in the public sector?

DAY 86

Jesus' life of prayer is a model for our lives

Jesus called disciples to share his life and ministry. The first step was *"follow me."* He placed highest priority on being with him. His life was his message. Why would his disciples ask him, *"Lord, teach us to pray"* if they had not seen him pray, been with him during some of his times of quiet prayer, and observed what he did following his prayer?

> *Then Jesus told his disciples, "If any want to become my followers,*
> *let them deny themselves and take up their cross and follow me."*
> (Matt 16:24)

This was an invitation to leave former lives behind (to die to self) and enter into the life Jesus wanted to share with them. *"Where I am, there will my servant be also"* (John 12:26). Rowan Williams calls this "being led to where Jesus is. It is living where Jesus lives."[26] This, says Williams, is the meaning of Christian baptism.

The decision to enter into Jesus' life also meant to enter into the lives of the people that Jesus loved, primarily Galileans. Their lives were simple, but very harsh. They were marginalized and abused by political leaders, Herod Antipas, Rome, and wealthy landowners and owners of storage houses and underground cisterns—where taxes paid with crops, wine, preserved fish, and other staples were stored for sale only when the market was to the owner's advantage. Because local people were weak and poor they were treated with shame and considered to be under judgment by God. Prosperity was a sign of God's favor. Galileans were poor, often unhealthy and lame, and held in low esteem. To follow Jesus meant to be with him as he brought good news to the oppressed. Jesus' ministry of healing, feeding, and teaching showed them that they are loved and cherished by God. Their problems were not solved all at once, but their personal integrity was restored and they were released from fear because the beginnings of the reign of God were tangible before their eyes. In order to live the message he preached, Jesus left his family and became itinerant, traveling with no money, food supply, or satchel, and depending totally on the hospitality

---

26. See Williams, *Being Christian*, 4–7.

of people he visited. He asked his disciples to do the same. It was risky, especially when Jesus was acting openly in the name of God in the territory of Herod Antipas.

How was it possible to follow Jesus like this? We are familiar with Peter's desire to leave all and follow him wherever it might lead. At first the cost seemed too much and during the trial of Jesus Peter disassociates himself with Jesus. Later he experiences remorse and is reassured by Jesus. But the question remains. What can we learn from Jesus himself about following him? How does following him today thrust us into the needs of other people in today's society? The following passages from the Gospels of Matthew and John give a partial picture of what this is like:

- *"Abide in me, as I abide in you"* is an invitation for union with Jesus (John 15:4a).

- *"Whoever serves me must follow me, and where I am, there will my servant be also"* (John 12:26). A disciple will live where Jesus lives, both in union with God and in compassionate engagement in society.

- *"I am the vine, you are the branches. Those who abide in me and I in them bear much fruit, because apart from me you can do nothing."* Bearing fruit will be the result of union with Jesus. A disciple will stay close to Jesus (John 15:5).

- *"And I appointed you to go and bear fruit, fruit that will last."* Following Jesus is for the "long haul" (John 15:16b).

- *". . . so that the Father will give you whatever you ask him in my name* [in the presence of and according to the will of God]." God's presence in Jesus will empower discipleship (John 15:16b).

- *"I am giving you these commands so that you may love one another."* Abiding in Jesus as a disciple will become the source of love between disciples (John 15:17).

- *"But when you pray, go into your room and shut the door and pray to your Father who is in secret; and your Father who sees in secret will reward you."* Be faithful to your intimate relationship with God. God will always respond (Matt 6:6).

Although the venues for following Jesus are different today from first century Galilee, the invitation to follow Jesus remains the same as well as the ways to remain close to him.

What in Jesus' life compels you to follow him?

What can be changed in you or pruned away in order to follow Jesus?

What are you called to offer Jesus as a disciple?

How do you remain with him?

DAY 87

Jesus life of prayer reveals the consequences of prayer

We have seen how often Jesus made important decisions, spoke wisely and with authority, and did amazing things following his times of quiet prayer or public worship. People often ask, "Does prayer work?" Their question relates to one of the highest values in modern society: results. There is no question that Jesus' prayer did "produce" results. But the production was not his own doing; it was the work of his Abba in his life. Yet the primary motivation behind the prayer of Jesus had little to do with "results." His prayer was "being present" to and with his Abba. That relationship with its exchange of energy was the source of his life of prayer. The Gospels do not equate Jesus' prayer with results. Yes, he was a unique example of the presence of God in the lives of people around him. But he was not always "successful." Some would say he did a lot of good for a while, but ultimately failed to overcome Roman rule, change the greed for money and power of the wealthy, and reform his religious community.

Jesus' idea of "results" was far more interior and substantive. He knew that all "successful" words and actions come from the heart, from inside a person. He also learned that God works through people. Here are a few of the interior consequences of prayer that we learn from Jesus:

- Our relationship with God in prayer is a source of joy: *"I have told you this so that my joy may be in you and your joy may be complete"* (John 15:11).

- Jesus passes on to those who entrust their lives to him the eternal dimension of his relationship with his Abba. If we are joined to God in prayer, that relationship is eternal because God is eternal. Speaking of himself, he addresses his Father, *"Father, the hour has come; glorify your Son so that the Son may glorify you, since you have given him authority over all people, to give eternal life to all whom you have given him. And this is eternal life, that they may know you, the only true God, and Jesus Christ whom you have sent"* (John 17:1b–3).

- In prayer Jesus encountered God's truth. We will experience that same truth in our prayerful listening and be able to share it with others:

"Sanctify them in the truth; your word is truth. As you have sent me into the world, so I have sent them into the world" (John 17:17–18).

- As we become one with God in prayer we will become one with each other. We become fully human when we are united with each other. *"I ask not only on behalf of these, but also on behalf of those who will believe in me through their word, that they may all be one. As you, Father, are in me and I am in you, may they also be in us, so that the world may believe that you have sent me"* (John 17:20–22).

- Through prayer we "know God" through experience of God's presence and will see things as Jesus saw them: *"Then turning to the disciples, Jesus said to them privately, 'Blessed are the eyes that see what you see! For I tell you that many prophets and kings desired to see what you see, but did not see it, and to hear what you hear, but did not hear it'"* (Luke 10:23–24).

How do the "results" of Jesus' prayer affirm or challenge your own expectations about prayer?

Why is prayer worthwhile?

What difference will prayer make in the way you live and the lives of the persons you hold in prayer?

DAY 88

For the life of the world

Jesus was a source of God's life for people and the world. He was very clear that any person who follows him shares his vocation.

> You are the salt of the earth; but if the salt has lost its taste, how can its saltiness be restored? It is no longer good for anything, but is thrown out and trampled under foot. You are the light of the world. A city built on a hill cannot be hid. No one after lighting a lamp puts it under the bushel basket, but on the lampstand, and it gives light to all in the house. In the same way, let your light shine before others, so that they may see your good works and give glory to your Father in heaven. (Matt 5:13–16)

In Jesus' culture the "glory" of God is the presence of God. Glory manifests God's being. There is no question about it. It fills a person or situation with wonder and awe. Jesus is saying that persons who entrust their lives to him are called to "good works" that embody God's presence. The works are good because their source is God, not because they are approved by human beings. They point toward God, not the person. Jesus said that only God is good. He declared that his "works" were not his, but the action of the One who sent him.

Being a source of life for others was the heart of Jesus' mission because abundant life is what God desires for every human being. When Jesus referred to himself as a good shepherd he was using an image ordinary Galilean people could understand clearly (John 10). He declares, *"I came that they may have life, and have it abundantly"* (John 10:10). He is not speaking about prosperity; he is talking about life where people are valued and treated with care rather than deceit. Their lives, like sheep in their own fold, will be centered in God, in one flock, and not scattered. But these wise words remain only words if they are heard without an active response.

Salt, light, a city on a hill, a lamp, a harvest, and a faithful shepherd are all metaphors with the same message. Each metaphor has power only when the reality it represents is used for its authentic purpose. Disciples of Jesus will be authentic disciples when they, too, become sources of life for others. This is a consistent message in the canonical Gospels, in the Thomas

Codex, and in Q because it is the central message of Jesus. The reign of God is love-in-action:

- *"No one after lighting a lamp puts it in a cellar, but on the lampstand so that those who enter may see the light"* (Luke 11:33; Q). The light is for everyone.

- "Jesus, said, 'A city built on a high hill and fortified cannot fall, nor can it be hidden.'" (Gospel of Thomas, logia 32)

- "Jesus said, 'What you hear in your ear, in the other ear proclaim from your rooftops.'" (Gospel of Thomas, logia 31a)

- "Jesus said, 'The harvest is large but the workers are few. So beg the master to send out workers to the harvest.'" (Gospel of Thomas, logia 73)

- *"My Father is glorified by this, that you bear much fruit and become my disciples."* (John 15:8)

Each person's life of prayer will have an effect on the world for good. It is not our doing. It flows from our intimacy with God in prayer. Prayer is a mutual presence in which the energy of God is transmitted. It is a mysterious gift that we accept and manifest through our openness, with no attachment, to the outcome.

Jesus did not rely on himself to be engaged in the needs of people around him. What were the sources of his passion to bring God's presence and power to the life of the world?

What have you learned from Jesus' life of prayer about the integration of contemplation and action?

DAY 89

Becoming part of God's field

Jesus used many images from nature. Like other children in Nazareth, he spent time in the vineyards and fields absorbing the beauty and noticing birds of the air, animals, and lilies of the field. He was present at the sowing and the harvesting of crops; he learned by watching. As a young adult he most likely walked across the countryside with Joseph from Nazareth to Sepphoris for work in homes of the wealthy or building their storage barns. He probably loved the shade and fruit of fig trees. He knew the process of pruning grape vines. One of the shrubs he must have known well is the mustard tree. Its tiny seeds were very unlikely candidates to produce thick shrubs that could become small trees. He must have noticed how popular this shrub was as a safe place for birds to build their nest and raise their young.

> He said, therefore, "What is the kingdom of God like? And to what should I compare it? It is like a mustard seed that someone took and sowed in the garden; it grew and became a tree, and the birds of the air made nests in its branches." (Luke 13:18–19)

When thinking of making God's desires tangible here "on earth as they are in heaven" it is possible to be overwhelmed. What difference can one person make? The challenges are great. Jesus' understanding of the kingdom or reign of God is not an exercise in triumphalism. It is not a "mega program." It is very simple. In Psalm 146 we see that the small seeds that we are can mature into the likeness of God, through justice for oppressed persons, food for the hungry, restoration of freedom for prisoners, new sight for the blind, hope for persons who are crushed by the weight of poverty, hospitality for strangers and refugees, and care for orphans and widows (Ps 146:5–9). The psalmist describes the "nests" that can be built in the tree that began as a tiny seed. Nests are wombs of life. Jesus says that we are called to be nests in the shrubs that grow in God's field. And it begins in the soil of prayer and germinates in the light of the presence and energy of God.

Not only does Jesus place great confidence in those who entrust their lives to him, he reminds them that the realm of God is a present reality in their lives. "Once Jesus was asked by the Pharisees when the kingdom of God *was coming, and he answered, 'The kingdom of God is not coming with things that can be observed; nor will they say, "Look, here it is!" or "There it is!" For, in fact, the kingdom of God is among you'" (Luke 17:20–21; Q).*

How is it possible for one person to make God tangible when the needs of the world are so complex and complicated in their scope?

Where can each person begin to "make a difference"?

DAY 90

Accepting and living with a mystery

The life of God we experience in prayer is a mysterious gift. When we go into our "inner chamber," as Jesus instructed, we have the opportunity to accept that gift and entrust ourselves to its presence in our lives. In our "inner chamber" we are invited to become part of the reign of God and share in God's active engagement with the needs of the world. In these daily "chapters" we have learned what this is like by looking at Jesus' life of prayer.

Jesus used many images to describe the reign of God as a mystery. The way the kingdom unfolds in daily life is mysterious, but its results are tangible and very practical. Here are two of his images:

> Again he said to them, "To what should I compare the kingdom of God? It is like yeast that a woman took and mixed in with three measures of flour until all of it was leavened." (Luke 13:20–21)

Jesus is using an example he experienced each day as a child. Jewish boys were under the care of their mothers until the age of seven. Mary went to the well in the morning. Wheat was ground in the home or using a common stone mortar in a courtyard. The water, wheat, and yeast were combined and set aside to rise before baking, usually in an outdoor shared oven. The ingredients and the method were known and the skill of the women was reliable, but in Jesus' day the "rising" was considered a mystery. In this example Jesus puts "three measures" of flour in the recipe—far more than is needed for one family—to emphasize what can happen in the reign of God. Just as baking is collaboration between the ingredients, the baker, the oven, and the mystery, so is our experience of God in prayer. How the "loaf" of prayer becomes tangible in daily life is a mystery. But our collaboration with God will "produce" more than we can imagine or control.

> He also said, "The kingdom of God is as if someone would scatter seed on the ground, and would sleep and rise night and day, and the seed would sprout and grow, he does not know how. The earth produces of itself, first the stalk, then the head, then the full grain in the head. But when the grain is ripe, at once he goes in with his sickle, because the harvest has come." (Mark 4:26–29)

Once again the growth of the kingdom of God is a mystery, but the harvest is tangible. *"The earth produces of itself . . . ."* The energy of God flowing through our lives produces God's self in our daily lives. In the same way that people in Jesus' time had no idea what caused a crop to sprout, grow, and reach maturity in the head, we do not know how the mystery of God's life becomes tangible in our lives.

Our first task is to accept the mystery. *"I appeal to you therefore, brothers and sisters, by the mercies of God, to present your bodies as a living sacrifice, holy and acceptable to God, which is your spiritual worship. Do not be conformed to this world, but be transformed by the renewing of your minds, so that you may discern what is the will of God—what is good and acceptable and perfect"* (Rom 12:1–2).

Even though the life of God in us is a gift and mystery beyond our control, we are invited to collaborate with God in the "harvest" of our own lives and the life of the world. *"Therefore, my beloved, just as you have always obeyed me* [listened and responded], *not only in my presence, but much more now in my absence, work out your own salvation with fear and trembling; for it is God who is at work in you, enabling you both to will and to work for his good pleasure"* (Phil 2:12–13).

Prayer is a journey to become a harvest of God's presence in the world. *"Every generous act of giving, with every perfect gift, is from above, coming down from the Father of lights, with whom there is no variation or shadow due to change. In fulfillment of his own purpose he gave us birth by the word of truth, so that we would become a kind of first fruits of his creatures"* (Jas 1:17–18).

What does the mysterious aspect of life teach you?

Where does mystery lead you?

What does mystery make possible in your life?

Desert Day Five

The risks and richness in Jesus' life of prayer.

Today is a Sabbath. Rest your mind from reading, studying, writing, and thinking. Being silent and less active will help you listen to the four Gospels in a unique way. When your mind and your heart are integrated you will begin to *experience* Jesus' life of prayer rather than study about it.

Today let your intellectual discipline be embraced and mentored by contemplative reflection on the risks and richness in Jesus' life of prayer. Using what you have learned thus far, try to enter into his adult ministry and let it speak to you.

Begin this day with twenty minutes of silent contemplative prayer. A simple method is described in Appendix E. Find a place that is as quiet as possible. You may prefer to walk to a quiet place and combine a silent walk with sitting once you have arrived.

You may not be able to make this Desert Day a full day. But do your best to make it an intentional part of your day. Set aside at least two hours, if possible. During that time let the four Gospels speak to you, rather than deciding what you want to learn from them. A simple prayer may help you, such as "Spirit, reveal what's true. . . . Spirit I bless you." Or "Come, Holy, Holy. . . . Come, Holy Spirit." Try to let go of the outcome of this day. Toward the end of this day recall what you have heard, learned, and experienced. Keep your reflections in a journal.

The following questions may help your reflection on the risks and richness in Jesus' life of prayer:

- In what ways did Jesus' life of prayer lead him to the conviction that his ministry was to "fulfill" the Torah?

- How was Jesus' prayer related to incidents in which he challenged the teaching of religious leaders and specific applications of the Torah in daily life?

- What have you learned from Jesus about the role of prayer in the midst of conflict?

- What role did Jesus' prayer have when he was challenged by religious and political authorities and when his life was endangered?

- What influence did Jesus' life of prayer have on his non-violent responses to criticism and the events leading to his arrest and execution?

- How was Jesus' life congruent with his teaching about loving one's enemies?

- What does Jesus require from persons who want to follow him?

DAY 91

(Summary Part One)
Knowing the Father

We have now completed ninety of our one-hundred days of reflection on Jesus' life of prayer. The last ten days will focus on a summary of what we have learned from trying to experience prayer from Jesus' point of view in the context of his culture. These last ten days provide opportunities to review what you have learned and reflect on its implications for your life.

The foundation of Jesus' prayer, in its variety of forms, is knowing the Father. This experience is the source of Jesus' desires, words, and actions.

> *Philip said to [Jesus], "Lord show us the Father, and we will be satisfied." Jesus said to him, "Have I been with you all this time, Philip, and you still do not know me? Whoever has seen me has seen the Father. How can you say, 'Show us the Father?' Do you not believe that I am in the Father and the Father is in me? The words that I say to you I do not speak on my own; but the Father who dwells in me does his works. Believe me that I am in the Father and the Father is in me; but if you do not, then believe me because of the works themselves. Very truly I tell you, the one who believes in me will also do the works that I do and, in fact, will do greater works than these, because I am going to the Father. I will do whatever you ask in my name, so that the Father may be glorified in the Son. If in my name you ask me for anything, I will do it." (John 14:8–14)*

"Whoever has seen me has seen the Father." Jesus has "known" the Father through his life of prayer. This "knowing" refers to intimacy so great that the conventional boundaries of "me" and "the Father" are dissolved. There is no dualism, no separation. Jesus made it clear that this same relationship is available to every person who entrusts her or his life to Jesus. To pray "in my name" means to enter into the presence of Jesus and share his energy; in this way what we "ask" will be congruent with what he desires for the life of the world. At the heart of Jesus' life of prayer is "knowing the Father" (the reality of God's presence) and remaining in that presence. Everything else comes forth from this presence.

Jesus experience of his Abba is deeply rooted in his piety as a devoted first-century Jew. On the one hand, he recognizes the transcendence of his

"Father, in heaven." The Father is creator, sustainer, and the source of justice and righteousness. Earth can never contain God and even the name of God may not be written or pronounced. At the same time, Jesus experiences "the Father" as *abba*, a personal title of both intimacy and respect. Jesus' experience of his Abba is tangible and the source of his words and actions. He does not experience Abba as "other." In this way, Jesus' experience of God is congruent with his Jewish heritage because his ancestors experienced God as both transcendent and immanent. It was a creative tension based on the different ways God was experienced in the lives of the Hebrews. God is both mystery and parent who cares for a child (Israel). This two-fold knowing is not a dualism, but two forms of the relationship between God and the people of Israel. The "knowing" is not knowledge, but mutual experience.

Jesus' "knowing the Father" expresses the prayers and piety of his Jewish heritage, although his personal experience of God as Abba is most likely unique. This two-fold experience of God in prayer was continued in the prayers of the earliest Christian communities and is still present in the liturgies of most modern Christian faith communities. Jesus' way of "knowing the Father" is a rich part of the Christian experience of personal and corporate prayer.

What have you learned about Jesus' experience of God in prayer?

How has this affirmed and changed your own life of prayer?

DAY 92

(Summary Part Two)
Fully engaged with life

In the same way that the fundamental aspect of Jesus' prayer was intimacy with God, the primary *consequence* of his prayer was that he became *like* his Abba; he made the Father's life *tangible*. The unwavering and passionate dimension of Jesus' manifestation of his Abba is his compassionate engagement in the lives of people, especially people who were hungry, marginalized, with various illnesses, shamed by society, sinful, poor, and without hope for change. Most of these people were considered "unclean" and to be avoided.

The Gospel of Matthew declares that after Jesus' extended period of prayer in the wilderness he wasted no time immersing himself in the lives of people:

> *Jesus went throughout Galilee, teaching in their synagogues and proclaiming the good news of the kingdom and curing every disease and every sickness among the people. So his fame spread throughout all Syria, and they brought to him all the sick, those who were afflicted with various diseases and pains, demoniacs, epileptics, and paralytics, and he cured them.* (Matt 4:23–24)

This is just one of many examples we have seen during the past three months of reflections.

Jesus' life of prayer challenges us to become fully engaged with life. He shows that intimacy with God, in prayer, is the womb of compassion, the wellspring of action, and is the motivation and energy prompting our words and deeds. Jesus, through his life of prayer, calls us to be generative and manifest the vitality and power of God in our lives. Prayer becomes tangible through responsible living, justice, caring for other people, generosity, and self-giving.

What have you learned about the ways Jesus' prayer influenced his engagement in the lives of people around him?

How has this affirmed or changed your understanding of the relationship between your prayer and your involvement in the lives of other people?

DAY 93

Summary (Part Three)
Another way of seeing

Jesus was very clear that he had no desire to abolish the Torah. He honored it as a path to fulfill the covenant his people had made with God. At the same time he claimed that he wanted to fulfill the Torah. His desire was to look into the heart of the Torah as a way to learn what God desires for human life and a path toward abundant living. As a faithful Galilean he followed the Torah and worshiped with his faith community. Yet often he could see a "disconnect" between what the Torah required and what many people actually did with their lives. Unlike John the Baptist, Jesus did not promote rash judgment from God as the means for transformation of people's lives. He spoke about God intervening in people's lives by a transformation of consciousness coupled with compassionate relationships with people whose needs were great and who were being ignored and abused. He knew it was possible to be "religious" (follow the teaching of the Torah) and fail to see what the inner dimension of the Torah desired. Jesus vision came from his intimate relationship with God in prayer and that vision enabled him to see the societal "disconnects" around him. He exhorted people to look at reality in its full spiritual dimension.

> *The eye is the lamp of the body. So if your eye is healthy, your whole body will be filled with light; but if your eye is unhealthy, your whole body will be filled with darkness. If then the light in you is darkness, how great is the darkness!* (Matt 6:22–23)

It is possible to follow every detail of what the Law requires to be a powerful leader, a successful land owner, or a hard working peasant and fail to see what God desires on earth. Jesus told parables to help people see a different way. Some understood, but most did not. Speaking to those who had entrusted their lives to him, Jesus said, *"But blessed are your eyes, for they see, and your ears, for they hear. Truly I tell you, many prophets and righteous people longed to see what you see, but did not see it, and to hear what you hear, but did not hear it"* (Matt 13:16–17).

Jesus' life of prayer shows that prayer involves listening, waiting, being aware, and being filled with wonder and gratitude. He offers the opportunity to experience truth so that our path is directed by what is real and does not become bogus or self-serving. Prayer is listening with the heart and being guided, sometimes driven, to see ourselves and the world with God's eyes and wisdom. Prayer enables us to see what is authentic in our lives and have the honesty to see our self-centeredness and sins so that we can turn and embrace our true selves. Prayer is vision.

How did Jesus' prayer help him discern his relationship with his Abba and his vision of God's desires for his life?

How has this affirmed or changed your understanding of prayerful discernment and self-knowledge as integral aspects of your prayer?

DAY 94

Summary (Part Four)
Prayer is an act of submission

Submission is not a popular word in Western societies, especially the USA. Yet it was a natural and essential part of Jesus' relationship with his Abba, and he exhorted his followers to submit control of their lives to God. He believed that submission was a matter of life and death. He saw submission as dying to self, abiding in his presence, and continuing in his word.

- *"Those who want to find their life will lose it, and those who lose their life for my sake will find it."* (Matt 10:39)

- *"Abide in me as I abide in you. Just as the branch cannot bear fruit unless it abides in the vine, neither can you unless you abide in me."* (John 15:4)

- *"If you continue in my word, you are my disciples; and you will know the truth, and the truth will make you free."* (John 8:31b–32)

Why is submission to the presence of God in Jesus important? Jesus makes it clear that placing our lives in God's hands is the source of authentic life. It enables us to bear the fruit of God's love—the fruit of the Spirit—and shows us what is real and true about life itself. Contrary to conventional wisdom, submitting our lives to God in Christ is the source of *authentic freedom*. Jesus' parable about the differing prayers of a Pharisee and a tax collector is a bold and transparent statement about the attitude of submission that makes prayer authentic.

> *Two men went up to the temple to pray, one a Pharisee and the other a tax collector. The Pharisee, standing by himself, was praying thus, "God, I thank you that I am not like other people: thieves, rogues, adulterers, or even like this tax collector. I fast twice a week; I give a tenth of all my income." But the tax collector, standing far off, would not even look up to heaven, but was beating his breast and saying, "God, be merciful to me, a sinner!" I tell you, this man went down to his home justified rather than the other; for all who exalt themselves will be humbled, but all who humble themselves will be exalted.* (Luke 18:10–14)

The Pharisee had "an attitude problem." The tax collector, knowing himself honestly, placed his heart and soul in God's hands. Submission to God is not willingness to be coerced or manipulated by God. It is an attitude of entrustment to the One who knows us better than we know ourselves. Submission is a threshold leading toward intimacy with God and a passionate *desire* to live a responsible and caring life.

Jesus exhorts us to give up anything that is less than our true selves. In this context, prayer is letting go of control and being open to God. Jesus reminds us that the path is narrow and demands wholeheartedness, persistence, and genuine desire. Prayer is "turning toward" [repentance] and offering our will and total self to God and our neighbor.

This is not easy! Jesus did not find it easy either. He found strength and wisdom for his life in his life of prayer, especially in the intimacy of his personal experience of his Abba. He teaches us that the inner resources we need for authentic life *are not our own*. That is good news! And it points to the fundamental need for prayer. If we want to be Jesus' disciples then it is essential to stay close to him and depend totally on God.

What have you learned about Jesus' total submission to the will of his Abba?

How has this affirmed or changed your understanding of submitting your life to God?

How do you submit your life to God?

What kinds of fear or anxiety arise when you contemplate dying to self? What supports you?

DAY 95

Summary (Part Five)
A three-fold pattern of prayer

Looking back at Jesus' life of prayer, the four canonical Gospels reveal a pattern that was the source of his life with God:

- Quiet listening: *"At daybreak he departed and went into a deserted place"* (Luke 4:42). The Gospels attest to Jesus' habit of finding time to be alone in prayer. He went into his "inner chamber" and exhorted his followers to do the same.

- Faithful discernment: *"Now during those days he went out to the mountain to pray; and he spent the night in prayer to God. And when day came, he called his disciples and chose twelve of them, whom he named apostles"* (Luke 6:12–13). Jesus' inner room was not a place of refuge for himself. His intimacy with God was a time to listen and respond to what he heard.

- Compassionate response: *"And he came down with them* [the disciples and the newly chosen apostles] *and stood on a level place, and a great crowd of his disciples and a great multitude of people from Judea, Jerusalem, and the coast of Tyre and Sidon. They had come to hear him and to be healed of their diseases; and those who were troubled with unclean spirits were cured. And all in the crowds were trying to touch him, for power came out from him and healed all of them"* (Luke 6:17–19). Jesus always found time to listen to God, the world around him, and his inner self. This listening heart was the source of the guidance and will that, along with direct experience of God's love, led and sometimes drove him into compassionate involvement in the lives of others.

All this took place in the context and in fulfillment of his religious community and its Torah. Jesus' life of prayer opened him to the vitality of God's energy and vision. He became what he sought and experienced in prayer. He loved what he saw. He transformed what he touched. He lived and shared what he spoke.

How do these three aspects of Jesus' life of prayer appear throughout his life?

How do these three patterns of prayer affirm or invite you to expand your life of prayer?

DAY 96

Summary (Part Six)
We shall become like he is

Although Jesus experienced unique intimacy with God that was manifest throughout his life, he did not see this relationship as exclusively his own. His passion was to share his life with God and include everyone willing to entrust their lives to God's presence in him. We have seen that he chose disciples to share his work. Jesus' life of prayer was not static! It was not a "closed system."

Yet it was not easy to follow him. Several times the disciples questioned the wisdom of his decisions or could not understand his parables. Some were discouraged because they could not cast out demons as he did. When opposition to Jesus' words and actions put him in danger the disciples resisted accepting Jesus' awareness that he would suffer at the hands of the religious leaders who opposed him. At one point James and John asked Jesus to allow them to sit on his right and left when Jesus came into his "glory." They were thinking of a nation-wide triumph, but Jesus knew they had little or no idea of the cost of sharing his mission. He asked them, *"Are you able to drink the cup that I drink, or be baptized with the baptism that I am baptized with?"* (Mark 10:38b). Later in his ministry the disciples continued to discourage Jesus from going to Jerusalem and avoid the conflict that ultimately led to his execution. In the midst of this uncertainty Jesus exhorted his disciples to stay with him and enter into the events and persecution that was certain to follow. When Peter enthusiastically declared his loyalty, Jesus knew Peter would give in to fear. The crucifixion brought dark clouds of failure and shame for the disciples. *"But we had hoped that he was the one to redeem Israel"* (Luke 24:21a).

Were the disciples failures? Why would Jesus choose such ordinary people? It is clear that in the earliest days of Jesus' mission he realized he would not accomplish all that was necessary to make the reign of God a reality. He knew it was both a present and future reality. That is why he chose disciples to share his mission. He knew they were ordinary persons and that it would take both time and experience for them to understand what was happening in his life. He knew, also, that if they placed their lives in the hands of his Abba, they would be transformed and filled with the same divine presence that energized his life.

> *Very truly, I tell you, the one who believes in me will also do the works that I do and, in fact, will do greater works than these, because I am going to the Father. I will do whatever you ask in my name, so that the Father may be glorified in the Son. If in my name you ask me for anything, I will do it.* (John 14:12–14)

This is hard to believe! Jesus' disciples will do greater works than he? Does this include twenty-first-century disciples? Can we really become as he is? Jesus shatters our efforts to make his life with God completely different from ours. He offers a path of endless transformation that includes (like his own spiritual formation) a discipline of personal prayer, corporate prayer in the context of a community of faith, and opportunities to embody prayer in words and actions. When we entrust our lives to Christ Jesus we will discern what to ask in his name because we will share his mind and intimacy with the Father. God's glory will become tangible in our lives. We will share God's unconditional love for humankind and the earth. But we will not do this on our own. Like the disciples, the Spirit will become our mentor and power:

> *If you love me you will keep my commandments. And I will ask the Father, and he will give you another Advocate, to be with you forever. This is the Spirit of truth, whom the world cannot receive, because it neither sees him nor knows him. You know him, because he abides with you, and he will be in you.* (John 14:15–17)

It was not until Jesus was raised from death that his disciples would begin to grasp the meaning of Jesus' life and mission and that it would continue through them. Saint Paul bears witness to the presence of God's Spirit in lives of persons who have experienced the risen Christ: *"Now we have received not the spirit of the world, but the Spirit that is from God, so that we may understand the gifts bestowed on us by God. And we speak of these things in words not taught by human wisdom but taught by the Spirit, interpreting spiritual things to those who are spiritual"* (1 Cor 2:12–13).

One of the early Christian desert fathers, Abba Pachomius, said, "For what is greater than such a vision, to see the Invisible God in a visible man, His temple."[27] This is the primary consequence of prayer. It was Jesus' desire for those who entrust their lives to him. We shall become as he is.

27. *S. Pachomii Vita graecae*, edited by Halkin, Subsidia hagiographica 19, Brussels,

What have you learned about Jesus' desire to share the presence of God in his life with other persons?

What will that good news make possible in your life?

1932, cc. 47–48, quoted in Chitty, *The Desert a City*, 28.

DAY 97

Summary (Part Seven)
Prayer combines personal intimacy with God and social responsibility

We have seen that Jesus' life of prayer—a mystical and personal relationship with God—was integrated with responsible interaction with the people and society that surrounded him. His words and actions included, but were not restricted to "religious issues" within his Jewish faith community; he was also outspoken about relations between employers and laborers, feeding the homeless and hungry, greed among public tax officials, oppressive treatment of persons who could not repay loans on time, inhumane treatment of persons with diseases, and many other "secular" issues in his society. Jesus' daily behavior reminded people that the reign of God included all aspects of human life. In Jesus' mind heaven is the place where God's nature of justice and righteousness prevail. *"Your will be done on earth as it is in heaven."* This begins inside a person:

"But whenever you pray, go into your room and shut the door and pray to your Father who is in secret; and your Father who sees in secret will reward you" (Matt 6:6). Jesus' personal prayer was a time to experience intimacy with God deep within his being.

"The kingdom of heaven is like yeast that a woman took and mixed in with three measures of flour until all of it was leavened" (Matt 13:33). Prayer is like the energy of yeast making bread dough rise. Jesus' time in his "inner room" was a flow of energy between his spirit and God's Spirit. This energy flowed out from his "room" into the words and actions of his daily life:

> Then Jesus went about all the cities and villages, teaching in their synagogues, and proclaiming the good news of the kingdom, and curing every disease and every sickness. When he saw the crowds, he had compassion for them, because they were harassed and helpless, like sheep without a shepherd. Then he said to his disciples, "The harvest is plentiful, but the laborers are few; therefore ask the Lord of the harvest to send out laborers into his harvest." (Matt 9:35–38)

Jesus' life demonstrates that prayer is at the same time a personal experience of God and an opportunity to make God's desires and presence tangible in ways that will transform society. When prayer and compassionate living are integrated they will bear fruit for the reign of God. The fourth-century Christian desert father Abba Moses reminded his colleague Abba Poemen that if a person's deeds are not in harmony with that person's prayer, he or she labors in vain.[28] Abba Moses' wisdom mirrors Jesus' words, *"Abide in me as I abide in you. Just as a branch cannot bear fruit by itself, neither can you unless you abide in me"* (John 15:4).

On the basis of Jesus' integration of his life of prayer with active engagement in his society, how would you respond to a person who maintains that religion and politics must remain separate?

How does your life of prayer influence your involvement in political and social issues in your community?

28. Paraphrased from a quotation in Keller, *Desert Banquet*, 14.

DAY 98

Summary (Part Eight)
Experience, through prayer, precedes theology

We have been exploring Jesus' life of prayer for over three months. What are the implications of his experience of prayer for our lives? After almost two-thousand years Christians still are not sure who he was, or at least we cannot agree on the best way to articulate his identity in words. Theology and conversations seem to have taken "center stage." Although theology is necessary, it is not where our life with God begins. Is it more important to declare who Jesus was or to live as he lived? Jesus was less interested in what people called him than in inviting them to follow him. His "good news" was that God was entering people's lives through his life and he invited people to share that same experience.

> *After this* [Jesus has just healed a paralytic and declared that his sins were forgiven] *he went out and saw a tax collector named Levi, sitting at the tax booth; and he said to him, "Follow me." And he got up, left everything, and followed him.* (Luke 5:27–28)

> *But if it is by the finger of God that I cast out demons, then the kingdom of God has come among you.* (Luke 11:20)

Entering into the life of Jesus does not begin with theological reflection or debate about right belief or right behavior. During his life on earth he was filled with the presence of his Abba. He was clear that when he left his disciples they would share the divine life present in his life. *"I will not leave you orphaned; I am coming to you. In a little while the world will no longer see me; because I live, you also will live. In that day you will know that I am in my Father, and you in me, and I in you. They who have my commandments and keep them are those who love me; and those who love me will be loved by my Father, and I will love them and reveal myself to them"* (John 14:18–21).

As we have seen, the disciples did not always *understand* what Jesus was saying or doing. And they were not always "successful" when they were sent out to heal in Jesus' name. But they learned through experience. Luke narrates a day when the seventy disciples Jesus sent out to heal and cast out demons returned with great joy. *"Lord, in your name even the demons submit to us!"* (Luke 10:17). Jesus' response is a profound statement about the role experience of God in the lives of his disciples:

> *At that same hour Jesus rejoiced in the Holy Spirit and said, "I thank you, Father, Lord of heaven and earth, because you have hidden these things from the wise and the intelligent and have revealed them to infants; yes, Father, for such was your gracious will. All things have been handed over to me by my Father; and no one knows who the Son is except the Father, or who the Father is except the Son, and any one to whom the Son chooses to reveal him." Then turning to the disciples, Jesus said to them privately, "Blessed are the eyes that see what you see! For I tell you that many prophets and kings desired to see what you see, but did not see it, and to hear what you hear, but did not hear it."* (Luke 10:21–24)

Entering into the risen life of the Anointed One comes by experiencing the same divine life that was present in him. We can learn what "experiencing the divine life" means by looking carefully at the life of Jesus of Nazareth. His life of prayer will teach us to pray. His compassionate involvement in the lives of people around him will inspire and empower our own involvement in the lives of people around us. That is his challenge to us. If we take his challenge to follow him, including following him into intimacy with God, we will experience the divine life in us. And this will transform our lives. It is not about theological correctness or studying wise sayings. It begins with experience of the Holy One.

As Jesus was growing up he valued the wisdom of wise teachers at the temple in Jerusalem and knew the sacred Scriptures of his tradition very well. Describe the relationship between Jesus' experience of his tradition's wisdom, his experience of God in prayer, and his involvement in other people's lives.

Today we live in "the age of information." How do you make room for experience of God and your neighbor?

DAY 99

Summary (Part Nine)
Prayer helps us embrace what is true

If you read the four canonical Gospels carefully and allow yourself to enter into the culture and life of Jesus (as best we can from our twenty-first-century point of view), you will discover that Jesus discerned and taught truth about God that challenged conventional knowledge and practice. It seems clear that the authority for his controversial innovations in thinking and action came directly from his life of prayer.

> *I can do nothing on my own. As I hear I judge; and my judgment is just, because I seek to do not my own will but the will of him who sent me. . . . The works that the Father has given me to complete, the very works that I am doing, testify on my behalf that the Father has sent me. (John 5:30; 36b)*

The "judgment" Jesus speaks about is the discernment he has received in the intimacy of his experience of God in prayer. The discernment enables Jesus to make some startling changes in the teaching of his faith community. Actually, Jesus referred to these "changes" as "fulfillment of the Torah."

> *You have heard that it was said, "An eye for an eye and a tooth for a tooth." But I say to you, Do not resist an evildoer. . . . You have heard that it was said, "You shall love your neighbor and hate your enemy." But I say to you, Love your enemies and pray for those who persecute you." (Matt 5:38–39a, 43–44)*

We have seen that Jesus touched lepers and ate with tax collectors, sinners, and prostitutes. Jesus' presence at meals with "unclean" persons was scandalous and made him unclean. This behavior contradicted the holiness code of his tradition. People are to be holy because God is holy. The leaders of Jesus' faith tradition were genuinely concerned that the corrupt religious influences coming from Roman society and culture would dilute or change their religious identity and the practices that kept them faithful to the Torah. They insisted that "separation" from all unclean influences, situations, and teaching was the way to preserve their religious purity.

Jesus learned from his Abba that God's holiness was embodied through compassion for one's neighbor, especially the poor, sinners, the homeless, the widows, the orphans, and persons with diseases that made them "unclean." God's intent, through Jesus, was to be with all these marginalized people. Jesus' taught—through his behavior—that if God's people are to be holy as God is holy they are to embody God's nature as one who loves unconditionally.

In his scholarly and very readable book *Jesus: An Historical Approximation*, the Spanish New Testament scholar José Pagola declares that Jesus' most significant clarification about God's nature is that God's holiness does not mean that people have to be separate from persons who are seen as impure in order to be holy. In fact, says Pagola, Jesus proclaims that God's holiness is compassionate love for every person.[29] This is a fundamental change from the accepted understanding of God in Jesus' day. Both the sources of this truth and the authority to declare the truth came from the intimacy of Jesus with his Abba in prayer. Experience of God's Spirit in prayer will lead us into all truth.

Christian denominations, local congregations, and individuals have not always been faithful to Jesus' understanding of holiness. When have you been frustrated or harmed in some way by this failure?

How have you responded?

29. See Pagola, *Jesus*, 192–201.

DAY 100

Summary (Part Ten)
Where it all begins

Every human being longs to know why he or she is alive. This longing is more than a search for knowledge It is a desire to experience fullness of life. Using the image of a gate into a sheepfold, Jesus said, *"I am the gate. Whoever enters by me will be saved, and will come in and go out and find pasture. The thief comes only to steal and kill and destroy. I came that they may have life, and have it abundantly"* (John 10:9–10). What did he mean? The meaning is embodied in his life. His life is his message! That is the great value of entering into Jesus' life of prayer as we have done these past ninety-nine days. What have you seen and experienced?

When the disciples asked Jesus to teach them to pray, Jesus responded by telling them to ask their *"Father in heaven"* to help them desire what God desires for life on the earth. Abundant life is asking only for what is necessary, each day, and no more. Abundance is embodied in a forgiving heart and reconciliation with people we have harmed or who have harmed us. Abundance is relying totally on God to guide us away from desires and situations that profane authentic human life for ourselves and for other people.

But who will teach us how to live like this? Where will we find the courage to choose the abundant life God offers? It is tempting to look here and there for ways to live full and meaningful lives and try to accomplish that goal on our own. Can life's authentic abundance and meaning be revealed in books, abstract thinking, or taking personal control over our lives? Jesus was very clear about the source of the way leading to truth and life. It is possible to know "the way." He invites us to look at the presence of God in his life and make a choice to entrust ourselves to that presence—as he invited his disciples to do. We do not create the reign of God; we are invited to enter. But where do we cross the threshold?

> *Once Jesus was asked by the Pharisees when the kingdom of God was coming, and he answered, "The kingdom of God is not coming with things that can be observed; nor will they say, 'Look, here it is!' or 'There it is!' For, in fact, the kingdom of God is among you."* (Luke 17:20–21; Q)

The place to begin is close to home. There is no need to search here and there. Jesus invited his disciples to go into their "inner chamber." He promised they would experience and be embraced by the presence of God in that spiritual center of their lives. The inner chamber of each person is the place where the reign of God begins:

> Do not store up for yourselves treasures on earth, where moth and rust consume and where thieves break in and steal; but store up for yourselves treasures in heaven, where neither moth nor rust consumes and where thieves do not break in and steal. For where your treasure is, there will your heart be also. (Matt 6:19–21)

> The kingdom of heaven is like treasure hidden in a field, which someone found and hid; then in his joy he goes and sells all that he has and buys that field. (Matt 13:44)

When we treasure the intimacy of God in prayer, we will experience that intimacy everywhere. It will transform our thoughts, desire, words, and actions, even in moments of life's darkness. We will be able to take the risk of loving because we have experienced unconditional love.

"Now during those days he went out to the mountain to pray; and he spent the night in prayer to God." This is where it all begins. We know from Jesus' life that this does not mean everything will be sunny and calm. But we will embody truth and we will be fully alive. This is the meaning of the words Jesus spoke to the Samaritan woman at the well:

> But the hour is coming and is now here, when the true worshipers will worship the Father in spirit and in truth. God is spirit, and those who worship him must worship in spirit and truth. (John 4:23–24)

Being a person of prayer and living a life of prayer is worship. Life's abundance is revealed in living and the purpose of life is discovered in unconditional love.

Desert Day Six

What have you experienced?

Today is a Sabbath. Rest your mind from reading, studying, writing, and thinking. Being silent and less active will help you discern what you have experienced these past one-hundred days.

Today let your intellectual discipline be embraced and mentored by contemplative reflection. Using what you have learned thus far, try to enter into Jesus' life of prayer and let it speak to you.

Begin this day with twenty minutes of silent contemplative prayer. A simple method is described in Appendix E. Find a place that is as quiet as possible. You may prefer to walk to a quiet place and combine a silent walk with sitting once you have arrived.

Try to make this last Desert Day a full day. During the time you set aside let the four Gospels speak to you, rather than deciding what you want to learn from them. A simple prayer may help you, such as "Spirit, reveal what's true. . . . Spirit I bless you." Or "Come, Holy, Holy. . . . Come, Holy Spirit." Try to let go of the outcome of this day. Toward the end of this day recall what you have heard, learned, and experienced. Keep your reflections in a journal.

The following questions may help your reflection on your experience of Jesus' life of prayer:

During these past three months how has your relationship with Jesus grown or changed?

- What have you learned about prayer?

- How has your life of prayer changed?

- Describe ways in which your prayer during this course has informed the way you study?

- How has your relationship with God changed during these past three months?

- What invitations or challenges are you experiencing in your life of prayer?

- During these one hundred days how have you experienced Jesus in a new way?

- How will Jesus' life of prayer influence the way you mentor other persons in prayer?

- What are the implications or direct influences from Jesus' life of prayer for personal and spiritual formation in your life, family life, and a local congregation?

- If you are, or will become, a spiritual director, how will Jesus' life of prayer influence: (a) Your relationship with your "directees"? (b) The way you listen to and offer guidance to your "directees"? (c) The role of prayer in your ministry of spiritual direction and in the lives of your "directees"?

- What has Jesus' life of prayer taught you about God's desires for human life?

- What has Jesus life of prayer taught you about being a Christian?

- How will you share your experience of Jesus with other persons?

EPILOGUE

Jesus' life of prayer today

Guard the good treasure entrusted to you, with the help of the Holy Spirit living in us. (2 Tim 1:14)

Modern Christian faith communities have been entrusted with a very simple message. It is Jesus' message, not the churches' message about Jesus. The message is embodied in the presence of the risen Christ in the lives of persons who have been gathered by the Holy Spirit into Christian faith communities. It is a way of life that makes the treasure of Jesus' life of prayer tangible in the twenty-first century. The message is the same gospel that Jesus, the first-century Jew, lived and proclaimed during his lifetime and the "good news" he continues to proclaim through his presence in the life of Christian communities throughout the world. It is a simple message about a good treasure.

We are created to participate in the nature of God

Jesus demonstrated that the true and authentic nature of human beings is divine. We are not God, or even gods. Yet the source of our being is the mysterious uncreated energy of God and our vocation is to become one with God. This authentic human nature unfolds in the context of creation, within time and space. At the same time, it is eternal because its source is the energy of God.

The lure of divine love

While our true nature is divine, the experience of living tells us we must discover and grow into our divine image and likeness. This is why we search for God with restless hearts. We experience an interior desire that longs for intimacy with God. Although it is our destiny and salvation, this unfolding of who we are is not forced on us. On the contrary, we can both ignore and reject the gift of divine life. Because the divine source of our nature is an eternal mystery, we cannot envision or attain the fullness of our being on our own or all at once. The gift is always present, but it is continually coming into being. The mystery unfolds, but is never consumed. Perhaps this is because we cannot fathom and embrace too much of the mystery at one time.

At the same time we seem, hopelessly at times, determined to control who we are and what we want to become. We limit the scope of our desires to the fulfillment of the temporal appetites and expectations which can addict us. These desires are not always selfish or bad, but if we become attached to them they lead us away from God and authentic human life. We cannot deny the reality of sin. Somehow, in our quest for fulfillment we settle for less than our true nature. The consequences of this self-centeredness can be horrific, filled with pain, injustice, greed, and lives wasted and destroyed.

Sin is losing sight of our divine nature and the consequences that blindness creates

When our self-centered control of life becomes a personal and societal norm we lose sight of what it means to be human. In essence, we create ourselves in our own image. This false self obscures our consciousness of the image we have in God. We create a barrier between ourselves and God. We do not cease to participate in God's divine nature, but we do not manifest our true nature. We choose to become a closed system and to live unto ourselves. We become less than who we are.

Jesus' life of prayer demonstrates a path of spiritual formation through which we have the opportunity to learn and become what we truly are. Taking the risk to follow the path wherever it leads is what is most important. Remaining on the path requires both vision and guidance. It demands, yes *demands*, a turning away from self and a letting go of control of both the journey and its destination. This is the meaning of repentance. Turning toward God is also turning toward our true selves, our divine nature.

Fertile ground for the growth of the seed of God's image in us

During his lifetime Jesus formed a community of disciples and shared his intimacy with God and his mission with them. He continues to gather followers today through the work of the Holy Spirit. Each assembly of modern disciples forms an environment of grace with sacraments that make the mystery of God's nature tangible.

The sacrament of baptism is an immersion into participation in the nature of God. It is a sacrament of vision. It is like an icon, a sacred window through which we glimpse an inner and more complete vision of ourselves. Baptism is the icon of the sacredness of human life. It presents us with the vision of our divine nature and exhorts us to follow the life of Jesus toward union with God and compassionate engagement in the lives of people around us.

But the treasure does not end with the icon of baptism. We need more than vision and we do not travel alone. Baptism takes place in the context of a community of persons who are also on the same journey, the church. These persons have been called together by the presence in them of the One who is both guide and source of life for the journey. Their union with God is nurtured by the sacraments, especially the Eucharist, and the wisdom of the Bible. The modern church has its roots in a biblical community.

Lord, teach us to pray

When Jesus of Nazareth was raised from the dead a community was formed called the "followers of the Way." During his lifetime Jesus became a living icon of the fullness of human life and vitality. His life was a vessel of divine energy. His openness to God was so complete that he experienced oneness with God that would lead St. Paul to say, later, that *"in him the fullness of God was pleased to dwell"* (Col 1:19).

Jesus realized that his experience of intimacy with God was the source of all his wisdom and actions. When he said *"I and the Father are one,"* he was showing his followers the depth and completeness of God's presence in his human life. This is the treasure he wanted to share with his disciples. Just before his crucifixion he prayed, *"I ask not only on behalf of these, but also on behalf of those who will believe in me through their word, that they may all be one. As you, Father, are in me and I am in you, may they also be in us, so that the world may believe that you have sent me"* (John 17:20–21).

Jesus did not demand that people agree with his teaching. He gave them the opportunity to entrust their lives to him and follow him into fullness of human life: union with God and with each other. It was Jesus' experience of God's love that enabled him to love others. He knew that human life is impossible without experience of God's love, a love that is mutual and bonding. This union, in love, is the source of all moral behavior, responsible living, and human compassion. Mirrored in Jesus' life is the wisdom that our journey into the heart of God is also a journey into community with each other. Personal transformation is an invitation to collaborate in the transformation of society. Jesus did not demand acceptance of theology or moral requirements. He offered a Way into the heart of God. He opened a path and he embodied the path which leads to fullness of human life and union with God. Jesus did not ask people to worship him, but to follow him. He knew that if people experienced oneness with God then clarity about life and courage for moral living would be the natural consequences. He lured people beyond themselves, saying, *"Very truly, I tell you, the one who believes in me will also do the works that I do and, in fact, will do greater works than these, because I am going to the Father"* (John 14:12). When Jesus invited the disciples to follow him into the life of God, Thomas asked, *"Lord, we do not know where you are going. How can we know the way?"* Jesus replied, *"I am the way, and the truth, and the life"* (John 14:5–6a).

Living the good treasure

The simple message of Christian faith communities is that the divine energy and vision present in Jesus is the same energy and vision God offers every person. But the message remains only words until it is heard and transformed into a way of life. This requires turning toward and remaining with the One who embodies the message. The Christian way is lived by faith: entrusting one's life into the life of Jesus, who is the way. The purpose of Christian faith communities in their variety of expressions is to incarnate this message in their common life. Their life must be their message. Only then will the One who is the way, the truth and the life, be embodied in each new generation.

The gift of Jesus' life of prayer today

During the past three months we have seen that Jesus did not believe that his way of life and the power present within him was a unique gift meant only for him. He proclaimed that every person who entrusts himself or herself to God will share this same gift for the life of the world. His deepest desire was to call others to experience the same intimacy with God that was the heart of his life. God's desires for human life were revealed in the way Jesus lived. But Jesus' life of prayer is more than an example to follow. Embedded in that example is the life-giving and uncreated energy of God that, through his risen life, makes it possible for us also to participate in the nature of God. This is the work of the Holy Spirit that Jesus promised would always be our companion and guide in prayer and living.

Although Christians continue to experience Jesus' presence in a unique way in their common life, his gift is not the exclusive possession of any institution. Just as death could not limit or end Jesus' presence among us and the power of God's life in him, no institution or religious tradition can contain his gift or presence. The gift of Jesus, a Galilean Jew, was given before his way of life became the core of Christian living. This does not diminish the integrity of the Christian path or the fruit of its faithfulness to Jesus. It proclaims that the gift of Jesus to humankind knows no limits and is available in a myriad of ways to every human being.

As we experience Jesus' presence and life of prayer today we can share the desire of the disciples whose lives were transformed as they followed him throughout Galilee and Judea in the first-century. We can begin one day at a time with this simple prayer: "Lord, teach us to pray. We want to be like you."

The Evolution of the Hebrew Scriptures and the New Testament

The priority of the canonical Gospels

Lord, Teach Us to Pray uses the canonical Gospels as its primary source. The Gospels of Matthew, Mark, Luke, and John are called "canonical Gospels" because they were accepted by the early church as "normative" in presenting the life, death, and resurrection of Jesus of Nazareth. The earliest Christians used the name "gospel" to refer to a document that included a "passion narrative," in addition to other details of Jesus's life. A gospel must include a narrative of the events that led to and included the last week of Jesus's life. Although there are other important early documents that contain sayings of Jesus and some details from his life and his relationship with Christians after his resurrection, they do not include a passion narrative. The title "gospel" has been given by translators and scholars to some early documents, including "The Gospel of Thomas," "The Gospel of Mary Magdalene," and "The Gospel of James." These codices give unique documentation for the theology, piety, and life of some of the earliest communities of Christians. They are a valuable part of Christian tradition, but they are not gospels.

The phrase "canonical Gospels" indicates that the Gospels of Matthew, Mark, Luke, and John were considered normative as representing both the oral traditions (memories) about Jesus' life and teaching as well as the teaching of the apostles as that teaching was transmitted to other teachers in the earliest Christian faith communities. Therefore, these gospels represent traditions about Jesus' life before his death and resurrection and traditions of his life from the point of view of Jewish followers of Jesus, Christians, and early Christian communities after his resurrection. One of the earliest references to these gospels was made by Ignatius of Antioch in 115 CE. He referred to them as "The Gospel." The next reference to these four gospels is in the Muratorian Fragment, dated circa 160 CE. Origen of Alexandria states that there was a consensus about the four Gospels in circa 250 CE. In 367 CE Athanasius, Bishop of Alexandria, compiled a list of the books of the New Testament that included these gospels and this list was approved in 393 CE at an ecumenical church council. The collection of the twenty-seven books now included in the New Testament and enumerated by Athanasius was officially approved in 405 CE. The canonical books of the New Testament went through a process of selection that lasted from 190 to 400 CE.

The Hebrew Scriptures at the Time of Jesus

Most scholars agree that during the revolt of the Maccabees against the oppressive and forced Hellenization by the Seleucid (Syrian) King Antiochus Epiphanes the collection of books (scrolls) now known as the Hebrew scriptures (Old Testament) was recognized by Judas Maccabeus around 164 BCE. This collection was divided into three sub-sections: The Law (the first five books of Moses, called the Pentateuch), the Prophets, and the Writings (although this last section had not yet been given a name and was referred to in the prologue of Sirach as "the other books of our ancestors"). The Law included Genesis, Exodus, Leviticus, Numbers, and Deuteronomy. The Prophets included four the historical books of Joshua, Judges, Samuel, and Kings, along with Jeremiah, Ezekiel, Isaiah, and twelve "minor" prophets. The Writings included the Psalms and what are now called the sapiential (wisdom) books, such as Job, Proverbs, Ecclesiastes, the Song of Solomon, and Lamentations.

The Law was accepted as "canonical" (i.e., accepted as the rule or correct collection) in the fifth century BCE, the Prophets in the third century BCE, and the Writings (also known as the Hagiographa) at a synod of rabbinic scholars at Jabneh (Jamnia) about 90 CE.

Languages Spoken at the Time of Jesus

Many scholars agree that Greek, Aramaic, and Mishnaic Hebrew were spoken in first-century Palestine (Judea and Galilee) and that Jesus was fluent in Aramaic and Mishnaic Hebrew and most likely acquainted with Greek. Mishnaic Hebrew and Aramaic were closely related languages, with some words almost identical. Mishnaic Hebrew was a common, every day form of Hebrew during this period and was different from the Hebrew in the scrolls of the Torah, Prophets, and Writings. Jewish sages and teachers usually taught and told stories and parables in Mishnaic Hebrew.

APPENDIX B

Some Insights Regarding the Father/Son Relationship in Jesus' Religious and Social Culture

Jesus lived in a patriarchal culture. Therefore, most images and metaphors referring to the relationship between God and human beings are male oriented. There are also some beautiful and powerful female metaphors for God's intimacy with humankind in the Hebrew Scriptures and the New Testament Gospels. Although the image of father/son is no longer a primary preference in the twenty-first century, we should avoid letting our preferences rob us of the significance of the first-century metaphor of the father/son relationship as we explore the relationship between Jesus and his Abba. Try also to let go of modern theological affirmations about Jesus as "Son of God." Looking at first-century meanings of father/son may give us new and valuable insights to our own understanding of Jesus and his mission.

First century patriarchal culture extended throughout the Roman empire and included Jesus' Jewish society. Much earlier, kings in the ancient Near East were often referred to as sons of the gods. The image of the Roman Emperor Augustus—who lived during Jesus' early years and died in 14 CE—was circulated on denarii used during Jesus' lifetime with the inscription "AVGVSTUS DIVI"—Divine Augustus. This Roman coin is mentioned in the Gospels and its value usually represented a day's labor. People in first-century Israel were familiar with kings and rulers who were presented as divine sons. This context sheds light on possible motives for using names and phrases in the New Testament that describe Jesus' relationship with God.

- Genealogies were important in the Hebrew scriptures and the New Testament because they refer to the continued legacy of men and women who were faithful to God's desires and to the people. Genealogies demonstrate connections and between past and present persons, often providing authentication and authority through lineage. Each of the four Gospels presents Jesus' identity at the very beginning. In John it is a prologue linking Jesus directly with God. In Mark it is a short, yet profound proclamation that Jesus is the Son of God. In Matthew there is a long genealogy linking Jesus with Abraham and King David and claiming he is the Messiah. In Luke's first two chapters there are narratives that describe the movement of God's Spirit in the events surrounding Jesus' birth. Then in chapter 3 Luke also includes a genealogy linking Jesus with David and Adam. These genealogies and prologue provide both a "foreshadowing" that gives authenticity to Jesus' life and sets the roots of his life within Jewish history and the activity of God in the lives of the people of Israel. They alert readers immediately to the person of Jesus and the significance of his life.[1]

- In Jesus' culture the relationship of father/son combined intimacy, delight, and respect. The same can be said for mother/son and mother/daughter. But in Jesus' day it was the relationship of father/son that was dominant and expressive.

- Sons were always known in reference to their fathers. They shared their father's lineage, work, characteristics, power, and legacy. Two of Jesus' disciples were called "sons of thunder," referring to the Hebrews' belief that thunder was the voice of God; these men reflected God's voice. In other words, sons were the image of their fathers, especially in vocation and agency; they had the qualities of their father.

- In the Hebrew Scriptures a father/son metaphor is often used to describe the relationship between God and Israel and demonstrates a corporate relationship of the people with God as father. It is a mutual and loving bond, with God providing loyal care. This is why God reacts with great emotion when Israel ignores or rejects that relationship.

- In the Hebrew Scriptures father/son is used often to refer to the relationship between God and the kings of Israel, especially David and his descendants. The king is chosen by God as a son. The king, as God's son, is anointed to reflect the nature of God's love and loyalty to the people. In a reference to Israel's king as God's anointed, the psalmist declares *"I will tell of the decree of the Lord: He said to me, 'You are my son; today I have begotten you"* (Ps 2:7). The king is entrusted by God to reflect the nature of God's love, justice, and faithfulness to

1. See Stanton, *The Gospels and Jesus*, 33–34.

the people. He is a shepherd and servant of Israel. The prophet Isaiah refers to a servant of God as one whom God upholds. He is *"my chosen, in whom my soul delights; I have put my Spirit upon him; he will bring forth justice to the nations"* (Isa 42:1). Both Jewish and Christian scholars speculate that this "servant" may refer to the nation of Israel, Israel's kings, or to an individual. Unfaithful and self-serving kings are seen as unfaithful "shepherds of Israel." Their actions as kings no longer reflect God's desires for the people. The prophet Jeremiah is unambiguous about the role of king as shepherd: *"Woe to the shepherds who destroy and scatter the sheep of my pasture! says the Lord. Therefore, thus says the Lord, the God of Israel, concerning the shepherds who shepherd my people. It is you who have scattered my flock, and have driven them away, and you have not attended to them . . . I will raise up shepherds over them who will shepherd them, and they shall not fear any longer, or be dismayed, nor shall any be missing, says the Lord"* (Jer 23:1–2a, 4). In an editorial comment describing Jesus' ministry, the evangelist Matthew describes Jesus' activities in a way that is congruent with Jeremiah's proclamation that God will *"raise up shepherds"* over Israel. *"Then Jesus went about all the cities and villages, teaching in their synagogues, and proclaiming the good news of the kingdom, and curing every disease and sickness. When he saw the crowds, he had compassion on them, because they were harassed and helpless, like sheep without a shepherd"* (Matt 9:35–36). There are other references to Jesus in the Gospels that mirror images of the king as God's son in the Hebrew Scriptures. In Matthew's account of the baptism of Jesus a voice from heaven said, *"This is my son, the Beloved, with whom I am well pleased"* (Matt 3:17). After describing incidents of Jesus' teaching and healing activities, Matthew adds an editorial comment that links Jesus directly with the description of God's servant in Isaiah 42. Matthew states that Jesus' activities fulfill Isaiah's words and then quotes directly from Isaiah 42 (Matt 12:15–21). Luke's account of the beginning of Jesus' ministry in Galilee narrates Jesus' return to the synagogue in Nazareth on the sabbath where he is asked to read and comment on the scroll of Isaiah (Luke 4:1–21). Jesus reads words that echo Isaiah 42 where the prophet speaks about God's servant being anointed with God's Spirit, giving sight to the blind, release of prisoners, and release for persons who sit in darkness. When he finishes he declares, "Today this scripture has been fulfilled in your hearing"

(Luke 4:21). Matthew describes an incident when John the Baptist sends disciples to Jesus to ask, *"Are you the one who is to come, or are we to wait for another?"* Jesus' reply mirrors words from several chapters in Isaiah that describe God's saving intervention in the lives of the people of Israel (Matt 11:2–6). Both Matthew's and Luke's choices of these incidents during Jesus' ministry in Galilee link God's presence in Jesus to the image of God's servant in Isaiah 42 and to messianic hope for the restoration of Israel.

- Faithful prophets were often called "men of God" (though not sons of God) in the Hebrew Scriptures because people recognized a divine soul in them. They were Spirit-filled men of God driven by the presence of God's Spirit to "spread holiness throughout the land."[2] Their intimate and prayerful relationship with God was the source of their words and behavior. They reflected God's desires for people and the world. These aspects of the Hebrew prophets are mirrored in the persona, words, and activities of Jesus in the four Gospels, although some of his opponents saw Satan as the source of his activity rather than the Spirit of God.

- The disciples of a rabbi were called the rabbi's sons. St. Paul calls Timothy his "son."

- At Jesus' baptism a voice declares *"This is my Son, the Beloved, with whom I am well pleased"* (Matt 3:17). In Jesus' culture this manifestation of God's presence would be seen and felt as a sign of an intimate bond between Jesus and God; Jesus is declared a person who will express what God is like in a unique way. After hearing these words Jesus is driven into the wilderness by the Spirit to discern their meaning prior to beginning his mission.

2 Johs. Pedersen, *Israel*, Vol 3, 111.

APPENDIX C

The Ancient Hebrew Understanding of the Human Soul

The origin of the human soul is the breath of God.

> *...then the Lord God formed man from the dust of the ground, and breathed into his nostrils the breath of life; and the man became a living being.* (Gen 2:7)

In the second creation account in Genesis (Gen 2:4bff.) we read that the human being (*'adam* in Hebrew) is linked with the earth (*'adama* in Hebrew). The human is formed from the ground. The human is physical but lifeless until the divine vital power—the breath of life—enters the human's body. Only then does the human become a living being. Body and life are united and the creation of the human is complete.

The Hebrew understanding of the human soul—a living soul—is the unity of the physical and psychic aspects of human life. The living soul springs forth from a life-less physical condition as a direct result of God's "breathing" the divine vitality into the human's nostrils.

The human being is a soul

The Genesis account declares that a human being is not simply a corporeal substance that God then "supplies" with a soul (*nephesh* in Hebrew). Rather, a human being *is* a living soul. The essence of a human being is her or his soul, and the soul encompasses and reflects every aspect of that person's life. "Soul" and "body" are not parts of a person; they constitute the totality of a living soul. The body does not "house" the soul. Rather, a human being *is* a living soul, and all the physical, emotional, psychic, rational, and spiritual aspects of each person's life are reflected and implemented in the way a person lives.

The example of Mary of Nazareth

When Mary of Nazareth proclaims to her relative, Elizabeth, "*My soul magnifies the Lord . . .*" (Luke 1:47a) she is telling Elizabeth that every thought, desire, action, and word in her life enlarges God's presence, both in her and in the world around her. As a first-century Jew, Mary knew that a "soul" is the totality of each human being—including the senses, characteristics, appearance, actions, demeanor, learning, wisdom, and even possessions.

Soul includes a person's heart and spirit

The Hebrews understood the *heart* as the operating force and center of the soul; it is the origin of volition. A person's volition—his or her desire or will—springs forth from the totality of the soul that includes both heart and spirit. The heart is the source of the soul's inner values and capacity for action. The spirit is the exercise of that same capacity through a person's words, actions, and influence in the world. "The heart and the spirit act upon the centre and urge it in a certain direction, towards action. 'Everyone whose heart stirred him up, and everyone whom his spirit made willing came and brought Yahweh's offering.' (Exod 35:21)."[3] The *spirit* of a person is the motivating power of the soul; it is the energy that springs forth from the soul and results in specific words and actions.

This is what is meant in the summary of the Torah in Deuteronomy: "*You shall love the Lord your God with all your heart, and with all your soul, and with all your might*" (Deut 6:5). It was at the heart of Jesus' relationship with his Abba and he embodied this great love with his whole being. It was the foundation of his life of prayer.

3. Pedersen, *Israel I-II*, 111.

APPENDIX D

The Ancient Hebrew Understanding of Blessing

What did it mean to bless or be blessed?

The Hebrews believed that the human soul was saturated with power. This power is present within a person as well as on the surface of her or his life—in words, actions, influence, etc. No person can live without this power. The Israelites called this life-giving power *berakha, blessing*. If the power of blessing is present within a person its presence will be manifested outwardly. You cannot have blessing without its outward manifestations. Blessing is the inward strength of the soul that becomes a source of vitality and happiness for others.

All life forms have blessing: "*Thus says the Lord; As the wine is found in the cluster, and they say, 'Do not destroy it, for there is a blessing in it,' so will I do for my servant's sake, and not destroy them all*" (Isa 65:8). It is the blessing of the grape to have juice and the potential of wine.

Blessing influences persons and situations

This understanding of blessing is far different from the modern sense that a blessing is "approval" or "protection." It is, rather, an investment with sacred power for the life of the world. The Israelites believed that a person's psychic identity influenced his or her surroundings. A strong soul supports the person's environment, including other persons and society. This "influence" was called a person's *counsel*. If a person was to have strong counsel, she or he must have appropriate blessing to make that possible. A person with strong counsel seeks the assistance of others. Israelite kings were seen as good when their power—their counsel—brought blessing to their people. Isaiah speaks of a coming perfect king as "Wonderful Counselor." This does not mean that the perfect king offers advice. It means that the king brings good counsel to the people through the blessing of his life-giving power.

Blessing is the transmission of life from one person to another

When God blesses a person, God transmits sacred power. It is a sharing of the life of the Creator and Sustainer. Thus, Abraham is the steward of God's power to bless "all nations." When Abraham blesses Isaac, his counsel (his ability to act according to the nature of the power that had been given) is transmitted from one leader of the clan to the next. The next leader derives his soul from the former. When Jacob wrestles all night with the mysterious person who dominates him he asks for a blessing—a portion of the mystery he has wrestled with and has left him lame. Jacob becomes Israel because he wrestled with God and prevailed long enough to receive a blessing that imparted power to Jacob as a patriarch of Israel.

This ancient Hebrew understanding of blessing may help us see the image of Jacob and the ladder as a mirror for our personal movement toward the mysterious power and presence of God in our lives and our plans for the future. It will also give deeper meaning of the blessings Jesus pronounces in the Beatitudes in Matthew 5:1–12.

APPENDIX E

A Suggestion for Contemplative Prayer[4]

Find a relatively quiet place in your home, your workplace, a church, mosque, or synagogue, a park, or another favorite place. You will need a chair, bench, or floor space to sit comfortably with your back straight and supported, but not rigid. With your eyes closed or partially open, begin breathing slowly in and out. Be conscious of your pattern of deep breathing. Let your body and your mind become as relaxed as possible. As your mind becomes relaxed you will experience many thoughts passing rapidly through your mind. These thoughts are normal. Let them come and go. Try, as best you can, to let your mind and inner being become empty. Let your whole being be an open vessel for God's presence and voice. Avoid expectations or hoped-for outcomes. Simply be present to God. You may find it helpful to repeat a word or short phrase silently to help let go of distracting thoughts and bring yourself back to quietness of mind. You can choose a word or short phrase that has special meaning to you. You might want to repeat a name for God, such as "Holy One," or a short request, such as "Come, Holy Spirit," but try not to think about the intellectual meaning of the words. When you have sat in silence for about twenty minutes, open your eyes, wait for a minute or two, and then give thanks to God at the end of your meditation.

4. Excerpted from Keller,. *Come and See,* 81.

Following Jesus through the Gospel of Mark

It will be helpful to place Jesus' life and ministry in its geographical context. It is necessary to "see" where he went. Use the outline of the Gospel of Mark that follows to work your way through Mark's account of Jesus adult life and ministry. As you follow Jesus' life and ministry, use the three maps that follow the outline and place each incident on one or more map geographically. It may be helpful to use a pencil and mark Jesus' path from place to place as the Gospel accounts unfold. This will give you an idea of Jesus' movement and the intensity of his ministry.

An Outline of Jesus' Ministry in the Gospel of Mark

Nazareth to Jordan River, East of Jerusalem (1:1–13)

- Baptism (intimacy with God)
- Temptations and desert retreat

Jordan River to Capernaum (1:14–28)

- Preaching (repent: kingdom of God is near)
- Calls disciples; prays in synagogue
- Teaching, with authority
- Heals the sick and demon possessed

Capernaum to various places in Galilee (1:35–45)

- Preaching; prays in deserted place
- Healing

Back to Capernaum (2:1—4:34)

- Heals and forgives sin (controversy) (2:10–12)
- Calls Levi (2:13–14)
- Associates with sinners (2:15–17)
- Controversy over fasting and Sabbath (2:18–28)
- Appoints the Twelve (3:13–19)
- Accused of having satanic powers (3:20–28)
- Teaching and sayings (Parables of Sower, Lamp on Stand, Growing Seed, Mustard Seed) (4:1–34)

Capernaum to Sea of Galilee (4:35–41)

- Jesus calms storm; "who is this?"

Sea of Galilee to Gergasa (5:1–20)

- Jesus heals demon-possessed man

Gergasa to lakeshore near Capernaum (5:21–34)

- Jesus heals daughter of Jairus
- Jesus heals a woman with chronic bleeding (great faith, astonishment)

Capernaum to Nazareth (6:1–6)

- Jesus teaches and is opposed; people show a lack of faith

Nazareth to various places in Galilee (6:7–13)

- Jesus teaches
- Sends out disciples to preach, heal, and drive out demons
- Disciples return; deluged by people

By boat to a solitary place (6:30–44)

- Jesus teaches
- The feeding of 5,000

Solitary place en-route to Bethsaida (6:45–50)

- Jesus prays on a mountain
- Jesus walks on water and calms the sea

Sea of Galilee to Gennesaret (6:53–55)

- Jesus heals the sick; many ill are brought to him

Gennesaraet to various places in Galilee (7:1–23)

- Jesus is confronted by the Pharisees about eating with unclean hands (what is truly clean and unclean, motives for religious practices, hypocrisy, institutionalism)

Gennesaraet to area of Tyre (7:24–30)

- Jesus heals daughter of a Syro-Phonecian woman (example of faith and the question of Jesus relationship with gentiles)

Tyre to Sidon to Sea of Galilee to area of Decapolis (7:31–37)

- Heals deaf man, tells people not to spread word of what he is doing
- Amazement of the people
- Feeding of 4,000 (Jesus' compassion and the failure of religious and political leaders of his day)

Decapolis to area of Dalmanutha (Magdala) (8:10–13)

- Pharisees demand a sign as proof of Jesus authority and unique relationship with God
- Jesus says "no sign shall be given"
- Beware of the leaven of Pharisees and Herodians (false wisdom)
- Depend on bread of life present in Jesus

Dalmanutha (Magdala) to "other side" of Sea of Galilee (8:13–21)

"Other side" of Sea of Galilee to Bethsaida (8:22–26)

- Jesus heals a blind man

Bethsaida to area around Caesarea Philippi (8:27—9:1)

- Peter declares Jesus is the Messiah
- Jesus speaks of his death a resurrection
- The cost of being a disciple
- Jesus speaks of the coming of the realm of God

Caesaria Philippi area to a high mountain (of transfiguration) (9:2–9)

- Jesus' transfiguration; awareness of his true nature and confirmation of his teaching and ministry as from God

Mountain of transfiguration to various places in Galilee (9:11–32)

- Jesus disciples argue with Scribes
- Jesus heals a boy with "evil spirit"
- Jesus teach his disciples in private
- Jesus speaks of his death again

Jesus arrives in Capernaum (9:33–50)

- Jesus teaches about greatness, servanthood, childlike openness
- Jesus emphasizes important of intimacy with and loyalty to God
- Danger of leading others to sin
- Jesus speaks of the need for the "salt" of God's presence in a person's life

Capernaum to area of Peraea (10:1–31)

- Jesus is tested by Pharisees about his interpretation of the Torah
- Jesus stresses the "motivation" or spirit of the Torah, rather than the strict letter of the Torah
- Jesus declares the need for a child-like openness and receptivity as the attitude for participating in the realm (kingdom) of God
- Jesus points to the cost of being a disciple
- Jesus speaks about stewardship of material things

Peraea to Jerusalem (10:32–45)

- Jesus speaks of his death for the third time and his inevitable confrontation with religious leaders
- Jesus speaks about the nature of power and greatness, showing that the true nature of power is in being a servant of others

A stop at Jericho en-route to Jerusalem (10:46–52)

- Jesus heals a blind man and speaks of the importance of faith

A stop in Bethany en-route to Jerusalem (11:1–11)

- Preparations for Jesus to enter Jerusalem on a colt
- Jesus enters Jerusalem from the Mount of Olives on a colt

Events in and near Jerusalem leading to Jesus crucifixion (12:1—16:20)

- Jesus teaches, uses parables, and comments critically on aspects of the religious leadership (in the area of the temple: 12:1—44)
- Jesus foretells the destruction of the temple, persecution of his followers, and desecration of holy sites; he exhorts his followers to have watchfulness (on the Mount of Olives, opposite the temple: 13:1–36)
- Chief priests and Scribes plot to kill Jesus (temple precincts: 14:1–2)
- Jesus is anointed with costly ointment (Bethany: 14:3–9)
- Judas plots with chief priests to betray Jesus (temple precincts: 14:10–11)
- Jesus celebrates Passover meal with his closest disciples (Mt. Zion in Jerusalem: 14:12–25)
- Jesus predicts his disciples will desert him (Mount of Olives: 14:26–31)
- Jesus prays with intense emotion in the garden of Gethsemane (Mount of Olives: 14:32–42)

- Jesus is arrested (Mount of Olives: 14:43–51)

- Jesus is taken to the palace of Caiaphas, the high priest, for a trial before the religious Council (Jerusalem: 14:53–65)

- Peter denies Jesus (outside palace of Caiaphas in Jerusalem: 14:66–72)

- Jesus is brought before the Roman governor, Pontius Pilate, for trial and condemnation (in Jerusalem at the Antonia Fortress next to the temple: 15:1–20)

- Jesus is crucified (outside the wall of Jerusalem at Golgotha: 15:21–41)

- Jesus is placed for burial in new tomb of family of Joseph of Arimathea (just outside wall of Jerusalem, near Golgotha: 15:42–47)

- Women visit tomb to anoint Jesus and are told to tell disciples that "he has been raised (16:1–8)

- Longer ending to Mark continues with Jesus' appearance to Mary Magdalene (16:9–12) and two disciples in the country.

- Jesus commissions disciples to proclaim the "good news" (16:14–18)

- Jesus "is taken up into heaven" (16:9) and the disciples go out to proclaim the good news (16:20)

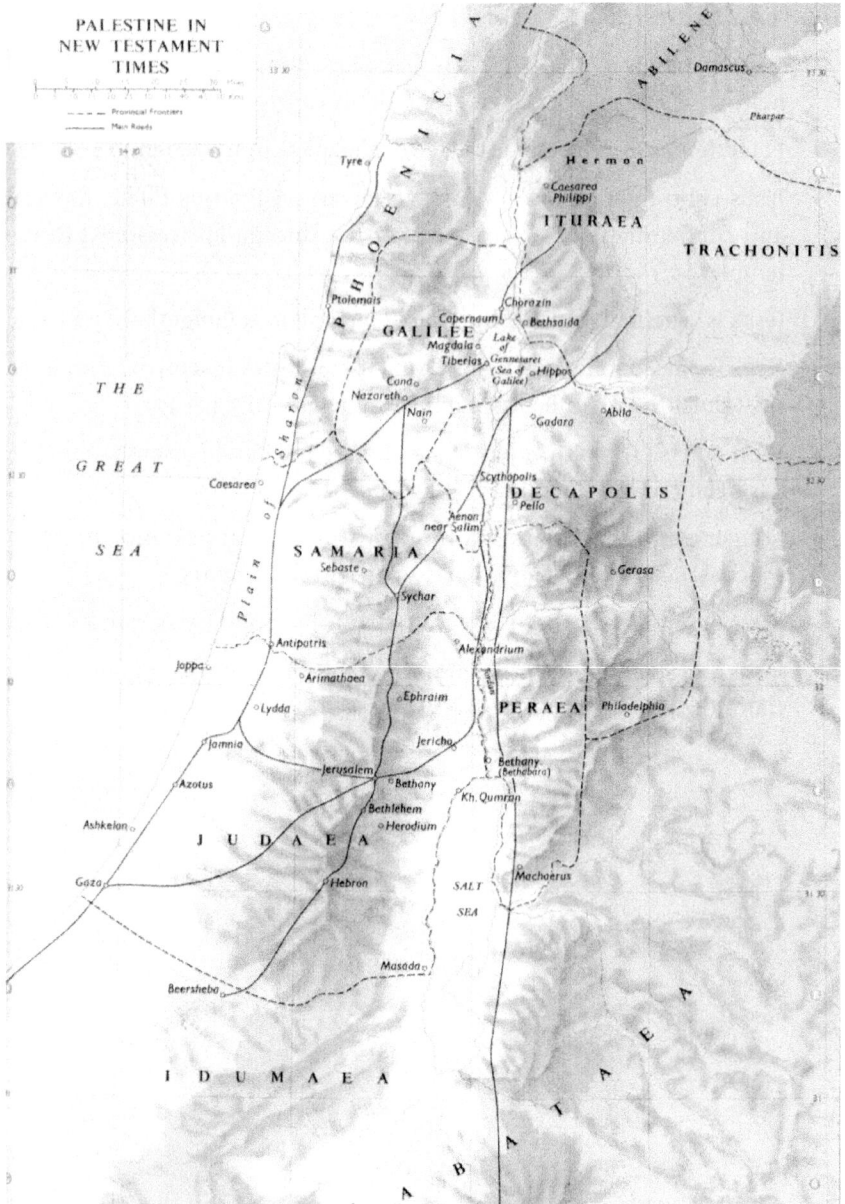

PALESTINE IN
NEW TESTAMENT
TIMES

Provincial Frontiers
Main Roads

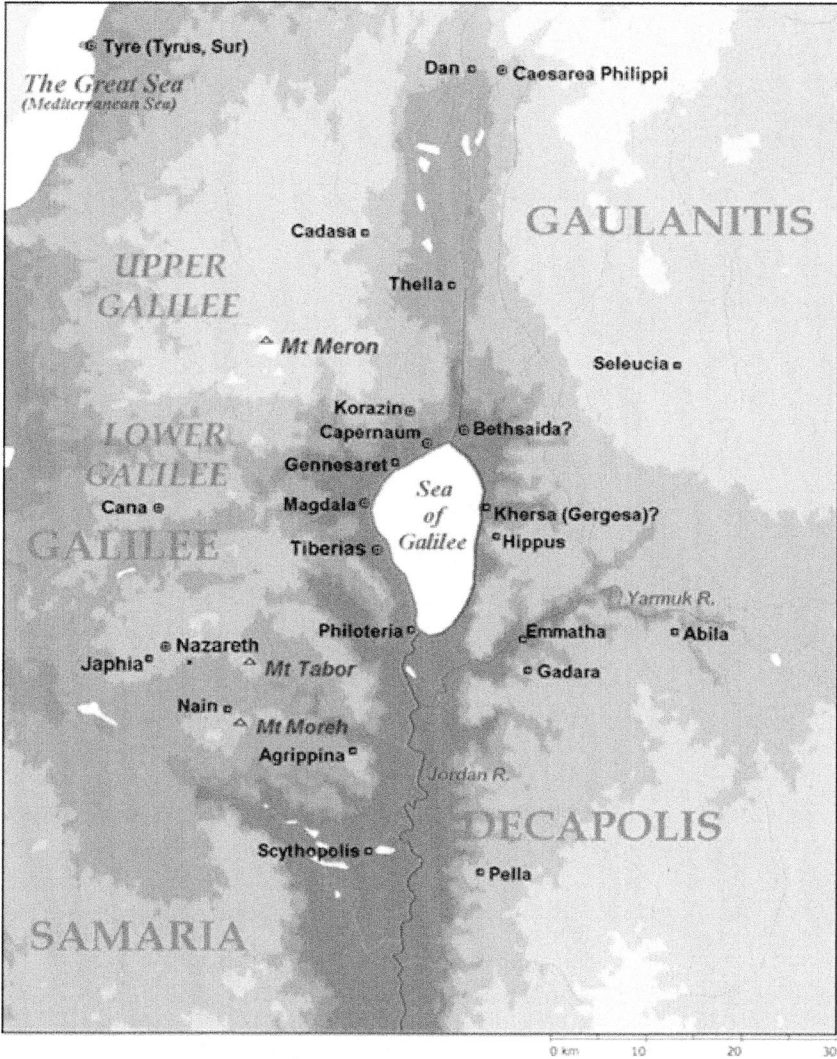

Tyre (Tyrus, Sur)

Dan   Caesarea Philippi

The Great Sea
(Mediterranean Sea)

Cadasa

GAULANITIS

UPPER
GALILEE

Thella

Mt Meron

Seleucia

Korazin
Capernaum   Bethsaida?

LOWER
GALILEE

Gennesaret

Cana

Magdala

Sea
of
Galilee

Khersa (Gergesa)?

Hippus

GALILEE

Tiberias

Yarmuk R.

Philoteria

Emmatha

Abila

Japhia   Nazareth

Mt Tabor

Gadara

Nain

Mt Moreh

Agrippina

Jordan R.

DECAPOLIS

Scythopolis

Pella

SAMARIA

0 km   10   20   30

Galilean Ministry of Jesus

Jerusalem: Events in Jesus' Life

Bibliography of Works Consulted

American Bible Society. *Revised Standard Version Synopsis of the Four Gospels.* New York: American Bible Society, 2010.

Bailey, Kenneth E. *Jesus through Middle Eastern Eyes: Cultural Studies in the Gospels.* Downers Grove, IL: IVP Academic, 2008.

Balentine, Samuel E. *Prayer in the Hebrew Bible: The Drama of Divine-Human Dialog.* Minneapolis: Fortress, 1993.

Bauman, Lynn. *The Gospel of Thomas: Wisdom of the Twin.* 2nd ed. Ashland, OR: White Cloud, 2012.

Black, Matthew. *An Aramaic Approach to the Gospels and Acts.* Peabody, MA: Hendrickson, 1998.

Borg, Marcus. *Jesus: A New Vision. Spirit, Culture, and the Life of Discipleship.* San Francisco: Harper and Row, 1987.

Bornkamm, Günther. *Jesus of Nazareth.* Minneapolis: Fortress, 1995.

Chilton, Bruce. *Jesus' Prayer and Jesus' Eucharist: His Personal Practice of Spirituality.* Valley Forge, PA: Trinity, 1997.

Chitty, Derwas J. *The Desert a City.* Crestwood, NY: St. Vladimir's Seminary Press, 1995.

Cooke, Bernard J. *God's Beloved, Jesus' Experience of the Transcendent.* Philadelphia: Trinity, 1992.

Crossan, John Dominic. *Jesus: A Revolutionary Biography.* San Francisco: HarperSanFrancisco, 1994.

Crossan, John Dominic, and Jonathan L Reed. *Excavating Jesus: Beneath the Stones, Behind the Texts.* San Francisco: HarperSanFrancisco, 2001.

Destro, Adriana, and Mauro Pesce. *Encounters with Jesus: The Man in His Place and Time.* Minneapolis: Fortress, 2012.

Dunn, James D. G. *Jesus and the Spirit.* Grand Rapids: Eerdmans, 1975.

———. *Jesus, Paul, and the Gospels.* Grand Rapids: Eerdmans, 2011.

———. *Jesus Remembered.* Grand Rapids: Eerdmans, 2003.

———. *A New Perspective on Jesus: What the Quest for the Historical Jesus Missed.* Grand Rapids: Baker Academic, 2005.

———. *The Oral Gospel Tradition.* Grand Rapids: Eerdmans, 2013.

Flusser, David. *The Sage from Galilee: Rediscovering Jesus' Genius.* 4th ed. Grand Rapids: Eerdmans, 2007.

Fredriksen, Paula. *From Jesus to Christ: The Origins of the New Testament Images of Jesus.* New Haven: Yale University Press, 1988.

Schüssler Fiorenza, Elisabeth. *Jesus: Miriam's Child, Sophia's Prophet: Critical Issues in Feminist Christology.* London: Bloomsbury Academic, 1994.

Hanson, Kenneth C., and Douglas E. Oakman. *Palestine in the Time of Jesus: Social Structures and Social Conflicts.* 2nd ed. Minneapolis: Fortress, 2008.

Harrington, Daniel, S.J. *Jesus and Prayer: What the New Testament Teaches Us.* Frederick, MD: Word Among Us, 2009.

Hartin, Patrick J. *Exploring the Spirituality of the Gospels.* Collegeville, MN: Liturgical, 2010.

Heinemann, Joseph, with Jacob J. Petuchowski. *Literature of the Synagogue.* Piscataway, NJ: Gorgias, 2006.

Jeremias, Joachim. *Jerusalem in the Time of Jesus.* Reprint. Philadelphia: Fortress, 1975.

———. *Prayers of Jesus.* 1978. Reprint. Eugene, OR: Wipf and Stock, 2006.

Keener, Craig S. *The Historical Jesus of the Gospels.* Grand Rapids: Eerdmans, 2009.

Keller, David. *Come and See: The Transformation of Personal Prayer.* Harrisburg, PA: Morehouse, 2009.

———. *Desert Banquet: A Year of Wisdom from the Desert Mothers and Fathers.* Collegeville, MN: Liturgical, 2011.

Koenig, John. *Rediscovering New Testament Prayer: Boldness and Blessing in the Name of Jesus.* San Francisco: HarperSanFrancisco, 1992.

Lee, Bernard J., S.M. *The Galilean Jewishness of Jesus: Retrieving the Jewish Origins of Christianity.* Mahwah, NJ: Paulist, 1988.

Lohfink, Gerhard. *Jesus of Nazareth: What He Wanted, Who He Was.* Collegeville, MN: Liturgical, 2012.

Malina, Bruce J. *The New Testament World: Insights from Cultural Anthropology.* 3rd ed. Louisville: Westminster John Knox, 2001.

Malina, Bruce J., and Richard L. Rohrbaugh. *Social-Science Commentary on the Synoptic Gospels.* Minneapolis: Augsburg Fortress, 2003.

Myer, Marvin. *The Gospel of Thomas.* San Francisco: HarperOne, 2004.

———, ed. *The Nag Hammadi Scriptures: The Revised and Updated Translation of Sacred Gnostic Texts.* Preface by James M. Robinson and Introduction by Elaine Pagels. New York: HarperCollins, 2007.

Murphy, Frederick. *Early Judaism: The Exile to the Time of Christ.* Rev. ed. Peabody, MA: Hendrickson, 2006.

Pagola, José A. *Following in the Footsteps of Jesus: Meditations on the Gospels for Year A.* Miami: Convivium, 2010.

———. *Jesus: An Historical Approximation.* Miami: Convivium, 2009.

Perrin, Norman. *Jesus and the Language of the Kingdom: Symbol and Metaphor in New Testament Interpretation.* Philadelphia: Fortress, 1976.

Pilch, John J. *The Cultural World of Jesus, Sunday by Sunday, Cycle A.* Collegeville, MN: Liturgical, 1995.

———. *The Cultural World of Jesus, Sunday by Sunday, Cycle B.* Collegeville, MN: Liturgical, 1996.

———. *The Cultural World of Jesus, Sunday by Sunday, Cycle C.* Collegeville, MN: Liturgical, 1996.

Perkins, Pheme. *Jesus as Teacher.* Cambridge: Cambridge University Press, 1990.

Riches, John. *The World of Jesus.* Cambridge: Cambridge University Press, 1990.

Robinson, James M. *The Sayings of Jesus: The Sayings Gospel Q in English.* Minneapolis: Fortress, 2002.

Rousseau, John J., and Rami Arav. *Jesus and His World: An Archaeological and Cultural Dictionary.* Minneapolis: Fortress, 1995.

Schottroff, Luise. *The Parables of Jesus*. Translated by Linda A. Maloney. Minneapolis: Fortress, 2006.

Schröter, Jens. *Jesus of Nazareth: Jew from Galilee, Savior of the World*. Waco, TX: Baylor University Press, 2014.

Senior, Donald. *Jesus: A Gospel Portrait*. Mahwah, NJ: Paulist, 1992.

Shoemaker, H. Stephen. *Finding Jesus in His Prayers*. Nashville: Abingdon, 2004.

Solle, Dorthy, and Luise Schottroff. *Jesus of Nazareth*. London: SPCK, 2002.

Stanton, Graham. *The Gospels and Jesus*. Oxford: Oxford University Press, 2002.

Stauffer, Ethelbert. *Jesus and His Story*. London: SCM, 1960.

Stein, Robert H. *The Method and Message of Jesus' Teachings*. Louisville: Westminster John Knox, 1994.

Thurman, Howard. *Disciplines of the Spirit*. Richmond, IN: Friends United, 1963.

Toledano, Rabbir Eliezer, ed. *The Orot Sephardic Weekday Siddur*. Lakewood, NJ: Orot, 1995.

Vermes, Geza. *The Authentic Gospel of Jesus*. New York: Penguin, 2004.

———. *The Religion of Jesus the Jew*. Minneapolis: Augsburg Fortress, 1993.

Von Rad, Gerhard. *Genesis: A Commentary*. Philadelphia: Westminster, 1961.

Williams, Rowan. *Being Christian: Baptism, Bible, Eucharist, Prayer*. Grand Rapids: Eerdmans, 2014.

Witherington III, Ben. *The Jesus Quest: The Third Search For The Jew of Nazareth*. Downers Grove, IL: IVP, 1997.

———. *Jesus the Sage: The Pilgrimage of Wisdom*. Minneapolis: Augsburg, 1994.

Wright, N. T. *The Challenge of Jesus: Rediscovering Who Jesus Was and Is*. Downers Grove, IL: IVP, 1999.

———. *Jesus and the Victory of God*. London: SPCK, 1996.

———. *Simply Jesus: A New Vision of Who He Was, What He Did, and Why He Matters*. New York: HarperOne, 2011.

Young, Brad H. *Meet The Rabbis: Rabbinic Thought and the Teachings of Jesus*. Grand Rapids: Baker Academic, 2007.

Printed in Great Britain
by Amazon

21943622R00158